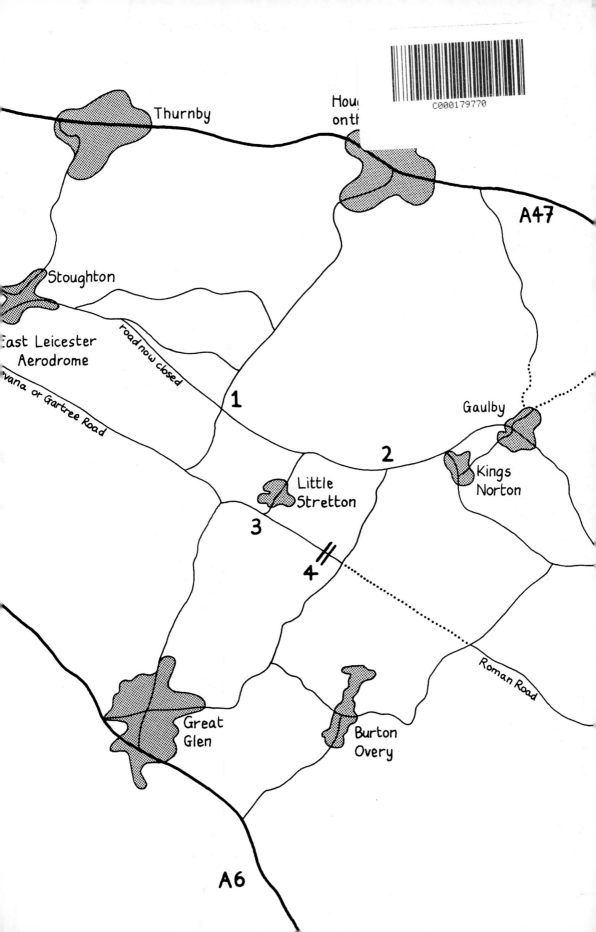

Thurnby

Hou
on th

A47

C000179770

Stoughton

East Leicester
Aerodrome

Road now closed

vana or Gartree Road

1

Gaulby

2

Kings
Norton

Little
Stretton

3

4

Roman Road

Great
Glen

Burton
Overy

A6

THE GREEN BICYCLE MURDER

C. WENDY EAST

ALAN SUTTON

This book is dedicated to the late
Sir Edward Marshall Hall K.C.

Inimitable, though some did try and were but a pale reflection;
much maligned in later years, though it would seem less so
in his own day, he left a void in a changing world
which was not, and now never will be, filled.

First published in the United Kingdom in 1993 by
Alan Sutton Publishing Limited · Phoenix Mill · Far Thrupp · Stroud · Gloucestershire

First published in the United States of America in 1993 by
Alan Sutton Publishing Inc · 83 Washington Street · Dover · NH 03820

British Library Cataloguing in Publication Data

East, C. Wendy
Green Bicycle Murder
I. Title
364.1

ISBN 0-7509-0372-4

Library of Congress Cataloging-in-Publication Data applied for

Typeset in 10/12pt Times
Typesetting and origination by
Alan Sutton Publishing Ltd.
Printed in Great Britain by
The Bath Press, Avon.

Contents

List of Illustrations   v

Acknowledgements   vi

Author's Note   vii

Introduction   ix

Chapter 1.   EARLY DAYS – ANNIE BELLA WRIGHT   1

Chapter 2.   FATEFUL MEETING   9

Chapter 3.   THE VIA DEVANA   15

Chapter 4.   INQUEST   28

Chapter 5.   BRIEF LIFE IS HERE OUR PORTION   35

Chapter 6.   HUE AND CRY   39

Chapter 7.   THE HAND OF FATE   49

Chapter 8.   ARREST   56

Chapter 9.   EARLY DAYS – RONALD LIGHT   62

Chapter 10.   'DAMN AND BLAST THAT CANAL'   71

Chapter 11.   POLICE COURT HEARINGS   73

Chapter 12.   THE STAGE IS SET   92

Chapter 13.   REX V. LIGHT – THE CASE FOR THE PROSECUTION   103

Chapter 14.   REX V. LIGHT – THE CASE FOR THE DEFENCE   125

Chapter 15.   REX V. LIGHT – CLOSING SPEECHES   144

Chapter 16.   REX V. LIGHT – SUMMING UP AND VERDICT   152

Chapter 17.   RONALD LIGHT – OFFICER AND GENTLEMAN?   161

Chapter 18.   *CORPUS DELICTI*   175

Chapter 19.   FATEFUL, BUT FIRST, MEETING?   186

Chapter 20.   AFTERMATH   195

Bibliography   199

Index   200

List of Illustrations

1. Bella Wright, *c.* 1914   xiii
2. Somerby School   3
3. Pupils of Somerby School   4
4. St Mary's Mill   5
5. Bella's parents   9
6. Bella's home   11
7. The murder scene   17
8. Joseph Cowell   21
9. Evington post office   29
10. P.C. Alfred Hall   33
11. Stoughton church   35
12. Bella's grave, Stoughton churchyard   37
13. Wanted poster   41
14. Bella Wright   47
15. The green bicycle frame and front wheel   50
16. The dragging of the canal   51
17. Local inhabitants join in the search for a revolver   53
18. Ronald Light, before the identification parade   59
19. Ronald Light, wearing the uniform of a Second Lieutenant in the Royal Engineers 67
20. No. 54 Highfield Street, Light's home   69
21. Ethel Tunnicliffe and Mary Webb   87
22. The green bicycle is taken into court   93
23. Crowds gather on Castle Green   96
24. Sir Thomas Horridge, the judge   99
25. Sir Gordon Hewart K.C.   103
26. The chapel at Little Stretton   107
27. Muriel Nunney and Valeria Cavan   110
28. George Measures   115
29. The murder scene, a recent photograph   121
30. Sir Edward Marshall Hall K.C.   127
31. Francis Sims and Edward Holmes   133
32. George Measures' cottage   137
33. Ronald Light in the dock   149
34. Ronald Light soon after his acquittal   155
35. Catherine Light   156
36. Ronald Light: the photograph given to the *Daily Sketch* reporter   165
37. Parkview, Granville Road   168
38. Ronald Light with his mother's dog   173
39. Shady Lane, Evington   187
40. Sunnyside Cottages, Isle of Sheppey   197

Acknowledgements

To the many archivists, librarians, superintendent registrars and registrars who patiently and with unfailing courtesy dealt with my numerous enquiries and applications I extend my thanks and appreciation.

To the many residents of Leicestershire, past and present, who took the trouble to contact me and to share their knowledge of and interest in the green bicycle case, I say thank you for many interesting hours of conversation.

I am grateful to Derek Charman for permission to quote from his unpublished history of Freer, Bouskell & Co., entitled *County Attorneys*, and to David M. Charman and Freer, Bouskell for permission to quote from William Wallace's unpublished work *Jack of All Trades*.

I am especially indebted to the following: Stewart Hall, Departmental Records Officer, Crown Prosecution Service for allowing me privileged access to the D.P.P.'s file, Rex v. Light; Miss Frances P. Grey for her kindness during my days of research at the C.P.S., Queen Anne's Gate; Miss Jill Adams, records officer and Terry Robson, librarian, both of the Lord Chancellor's Office; Aubrey W. Stevenson, Leicestershire County Record Office for their help over many months of research; Pat Burford of West Bromwich Central Reference Library; Angela Atton, Archivist and Mr T. Wood of the Leicestershire Constabulary; Dr Jacqueline Bower of the Centre for Kentish Studies, Maidstone; Mrs M. Magnusson of the Institution of Royal Engineers Library, Chatham; Brigadier K.A. Timbers, Historical Secretary of the Royal Artillery Historical Trust; Mary Murphy and Amy Rachlin of the Institution of Civil Engineers; S.G. Fowler, Bursar at Dean Close School, Cheltenham; Joyce M. King, Registrar, Charing Crematorium; David Bromwich, Local History librarian at Taunton; Catherine McCord at Kensington Library; the staff of the Probate Sub-Registry, York; the staff of the Guildhall Library; the staff of the British Library at Colindale; the staff of the Public Record Office, at both Kew and Chancery Lane; Janet Edgell, Keeper of Records, Middle Temple; staff of the National Maritime Museum, Greenwich and staff of the National Army Museum, Chelsea, also Mr A.W.P. Mackintosh.

My grateful thanks go also to Peter, the son of Gertrude Ward for permission and indeed encouragement to incorporate in my text his mother's account of the Ward family's involvement in the case.

A particular word of thanks must go to David Buxton and Simon Fletcher, editors at Alan Sutton Publishing, for their help throughout the production of my book.

There are a further five people to whom I owe a special debt of gratitude: firstly to Tony Duggan, for having faith in my book and for ensuring the backing of Leicestershire Museum, Arts and Records Service in bringing the book to the attention of Alan Sutton Publishing. My own load was considerably lighter for Tony's involvement from an early stage.

To Bill Richardson for quite unselfishly sharing with me his interest in the early life of Bella Wright and for the supply of several photographs.

To Major (Retd) John R. Oldfield of the Weapons Museum, School of Infantry, Warminster whose warmth, humour and hospitality coupled with his extensive knowledge of the fascinating subject of weaponry has been of tremendous help. I am particularly grateful to him for his constructive suggestions about Chapter 18.

To Robin P. Jenkins, Keeper of Records for Leicestershire, who first suggested that my research might appropriately lead to a full review of the case rather than form an odd chapter in my planned and temporarily shelved biography of Sir Edward Marshall Hall. My gratitude goes to Robin for bringing my book to the notice of Tony Duggan. I have also been inspired by his constant support, friendly encouragement and faith in my work. I am particularly mindful of the many hours that he spent in reading my first draft, his constructive criticism of which was influential in my preparation of the final draft.

Finally, to my husband Leslie, who has with patience and good humour ridden the green bicycle in tandem with me to the extent that holidays were always spent in places appropriate to my research. I say thank you for that support and encouragement and for much more which cannot be appropriately mentioned here.

* * *

Illustrations are reproduced by kind permission of the following: the British Library: pp. xi, 47, 67, 127, 149, 156, 165; Leicestershire Record Office: 17, 50, 51, 53, 59, 93, 96, 99, 187; the *Leicester Mercury*: 21, 87, 110, 115, 133; Leicestershire Constabulary: 33, 41. All other illustrations are from the author's collection.

Author's Note

I would wish to make it perfectly clear that while I believe the loss of the case papers concerning the green bicycle case from the archives of the Leicestershire Constabulary to be entirely regrettable, I know of no reason to suppose that any blame for that loss attaches to any member of the force past or present. Any criticisms that I make of the Leicestershire Constabulary or of individual past members of that force involved in the investigations into the death of Bella Wright and the eventual apprehension of Ronald Light cannot and do not pertain to the present-day force which, in a county that saw the pioneering development and introduction of genetic finger printing, must be regarded as one of the most go-ahead police forces in the county. If the body of Bella Wright were now to be discovered lying in a Leicestershire lane, it might be expected that with all the technology and skills at the fingertips of today's officers a very different investigation would ensue and in consequence a far more satisfactory conclusion be reached.

'Let guilty men remember their dark deeds
Do lean on crutches made of slender reeds.'

John Webster, *The White Devil*. Act V.Sc.6

Introduction

The death of a young Leicester millworker Annie Bella Wright in a leafy and little-used lane at Little Stretton in the summer of 1919 might, but for the initiative of one police constable, easily have passed into history as just another unexplained bicycle accident. It was the best part of twenty-two hours after the discovery of the young girl's body before the Leicester County Police Force began to treat the case as one of murder. In a county blessed by an above average number of amateur historians and local history researchers, this is one incident in the criminographic and forensic history of the county on which those who know of it, and the ever dwindling few that actually remember it, seem to hold very definite views. Those views may vary from individual to individual but the certainty with which they are held seems surprisingly universal. This sureness of opinion is all the more surprising when we consider that the manner in which death came to young Bella Wright was and never has been satisfactorily explained. No indisputable evidence of events surrounding the last few minutes of her life has ever been publicly adduced, though it is clear that at the time of her death much was known which has until quite recently lain undisclosed.

The weapon that was fired to kill young Bella Wright has never been produced though at the subsequent trial of a Leicester man, Ronald Light, the prosecution, with a strong if totally circumstantial case, offered a decided and to this day frequently upheld theory based on police findings that Bella Wright was killed by a bullet fired from a .45 service revolver. It is a fact of the case, however, and not out of keeping with the remainder of the 'expert' evidence presented, that the one real ballistics expert of the day (in what was still in 1920 a relatively new science) was not called by the prosecution to give evidence in support of their theory. It is also a fact that a written suggestion by the local physician who carried out the autopsy that an expert forensic pathologist should be called in was overruled. From the police in Leicester to the Department of the Director of Public Prosecutions and to the then Attorney-General, there was an apparent consensus of opinion about the calibre of weapon that was used in the killing of Bella Wright. It was a consensus that was to be strongly contested by the defence. As will become evident that was a very necessary line of defence to take, but there was more to it than that. Leading defence counsel Sir Edward Marshall Hall was himself greatly interested and extraordinarily well versed in the use of firearms, having from the age of seven owned and regularly used many different calibre pistols and revolvers as well as sporting guns. He well knew the sort of damage one can expect to inflict with a weapon of a given calibre. It was never his opinion, at the time of the trial or indeed in later years, that Bella Wright could have been killed by a bullet of the calibre indicated by the prosecution. Recent research suggests that his scepticism was well founded.

At the eventual trial of Ronald Light the prosecution could not prove, indeed could barely suggest, any motive for the killing. It was not then as now a necessary part of prosecution to prove motive, but there is little doubt that when a case, especially one of murder, is presented to a jury with no motive seriously suggested, that case is weakened. There was, however, a veiled suggestion by the eminent leading prosecution counsel Sir Gordon Hewart of what the motive might have been, but there was never the slightest indication in that courtroom that the suggestion could have been anything more than sheer speculation.

Why then has this particular murder, usually dubbed the 'case of the green bicycle', so caught the imagination of three generations, not only in Leicestershire but also country-wide?

Why has this case so frequently over the years appeared in forensic case histories, despite the fact that for over seventy years, given an almost total dearth of new information regarding the case or its central characters, writers have seemingly been content with inventing new theories based on old and not always totally factual accounts? Perhaps the answer to that question lies in how the case was laid before the public from the outset.

The death of any young girl is a tragedy for her immediate family and friends, all the more so when death is neither expected or explained, and even among those who merely read of the events surrounding that death there are many who are understandably and perhaps inevitably drawn by their own imaginations and emotions into sharing to some extent the misery of those more directly involved. In this, undoubtedly Leicester's best-known murder case, the pathos surrounding the death of such a young girl was and is still quite evident, but the case had much more than that to commend it to the public imagination and memory. It is from there that the apparent fascination with the case stems, and over the years over thirty writers have put pen to paper in an attempt to satisfy a thirst for the truth.

From the outset the case of the green bicycle has been fraught with red herrings, and in this case especially a black raven. From day three the hue and cry went up for a mystery cyclist who had been seen in company with the girl only minutes before her death, and who had by nightfall, without any proof whatever, been irrevocably linked in the public mind to the young girl's death. The resultant chase took many months and involved the police of many counties in England and Wales. It was a chase that culminated in a discovery which, just as the public memory had begun to fade, once again set the newspaper presses working overtime. No novelist would have thought the circumstances that surrounded this discovery would be credible.

The subsequent trial might easily have been an anti-climax but in the event was as dramatic in a variety of ways as anything seen in those post-war years. The defendant Ronald Light exercised his rights and reserved his defence until the very last moment; the trial was well under way before even an inkling of what that defence might be became evident to those in court. One leading counsel, Sir Gordon Hewart, curtailed his part in the proceedings before the trial was half over under circumstances that have never been fully explained, and to further titillate readers, the contemporary newspaper reports were lavishly supplemented by photographs taken of the courtroom proceedings.

If the very mix of personalities in that courtroom, albeit depleted by the third day, did not promise to put fire into the proceedings, then perhaps one man present could be relied upon to do just that. Leading defence counsel Sir Edward Marshall Hall was in 1920 at the peak of his incomparable and much misunderstood forensic career, and, love him or hate him, the general public, in common with many within his own profession, was quite simply powerless to ignore him. The mere promise of his presence at a major trial throughout the early years of the century was guaranteed to pack any courtroom to the rafters. He came to Leicester with a string of well-publicized successes under his belt, but those who filled the court to see him did so not simply to witness a successful defence, but rather in the hope of seeing the fireworks or the tears that were indicative of Marshall Hall's nature and the very synthesis of his highly individual defences in every capital case in which he appeared.

Even given the presence of Marshall Hall, the outcome of the case was not as expected. Anyone in Leicester in June of 1920 rash enough to wager a fiver on an eventual acquittal would have had to accept very poor odds. Of those people who appear at the time to have been satisfied by the verdict, many are, strangely, to be found on what might be loosely termed the losing side. It is a fact that a surfeit of congratulatory messages on the handling of the case passed between the officers of the local police force and the office of the Director of Public Prosecutions.

Bella Wright, c. 1914

To date there has been published but one full-sized volume on the case. It appeared in 1930, the work of the Rt Revd H. Russell Wakefield, the then Bishop of Birmingham and was predictably enough entitled *The Green Bicycle Case*. Russell Wakefield wrote almost entirely from contemporary newspaper reports, and in places his words are exactly word for word those that appeared on the breakfast tables of the newspaper-reading public in the Leicester of 1919 and 1920. He was admittedly hampered, as indeed many writers in subsequent years have been, by the surprising but simple fact that no trial transcript of this remarkable case, unquestionably Leicester's most celebrated murder trial, exists. There is no trial transcript it appears because no one thought it necessary, or someone thought it for some unexplained reason unwise, to have the original shorthand notes transcribed. It has been suggested that the real reason was that the case did not go to Appeal, a suggestion that would be laughable if it were not so ridiculous. Since 1907, when the Court of Appeal was first established, there have been countless perfectly good and complete trial transcripts taken from the original shorthand notes relating to cases that were not referred to the Court of Appeal, and indeed could hardly be so, the defendant having already been acquitted. Given that for whatever reason the shorthand note of these proceedings was not transcribed, then it ought still to have survived, but it does not appear to have done so.

Russell Wakefield may well have been hampered by the lack of a copy of the whole proceedings at trial, but he was apparently to some extent aided by Det. Supt. Taylor, who was as familiar with the case and its locale as anyone in Leicester at that time. It was he who shepherded Russell Wakefield around the route that Bella Wright took on her last cycle ride; it was he who pointed out the various places of interest connected with the case, most of which are little changed today – a point on which today's writer is hardly less well served than was Russell Wakefield all those years ago. It may also have been Det. Supt. Taylor who gave Russell Wakefield an impression of how efficiently the case had been handled and the suspect tracked down. There seems to be scant evidence of that today.

Whatever the case in mind, if there exists no trial transcript then there is necessarily far less information on which any researcher might base his own enquiries, but in this particular case the lack or loss or destruction of that transcript is compounded by the loss of other vital papers concerning the case. Papers presented by the Treasury to the defence lawyers are no longer extant in the D.P.P. file. Marshall Hall's own papers on the case, along with all his personal and forensic papers, were destroyed a year or so after his death in 1927, in precise accordance with his wishes. Any paperwork on the case which may have been preserved by Sir Gordon Hewart, then Attorney-General, who led for the prosecution, was lost when a deed box belonging to his widow was stolen some time after Viscount Hewart's death in 1943. The deed box has not been recovered. In June 1956 the then Assistant Chief Constable of the Leicestershire and Rutland Constabulary, John R. Webster, wrote to the Director of Public Prosecutions, Theobald Mathew, requesting that 'for the sake of posterity' the D.P.P.'s copy of the Attorney-General's brief should be sent to Leicester for copying 'by the force photographer' in order to complete the police files. The brief was duly supplied to the Leicester force. If that brief was ever returned, and information indicates that it was not, it certainly is no longer extant in the appropriate file. If relevant documentation on the case, once preserved in the capital, seems somewhat depleted then it is no less so in Leicestershire itself. Staff at the Leicestershire Constabulary Archive are unable to locate the original case papers; they may have been 'mislaid' or even destroyed. A similar fate may have befallen the inquest papers pertaining to the death of the victim. Previous and subsequent years are lodged as might be expected in the Leicestershire Record Office, but those for 1919 are not. One might therefore think there to be very few original documents pertaining to the case still extant and available to today's researcher. Fortunately sufficient material does exist, much of it previously untapped, making resort to earlier accounts for anything other than comparison and comment unnecessary.

After the passing of more than seventy years no writer need feel under any obligation save that to relate the truth of the case as presented by his or her own original research. Writing of the case in 1930, Russell Wakefield must have been to an extent disadvantaged by the fact that those whose lives had been most affected by the case were alive and still living, for the most part in and around Leicester. Yet if there was difficulty in Russell Wakefield's position there must also have been tremendous opportunity, for after all the public memory was still comparatively fresh. Events had hardly had time to fade from the minds of those on the fringes of the case, and many who, though not directly or even indirectly involved, must by their own ingenuity have put two and two together and actually come up with four. Many fervent readers of their daily newspapers, national as well as local, must have had a shrewd idea of the circumstances which surrounded the case and its main character, the eventual defendant Ronald Light (incidentally the only real suspect, for the police seem not to have sought anyone else after Light's acquittal). Those contemporary newspaper readers would have put a completely different complexion on the whole proceedings from that which has so often been offered as a fair assessment of the case in later years. Yet if Wakefield took advantage of the opportunity afforded by one of the earliest attempts to write at any length on the case, there is no hint in his book that he ever learned the elusive truth behind the actions and activities of Ronald Light. If he did gain an inkling of that truth then he chose not to share it with his readers.

The green bicycle case surely left more questions unanswered than it originally posed. Questions that were not addressed in Russell Wakefield's book, and which later writers did little to answer, despite some of those answers always being available to those who cared to seek them out. Questions not only concerning motive or the lack of it but relating to the main characters in the case have abounded, and the mystery concerning the past life and character of Ronald Light has certainly been, if not the principal reason for the continued public interest in the case over more than half a century, then at least a major contributory factor to the growth of that interest. That is one mystery on which I am in the course of this book to shed a little long overdue light. However, in writing these chapters I feel that it is inevitable that I shall fuel other mysteries and awaken other ghosts that have for more than seventy years lain undisturbed.

CHAPTER I

Early Days

BELLA WRIGHT

High Summer 1919, and the younger men of rural Leicestershire, volunteers and conscripts alike, were enjoying their homecoming from the trenches of France to the quieter and infinitely more pleasant fields that some seventy odd years ago skirted the east of the city of Leicester. During their absence the economic and political structure of Britain and indeed the whole of Europe had altered almost beyond recognition. Homes and jobs were scarce: those returning to take up the work that they had left off when the call to arms came were frequently sadly disappointed; and those in work were not always much better off. High prices and low pay increased the unrest of a nation that had looked forward to the end of hostilities and a resumption of a normal life. Now, as peace returned, it seemed to many that the enemy was once again the establishment. Men felt once again the need to unite and the so-called triple alliance of pre-war years was taken down and dusted off from the shelf where it had been laid, while a more dangerous common enemy had been defeated. Miners up and down the country faced the prospect of Lloyd George's government handing back the mines to their owners, and the subsequent increase in working hours and cuts in pay. There were many men, not all of them from the poorest classes, who by the summer of 1919 found themselves idle and disillusioned. Their thoughts and temptations, if not entirely coloured by their service overseas, for many took on a new and sinister significance, and the time that they found on their hands afforded opportunity to turn those thoughts into reality.

Bad as times were for those that worked on the land rather than under it, at least they had some small compensation of a pleasant and familiar landscape upon which to gaze. The landscape to the east of Leicester even now is hardly changed; to some of those men returning from war torn France it must have seemed as though they had been away but a week or two. The memory of that landscape and their loved ones back home in those quiet villages, carried with them like a talisman through those years of sacrifice and deprivation in the turmoil of warfare, had seen them through. They returned to those softly undulating fields and warm summer evenings spent watching the sunset redden the grass and the hedgerows, and remembered those Flanders poppies that had been but another reminder of better days before the outbreak of hostilities. The glorious red drifts that brightened the fields and lanes around familiar Leicestershire villages in those days do so even now.

In the absence of the younger men their work had been done by those who were too old or infirm to serve the colours in any military capacity, but who had nevertheless made a not inconsiderable contribution to the war effort. Such a man was Kenus Emblin Wright. A farm labourer all his life, he had been employed as a cowman for the previous three years by two local landowners. The father of seven children, four boys and three girls, he had lived since April of 1919 with his family in a cottage in the village of Stoughton (locals say Stoat'n), two or three miles to the east of Leicester. Kenus Wright was forty-eight years of age at the outbreak of the Great War, and by 1919 he must surely have believed along with many of his contemporaries that 'the war to end all wars' being over, he could look forward to happier times. How could he know on that summer Saturday of 5 July that for him and his family, and especially for his wife, life would never be quite the same again; that the closing six months of

1919 and most of the following year would represent the saddest and probably the most bewildering and apparently frightening time of their lives? When finally the law had ground its inevitable course, and that in itself would take a little over twelve months in all, no doubt Kenus Wright would ask himself 'Why? Where was the reason for it all?', and where was that justice of which the English so proudly boast? For by nightfall on that July day he would have lost his eldest daughter, and over twelve months later he would still not have been given a satisfactory explanation of how she met her death. Nor would he ever receive any such explanation. But in common with many of those living in his own and neighbouring villages, in the city of Leicester itself, and indeed along with interested parties all over the country, he would form his own opinions about what had occurred in that short time between his daughter's departure from his sister's home and the finding of her body in a quiet lane. Time did nothing to change those opinions or the sense of grievance that was felt by Kenus, his family and their close friends. That the full process of the law had been invoked was of no consequence to them and of even less consolation. The circumstances of Kenus Wright's daughter's death remained as a source of sadness for her family. It has subsequently been a source of fascination and conjecture for three generations.

*   *   *

In July 1919 Annie Bella Wright was twenty-one years of age; had she lived she would have celebrated her twenty-second birthday on the fourteenth of the month. The eldest of the Wright children by two years, Bella, as she was always known to family and friends alike, had been born in Jubilee year, 1897. The birth was registered by her mother Mary Ann Wright at Melton Mowbray, and the place of birth was entered as Somerby. Many people living in the area, however, now believe Bella was born at Newbold, another small village quite near to Somerby, in a cottage now long since demolished – one of three which once stood on a hillside, where now only a heap of rubble and part of the original foundation remain. That belief may be correct, the family certainly living for six years at Newbold, but not apparently immediately after Bella's birth. It seems probable that this may have been at the home of a relative. In any event it would appear that Bella's parents settled at Somerby very soon after the birth, which probably accounts for the fact that it was registered three weeks or so later in August as being at Somerby. Of course the actual place of birth ought properly to have been registered, but if there was confusion it may be explained in that Bella's mother was very young and she may have misunderstood the questions put to her by the then registrar, John Jackson. It is quite understandable, and especially so in those days, that a young countrywoman registering the birth of her first child at the same office she herself had attended for her marriage a little over four months earlier, might feel some uneasiness and apprehension in doing so; which may in turn have led to some confusion. Mary Ann Beaver, the daughter of John William Beaver, a farm labourer of Pickwell, had in March 1897 married Kenus Wright, the son of Philip Wright, another farm labourer from Somerby. At the time of the marriage Kenus's age was given as twenty-nine and Mary's as nineteen, though their gravestone at Markfield would seem to indicate that at the time of their marriage Kenus was in fact thirty-one years of age and Mary Ann was just seventeen. Kenus and his growing family were to have many homes over the years, all located in and around Leicester, but for about eighteen months he, Mary and their first-born daughter Annie Bella resided in Somerby, moving on to nearby Pickwell where they lived for just a year. Their second move took them to neighbouring Newbold where they would remain for about six years.

Bella was seven years old on the day that she began her education at Somerby school in

Somerby School, Leicestershire

February 1904. On that same day her five-year-old sister Louie also attended for the first time, which would seem to indicate that Bella was somewhat late in starting her education, but that was not all that unusual for rural areas in those days. Another factor may have been that Kenus Wright was himself unable to write and may have placed his daughter's education low on his list of priorities. Another complication may have been that by 1904 more children had been born to Mary Wright, and she may have been apprehensive of sending such a young child as Bella to school alone along quiet country lanes. It may be that she kept her eldest daughter at home until her second-born was of an age to accompany her elder sister to the nearest school. Certainly no record of previous education seems to exist, for when the two children were entered at Somerby school, any previous attendance at other schools was given as 'nil'.

Although the family was living within the catchment area of Somerby school there was still a good walk to and from school each day, especially for two such young children. This is known because the mother of another child at the school, young Arthur Hayes, who entered the school just a month or so later than the two sisters, took a kindly interest in the farm labourer's daughters and saw to it that they had some tea each school day before starting the long walk home.

In November 1906, when Bella was a little over nine years old, the family once again moved house. The school record gives the somewhat ambiguous entry in the withdrawals column: 'Gone to Knossington'. Mary Wright said in later years that at that time, and indeed in 1910 when Bella finished her schooling, the family were living at Owston, which would seem to indicate that both girls probably moved from Somerby school to complete their education at a school in or near Knossington.

In common with so many girls of those days who had received only an elementary education, when in 1910 the time to leave school approached, Bella had little choice before her. She was thirteen years of age, and might find work on a local farm or in domestic service in one of the towns; neither alternative would be well paid and both necessitated hard work and long hours. In 1910 factory work was not the lucrative alternative for women that it would become during the years of the Great War; indeed, the coming of war would change the working patterns for women forever. Bella's first job was with a Mr Kerr of Keythorne Lodge at Tugby, another village not too far from her home. It seems probable that the work was for the most part of a domestic nature. In all events, Bella must have been reasonably happy there because she stayed for three years, leaving only (in her mother's words) 'to better herself'. Her next move seems to have been something of a mistake, for she disliked the work with Mr Parker of Stocking farm, Belgrave and stayed for only two months. Obviously feeling the need for a complete change, Bella's next place of employment was in the Spinney Hill district of Leicester, where she was employed as a shop assistant in Saint's Dairy. But again she was to stay there for only a few months. Once more Bella went into service, this time as a maid in the home of a local boot manufacturer, John Compton Rawson, at No. 5 Seymour Street, Leicester. Bella had probably found working in Leicester itself convenient because it gave her the opportunity to visit her family on her days off. She was by all accounts reasonably well paid for this type of employment, parlourmaids in those days earning something less than a pound a week, and the Rawsons were pleased enough with Bella's services, finding her a hard-working girl who was always eager to help out around the house. Indeed, as late as 1970, following the publishing of

Pupils of Somerby School with their teacher Miss Mantle c. 1905. Bella Wright and her younger sister Louie (left) circled

St Mary's Mill. A recent photograph showing Bella's last place of employment

an article on the green bicycle case, the daughter of the house, who remembered Bella as a girl of about her own age, felt interested enough to telephone a Leicester newspaper to say how well she remembered Bella. After eighteen months Bella felt it was time for another change, to domestic service with a Mrs Allen of Hinckley Road, Leicester.

It may have been on trips into the city from Mrs Allen's home or on trips to her parents' home from Seymour Street that Bella first formed the idea that she would be better paid if she gave up her domestic work and found employment in one of the numerous local factories which she passed on her cycle rides. By the early war years, women, who before the outbreak of war had been happy enough to work in a domestic capacity, were streaming into the factories of the industrial areas up and down the country, taking up the work previously carried out by the thousands of men who had gone to the front, though Leicester with its hosiery factories had always had fewer female domestic servants than many other towns of comparable size. Bella was one of an estimated 400,000 women who at that time took up the more lucrative factory work. Perhaps some of the best paid were those girls and women who worked in the dangerous munitions factories, 'Lloyd George's canaries' as they became known – because of the discoloration of their skin that they suffered as a result of contact with TNT. The shift in employment patterns also gave women the chance to feel that they were contributing to the war effort and supporting their menfolk. Bella's trips to the city from the Hinckley Road area would have taken her past the mills and warehouses which crowded the Old River Soar area of Leicester, and she may have seen the groups of young factory girls making their way home to the city over the bridges and locks that cross this stretch of the Old River Soar, giving it the local name of Twelve Bridges. Here the river had earlier been divided, forming a navigable canalized section which, together with the nearby railway, served the wharfs, warehouses and mills that in the early part of the century still flourished to the west of the city centre. Perhaps Bella envied the mill girls their greater freedom and their opportunities to meet both young men and women of their own age which, tied as she was by domestic service, she would have found much more difficult. Whatever her reason, Bella took her leave of Mrs Allen and the Hinckley Road to begin new and totally different employment as a machinist in the Havelock Shoe Works of Messrs Coleman & Lewitt, which was situated in Havelock Street, Leicester. There she was to stay for about twelve months leaving, in her mother's words, 'of her own accord'. For some time after this Bella was employed in lighter work at the factory of B. Russell & Sons, fancy hosiery and glove manufacturers of Eastern Boulevard, Leicester.

Many references state that Bella began working at her final place of employment in May 1917, but that seems to be simple reiteration of an early mistake in a local newspaper report of her death. Mary Wright actually told the police at the time of Bella's death that her daughter had begun working there as late as February 1919. The work was not the dangerous work of the 'canaries', but we may suppose that it was rather heavier and dirtier work than had been required of her in the hosiery trade. Throughout those last few months of her short life Bella was employed on a five day week as a rubber hand with W. & A. Bates at their St Mary's Mill factory, in the manufacture of pneumatic tyres. Although the registered offices of the company were on Narborough Road, St Mary's Mill was actually situated to the east of the London and North Eastern railway line, backing on to the canalized section of the River Soar, near to where it passed the gas works.

Bella appears to have been a reasonably sensible girl. Not the sort to act without thinking, she seems to have changed her place of work a little frequently but for all the more usual reasons, to better herself or because the work was unsuitable. There has never been the slightest suggestion that on any occasion Bella was required to leave by any of her several employers; always the decision was her own. Some have said that she was rather reserved in her manner, quite happy to keep herself to herself, which may indicate a capability to keep her own counsel, not finding it necessary to confide her every thought and activity to her friends and relatives. She may have been, despite her limited formal education, very much her own woman, and probably she had learned, as do many elder children, not to lean too much upon her parents, who with a large family probably had more than enough to do to cope well financially. Rather, Bella may have learned early to make her own decisions. Sadly one such decision may indirectly have ended in her death. In total contrast to all other reports one writer in recent years referred to her as chatty, a description which though not particularly apt does point to what may have been a more outgoing personality than had hitherto been suggested. The precise nature of Bella Wright must remain something of a mystery. While it does seem apparent that she could on occasions keep her own counsel, she was certainly not secretive or unfriendly and appears to have been quite ready to join in the fun of those times. There can be little doubt that she was popular with her workmates.

On 28 June 1919, only a week before her death, Bella, along with a party of her workmates from St Mary's Mill, had enjoyed what was referred to as a 'shops outing', probably organized at least in part at the expense of their employers W. & A. Bates. The party had been transported by wagonettes to a popular local haunt, Foxton Locks on the Grand Union Canal, which lie just off the A6 between Kibworth and Market Harborough. Bella had joined the party at ten o'clock on that Saturday morning at Oadby. The party having clearly enjoyed the day, and all feeling a little merry, arrived back in Oadby at ten in the evening. Bella, no less merry than the rest, alighted here, a mile or two from her home at Stoughton. As Bella climbed down from the wagonette one of the other occupants shouted to two brothers, Norman and William Bertie

Wood, who were standing nearby at the crossroads of the London Road and Stoughton Lane, and asked one of the two to see Bella home. Norman, a twenty-nine-year-old soldier, stayed put but William, a twenty-five-year-old unemployed blacksmith, who at that time filled his days as a jobbing gardener, duly obliged and accompanied Bella as far as the church of St Mary and All Saints in the village of Stoughton, just a short walk from her home. That young man may very well have regretted his chivalrous deed when he read only a few days later that the police wished to interview a young man who had been seen in the company of Bella Wright on that particular evening, and whose description he fitted reasonably well. William Wood told his story to the local police on 16 July and was immediately eliminated from their enquiries. He had not previously met Bella and he had not seen her after that Saturday evening; she had not told him her name and on that short walk as far as Stoughton church he had passed several people that he knew and knew him, and was able to give their names to the police. The incident, however, did little for his peace of mind or that of his family. Following a report of his association with Bella Wright, his mother wrote a letter to the press, thus ensuring that a short article detailing the events of that evening appeared in a local newspaper on the day that the inquest into Bella's death was first reopened. Mrs Wood's letter pointed out quite clearly that her son who was not named in the article, had already been in touch with the local police force and was in no way connected with Bella's death, merely having escorted her home on that one occasion and then only because he had been requested to do so by Bella's friends.

Two sisters, Sally and Gertrude Ward, were especially good friends to Bella. Sally was employed alongside Bella at St Mary's Mill, while Gertrude was employed elsewhere in the factory. Sally, the older of the two, was about Bella's age and Gertrude was younger. The two sisters were not only workmates to Bella, as their brother Archibald had already been introduced to Bella by her brother Philip. By July 1919 Bella, though not exactly engaged to Archie, had what has been described as an unofficial understanding with him that they would eventually marry. They had indicated to their friends that they were waiting for the day when Archie would be demobbed, which they expected would be sometime during August 1920. Their friends looked on them as a courting couple, as had villagers at Stoughton when before his Navy service and probably because he had had a minor tiff with his own parents, Archie had stayed for a short time with Bella and her family. Archie had joined the Navy in May 1919 and was seeing his short naval service out as an assistant stoker aboard the somewhat antiquated HMS *Diadem*, an old protected cruiser which since December 1914 had been a training ship for naval stokers. On that fateful Saturday of 5 July 1919 *Diadem*, with Archie Ward aboard, was at her permanent mooring at Portsmouth. Archie Ward, probably as a result of the events in Leicestershire following Bella's death, received his demobilization papers in June 1920, a few weeks earlier than he had anticipated.

Quite what Archie Ward intended to do when he finally received his demobilization papers is not known, but there is some indication that he had for a very short time also been employed at Bates's Rubber Mill. The increase in demand for pneumatic tyres could surely be expected to keep pace with the increasing popularity of the motor car, and with so many men returning to their wives after being parted for something like four years it is only reasonable to suppose that a baby boom would create a need for experienced hands returning from active service to take over in the factory, while their wives and girlfriends returned to domesticity. For many women, though, the die was cast and they would never again see themselves as simply wives and mothers. Quite what sort of life Bella would have chosen to lead we cannot know, and we can only speculate whether or not she and Archie Ward would in the end have married. One official document from 1919 puts Archie's age in that year as eighteen, some three to four years Bella's junior, a fact which seems to be borne out by contemporary photographs of him. But despite their apparent age difference the pair probably had much in common. They came from the same area of Leicestershire and from similar backgrounds, both their fathers being farm labourers, and Archie himself had been employed by Joe Chapman, in Archie's words 'a proprietor of threshing machines at Enderby', before entering the Navy in the previous May.

We can only speculate about what future, together or separately, there may have been for Bella and for Archie. There is only one certainty, that any choices which lay before Bella were to be rudely snatched from her on that fateful July evening in 1919.

CHAPTER 2

Fateful Meeting

During the week ending 5 July 1919 Bella was employed on what has usually been referred to as the night shift at St Mary's Mill. The shift would be better described as a late shift, beginning as it did at 2 p.m. and ending at 10 p.m. After her shift on Friday, the last of the week, she had still to cycle through Leicester and out to her home to the east of the city, for by then the last of the Wright family moves which need concern us had taken place and Kenus and Mary Wright together with their remaining children were living at Stoughton in a small cottage attached to a schoolroom. The entire building, externally little altered, is still in existence today and has been converted to form just one house. It seems that by that time Bella's younger sister Louie was no longer living at home. Both Kenus and his son Philip, aged seventeen in 1919, were employed by Mr Key who farmed at Stoughton, Kenus as a cowman and Philip as a wagoner.

To many, Bella's ride home of three or so miles would have been a tedious journey after a full shift at the factory in conditions which could be hot and dirty and, for a young girl born and bred in the countryside, particularly noisy. It may be that Bella enjoyed the ride home for, in company with many girls of her generation and perhaps through necessity, she had become an

Kenus and Mary Wright, Bella's parents: a photograph
taken at the time of Ronald Light's trial

enthusiastic cyclist. The pneumatic tyre had made the whole thing so much more enjoyable, despite the fact that the condition of country roads in those days seems to have ensured that regular punctures were the expected accompaniment to every cyclist's life. The opportunity to purchase cost price tyres from her employer probably did much to nurture Bella's interest in cycling, without which her life would have been much more restricted – though it ought to be mentioned that after her death it was pointed out by her mother that she only ever cycled within a few miles of home.

At this point in our story it may be of value to familiarize ourselves with the locality in which Bella Wright lived and died. To the east of the city of Leicester lies a segment of countryside bounded to the north by the present day A47 trunk road, to the south by the A6 and to the east by the B6047. Mainly rural to this day, the most significant change has been in the establishment of the Leicester East Aerodrome which is situated directly on the old route from Stoughton to Gaulby. The countryside to the east of Leicester is of sleepy undulating pastures punctuated by the rising spires of village churches, a peaceful corner of the English Midlands. In 1919 there were practically no ploughed fields to be seen largely because that area enjoyed a reputation as good hunting country and for many years had attracted many enthusiastic huntsmen, among them Edward VII when still the Prince of Wales, who probably best remembered the place for the tumble he once took while in the hunting field. The farming communities in the area were chiefly occupied in the rearing of beef cattle, though there were some dairy herds.

Having arrived home very late on the evening of Friday 4 July Bella retired to bed, and enjoyed her customary lie-in on Saturday morning. By about half past two on Saturday afternoon she was up and about again, and spent the afternoon in writing letters. Her mother recalled that she wrote three. One of them was addressed to Archie Ward, and would reach his ship after he had been called back to Leicester by the local police. The letter was sent on to him at the Ward family home causing great upset, arriving as it did several days after Bella's death. When her letters were finished, Bella sat down to eat tea after which she said to her mother: 'Mum, I am going to Evington to post these letters and have a run round on my bike.' Evington was the nearest post office and is a short ride back in the general direction of Leicester so there can be no doubt that Bella was hoping to catch the evening post. There was some talk at the time that Bella's eldest brother Philip accompanied her on that trip, but as his statement to the police shows, although Bella did ask him if he intended to go for a ride that night, he told her he did not. She replied that she thought she would because she had 'been down in Leicester all the week' which he took to mean that she had been working in Leicester all the week. As Bella reached Evington church she met Mrs Kathleen Power, who was employed at the post office and was making her evening round of postal deliveries. That meeting saved Bella the trouble of going on to the post office: from Mrs Power she was able to purchase some stamps, and Mrs Power took the stamped letters from Bella for posting. From Evington Bella retraced her route back to the cottage in Stoughton, apparently popping into the cottage for a short time, but it seems that she did not see or at least was not seen by her mother who later stated that she last saw Bella alive when she left to post her letters.

By about 6.30 Bella left the cottage for the last time, riding up through the village and past Stoughton church in the general direction of her uncle George Measures' cottage in the village of Gaulby, some three miles further to the east. She took a route that today would be impossible, part of the road being fenced off where it crosses Leicester East Aerodrome. Somewhere along her route, for they were together by the time they reached George's home, Bella met another cyclist, riding a green bicycle, a man of about thirty-five who would

Bella, her parents and siblings occupied the smaller of these two cottages, which now form one dwelling

feature to a greater extent than would Bella herself in what to this day is known as the green bicycle case: as so often happens in such cases, the young victim was nearly forgotten in the hunt for the person responsible for her death. That man, Ronald Light, when eventually charged with her murder, would say that they met where the road from Stoughton crosses the road to Houghton on the Hill, a mile or so to the north. He would say that he had approached the junction from Great Glen, to the south, and that when he first saw Bella she was bending over her machine inspecting it. He said she asked if he had a spanner but he carried no tools with him, and although he did detect a little play in the free-wheeling system of her bicycle he could do nothing to correct it. They may or may not have met on this road, we have only the word of Ronald Light for that, but they certainly rode along it, and at least George Measures was satisfied in his own mind that his niece had travelled to Gaulby by this route because she arrived at his cottage carrying an armful of gorse which grew in abundance along that particular stretch of road. Wherever they had met, apparently they cycled on more or less together, not as it turned out completely unnoticed, until they came to Gaulby. Bella, as had presumably always been her intention went into her uncle and aunt's cottage, her cyclist companion of whatever acquaintance waited around outside. He would later state that he hung about the village because before Bella entered her uncle's cottage she had said to him that she would only be ten minutes, and he took that as an invitation to wait for her to leave. He would also claim that he spent some of the time during which Bella was inside the cottage, which clearly extended to more than an hour all told, in trying to repair a puncture to his bicycle tyre. From this point the versions of what really happened begin to diversify.

* * *

Bella's uncle, George William Measures, was a well-known figure in the locality, not only because he sported a large and bushy beard and was employed as a local roadman by Billesdon R.D.C., but sadly because he had lost his right leg below the knee and walked with the aid of a walking stick and a peg leg. George was married to one of Kenus Wright's sisters. On that July Saturday George, despite his wife being out for the afternoon, was not alone. One of their daughters, Margaret Louisa, and their son-in-law James Evans, together with their two children, one a babe in arms, were down visiting from their home at 6 Grove Terrace, Leslie Avenue, Maltby, near Rotherham, where James Evans was employed as a miner at nearby Maltby Main Colliery. Apparently James Evans, who was twenty-two, had met with a minor accident to his foot and probably for that reason only was on that particular day down in Leicestershire. It was a tremendously lucky break for the local police force that not only was James Evans a particularly observant man, but more importantly was a keen cyclist with an interest in the mechanics and design of the bicycle. His own enthusiasm for cycling is demonstrated by the fact that, despite his injured foot, he had brought his own cycle down to Gaulby for the duration of his stay, which in the event turned out to be longer than he had expected.

Precisely how long Bella stayed with her family in the cottage is not known, but it seems a fair estimate to say that she arrived some time around 7.15 p.m. and finally passed out of sight of her family at the earliest a few minutes before nine o'clock. It may, though it seems unlikely, have been as late as nine. She had been inside the cottage for only a short time when George went to the door to speak to a carrier by the name of Charles Palmer of Illston on the Hill, who had called at the house together with his wife Elizabeth to deliver groceries. As George dealt with the Palmers he looked out of the doorway of the cottage to his right, where about forty or fifty yards away, slightly uphill and near to Gaulby church, he noticed a stranger standing beside a green bicycle, a man whom he would later identify as Ronald Light. Given that strangers to the village were not too numerous, he enquired of Palmer if the man was with him and received a negative reply. In his mind he linked the man's presence with the arrival of his niece, who had arrived unexpectedly and who did not seem to have been in the habit of frequently visiting her uncle and aunt. Bella had not been to the cottage since a fortnight after the previous Easter, which, since Easter Sunday fell on 20 April in 1919, means that her last visit to the cottage had been during the first week of May. On that occasion she had taken along Archie Ward, and they had had tea with her aunt and uncle, a visit that perhaps was precipitated by Archie's impending departure for Portsmouth to join HMS Diadem. Perhaps Bella's visit on that particular July evening was in order to see her cousin Margaret and her husband and children. Not since Bella was fourteen had the two girls met, while she had never met James Evans and had probably not seen the Evans's youngest child. George seems to have taken an instant dislike to the stranger who waited in the lane outside, perhaps partly because the village was a quiet place and strangers were distrusted. George Measures went back inside his cottage and informed Bella of the man's presence, and of the fact that he was unknown to the carrier Palmer. Bella told her relatives that he might be a man who had overtaken her on the road and had said that he had come up from Great Glen. Once again, at about eight o'clock, George Measures went to his door and checked to see if the man was still outside. Bella was then on the verge of leaving, but when her uncle told her that the man was there she sat down again, saying: 'Well, I'll sit down for a few minutes and perhaps he will be gone.' There must also have been questions about who the man was and how well, if at all, Bella knew him, for her uncle and Margaret Evans would say that when George Measures said to his niece: 'You must know something about him, I know,' Bella simply replied that he was a perfect stranger to her and that they had met for the first time on the ride to the cottage. He had asked, she said, directions to a village she had never heard of and then had ridden along with her until she reached Gaulby. Apparently there was some less than gentle chiding because the stranger looked to be about thirty-five to forty years old and in fact George, obviously not a man to mince his words, told his niece that the cyclist looked old enough to be her father. Bella only laughed and did not seem to exhibit any nervousness as far as the cyclist was concerned. Whether or not her uncle had any idea of the informal arrangement that Bella had with young Archie Ward, if he had liked young Archie he would probably not have wished to see another man taking up with his niece, and Bella herself would not have wished them to think that that was even a possibility; but it would seem that of them all it was Bella herself who was the least disturbed by the man's presence. During her visit she had sat cuddling her cousin's baby and had chatted to James Evans about her work at the Rubber Mill and the fact that she could get cost price cycle tyres. She also talked of some repairs that had been done to her own bicycle, a point which as will be seen later may have been of considerable significance. Bella apparently stayed at the cottage longer than she had intended, no doubt her original intention being to get back home before nightfall. She would have been well aware of the state of the country roads on her route back and of the dangers to cyclists that unseen potholes might represent, cycle lamps leaving a lot to be desired; she would almost certainly have wanted to complete the greater part of her journey before the light began to fail significantly. That she would not have left the cottage too late is apparent from an interview, given many years later to a local newspaper by one of Bella's brothers, who said that she invariably used to get home before nine o'clock whenever she went out for the evening. We can rest assured that this was probably no exaggeration; in 1919 girls of Bella's age and already earning their own living still abided by their father's decisions on such matters, at least as long as they stayed under their father's roof. George later said that it was about 8.30 p.m. when Bella first got ready to leave. It may have been at that point when it was noticed the cyclist had walked down and was standing near to the gate. If Bella had left her uncle's cottage at 8.30 p.m. she could have arrived home easily around her usual time, assuming that she had gone straight home. However, when told that the man was still outside, Bella had sat down again, and it was some minutes to 9 p.m. before she made a final move to leave the cottage, and even then her departure was far from immediate. Apparently the cyclist did for some time move away from the cottage because James said to Bella: 'I think the man is gone,' and she replied: 'I'll be getting off.' It became patently clear, however, to Bella and her family as they left the cottage that the man had not gone, and he came up to the group and addressed Bella in words, the exact form of which would be hotly disputed at the subsequent trial of Ronald Light. The gist of what he said was that he thought he had missed her and that she had gone the other way, which would seem to indicate that he was not a complete stranger in those parts, and may have known where Bella would be headed when she left the cottage. All those present at the time swore that Bella made no reply, a point on which Margaret Evans would elaborate with what can only be referred to as feminine intuition. However, the indications of those brief snippets of conversation from the stranger and Bella's response to them were not lost on James either, yet strangely, George would in the end take a slightly different position from his daughter and her husband. At this point Bella went back into the cottage to get a spanner and James engaged the stranger, or it may have been the other way round, in conversation. They seem to have chatted for a few minutes and apparently discussed the man's rather distinctive bicycle and the repairs which he had just had done to it. Bella had still not left the cottage at 8.45 p.m. when George's younger daughter, twelve-year-old Agnes Olive returned home, for she told the police that Bella and the cyclist spoke together in a low tone and smiled at each other. Then she heard him say, apparently it would seem to James: 'This is a rather heavy machine.' Presumably at this point the man was in the process of turning his cycle around, for both he and Bella finally left the cottage walking uphill towards the church and pushing their bicycles. That was not before George had given Bella a word of warning, presumably out of earshot of the stranger. As he later repeated to the police he didn't like the look of the man and he told his niece so, advising her to make haste and hurry back home. Her reply is nothing if not puzzling for a girl who had shown no fear of the man while she waited in the cottage: 'I'll try and give him the slip. I can easily get in front of him on my bicycle.'

To reach Stoughton, Bella might have turned either to her left or to her right as she left the cottage, and unless her companion had been standing in the immediate vicinity of the cottage and keeping a sharp look out he would not necessarily have been able to observe anyone leaving the building, for in either direction the road curved away from the cottage, the view being restricted by the sweep of the road and the hedges bordering it. It is fair to say that the cyclist could have been waiting quite close by and still have missed her. Clearly he had been prepared to take that risk, for he had indeed waited throughout the time Bella was with her family, in all something well over an hour and presumably when Bella finally decided to leave he must have been, for that moment anyway, out of sight of the cottage window. James Evans would later be called upon to give a description of both the man and his machine, and of the latter he would be most informative. It was a B.S.A. machine, the frame of which was green in colour, not all that rare a colour for a bicycle in those times, but nowhere near as common as the more familiar black machines. James also noticed that the bicycle had a back pedalling brake operated from the crank, which was of an unusual pattern, while the saddle was made by Brooke's of Birmingham. Among various other things, he saw that the three speed control had recently been repaired with a length of new cable, though it is possible that this particular repair was actually pointed out to him by the rider. If at that time any evidence of a puncture or its recent repair was visible, the observant Mr Evans failed to notice it, but it was evident to him that the machine was of a sophisticated design, one which he coveted, the odd thing being that for some reason Bella seemed to think that she could easily outrun the man on her own cycle, certainly an inferior machine, the condition of which will be discussed in a later chapter.

Whatever her feelings may have been toward riding back with the cyclist, Bella was in no position by the time they met at the door of the cottage to avoid it without causing more embarrassment to either herself, the man on the green bicycle, or indeed her family. If she had really sensed any danger in making the trip in his company surely any embarrassment would have been justified, and doubtless she would have overcome that feeling. After all she could easily have made some excuse not to leave at that time, for example saying that she had decided to stay the night at her uncle's cottage. No such excuse was made and probably no such excuse was contemplated. George would say later that if Bella had felt it necessary she could have been escorted home by James, who had his bicycle with him at the cottage. That may have been so, but James would say that he did not offer to escort Bella home. By all accounts she said farewell to her family apparently in good spirits, and the couple set off together on what appeared to be friendly terms, pushing their cycles up the short hill until they came to more level ground. Doubtless her family were left outside the cottage with somewhat mixed feelings, but it was Bella's cousin with that much maligned female intuition who felt most strongly about the unknown cycling companion. Margaret Evans watched as Bella walked away from the cottage, out of her sight and out of her life for ever. It is regrettable that of the three adults left at the cottage as Bella left, Margaret would be the only one not to appear in the witness box at the subsequent hearings. Had she had that opportunity, and had she given her version of events in her own words, then the green bicycle case may not have become quite so much of a mystery. As it is, simply because Margaret did not give evidence, her deposition has been totally ignored and has never received the interest that it so obviously deserves. Her instincts concerning the stranger who waited for her cousin in Gaulby were entirely correct in one particular and may well have been not entirely inaccurate in all other respects.

CHAPTER 3

The *Via Devana*

The events which took place between the time when Bella and her cyclist companion left the home of George Measures and the discovery later that evening of her body on the old Roman road, known locally as the *Via Devana* have undoubtedly over the years put some of the mystery into the green bicycle case. Was the death of Bella Wright accidental? Did the person responsible even know that he or she had caused a death? Was Bella murdered? Was it in fact not a case of murder but of manslaughter? This last possibility was not an option ever seriously considered by the police or the office and representative of the D.P.P. Each possibility has its adherents and the theories of precisely how Bella met her death are legion; I will say a little more of them and other possibilities in a later chapter. It will suffice for the moment to say that at the time of Bella's death in July 1919 and for some time afterwards the great mystery was not how she had met her death, but rather, who was the man on the green bicycle? Who that man might be was the talk of not merely Leicester but of the whole country.

In the few years from 1919 through to 1923 there was hardly a time when the national newspapers were not reporting some sensational murder case or other. It was criminographically an extraordinary decade, undoubtedly in some degrees at least attributable to the brutality of war that a whole generation had experienced for the first time. Few cases, however, caught the imagination of the general public in quite the way that the green bicycle case seems to have done. Perhaps the Thompson/Bywaters case of 1922 would in the long term have a greater impact on both the general public and amateur criminologists alike, but that is mainly because Edith Thompson was executed along with her lover Frederick Bywaters in what these days is usually seen as a moral if not in a legal sense a miscarriage of justice. Without a doubt Edith Thompson paid the price for her infidelity, and not for her involvement in the actually killing of her husband. But for a case which stirred the imagination, for something that brought the thrill of the chase and eventual capture to the reader, look no further than the death of Bella Wright in 1919. Not since 1910 and the flight of Hawley Harvey Crippen with his paramour Ethel le Neve, when the newspaper-reading public waited with bated breath to see if Inspector Dew aboard the *Laurentic* would outrun the *Montrose*, thus enabling the officer to arrest Crippen and his alleged accomplice before they reached the comparative safety of the Canadian coast and possible freedom, had there been anything to compare with the green bicycle case. At quite an early stage there were those in Leicester who believed they knew the identity of the man on the green bicycle – later and in one case – repeatedly, they would say that they had always had their suspicions but nothing would be confirmed and certainly the general public would remain in suspense for several months to come. There have been other mysteries and suspicions connected with Ronald Light who must be termed the main character in the case. The man on the green bicycle assumed that role almost from the outset. I shall return later to those mysteries and suspicions which in essence were well founded. However, to all intents and purposes when people have spoken of the 'mystery' of the green bicycle case, they are generally referring to the time for which we have had to date no definite account of events, no absolute proof of what took place, no eye-witness accounts, quite simply nothing but the body of Bella Wright and the circumstances in which she was found to guide us. From the time that Ronald Light and Bella walked away from George Measures' cottage until the time when her body was found by a local farmer driving cattle along the *Via Devana*, nothing that could be classed as evidence has ever been brought to public attention; not one single witness was found who could say that the couple were together at any point after they walked out of sight of Bella's family, which contrasts strangely with the number of witnesses who saw them together on their way into the village. With the exception of Light's own admissions, given some would insist belatedly, at the subsequent trial, and the discoveries of one policeman at the scene, together with the exhibits stumbled upon in the following year, there has to date been no clue about the crucial time when Bella Wright met her death. All has been theory; all evidence offered at trial was absolutely circumstantial.

Quite why Ronald Light thought it worth waiting for Bella has always been a matter for speculation. She was not an unattractive girl, variously described in accounts of the case over the years as either plain or pretty or countrified, which if nothing else goes to prove that amateur criminologists have as diverse a taste in women as any other section of British manhood, since all those varying descriptions are apparently based on just two published and much copied photographs. Bella was quite definitely dark haired, a brunette with a pleasing, open countenance, one might say altogether an honest looking type of face. She was not a great beauty nor, by the standards of the day, particularly slim. Bella would later be described by the police surgeon who carried out the autopsy as well nourished. If she had one outstanding attribute it was most definitely her complexion and skin colouring, which was described by the same medical man as 'peculiarly fair and white'. Bella had spent the last two or so years of her life working in various factories, but she still took any opportunity that she had to get out in the open air and enjoyed the rides to and from her work. She was never happier than when cycling along the local and familiar Leicestershire lanes, cycling said by her family to be at the time her chief hobby. It was more fashionable then to wear a hat, and the two photographs of Bella Wright which have passed into the public domain show her wearing hats with large brims; if she had a preference for that type of hat it might explain, at least in part, her fine complexion. As to Bella's character and attitude to life, that is more difficult to access. At the time of her death she was described as being rather quiet and reserved; more recently she has been blessed with the epitaph 'a bit of a flirt'. It may be supposed that in defence counsel's words at the subsequent trial, 'the sex attraction' was as strong as it may be in the mind of Ronald Light as he waited in Gaulby for over an hour, but there may just as easily have been an altogether more mundane reason why that particular man should have considered it worthwhile to wait so long. Nevertheless, that 'sex attraction' would seem to be the most likely explanation of why a man, particularly that man, should wait so long for a young girl to reappear, especially when we consider that he also said he was expected home for a mid-evening meal, that he had also had a puncture which he had unsuccessfully tried to repair and caused him trouble all the way back to his home, where he eventually arrived much later than expected. If indeed he did have a genuine puncture, and there was no other witness to that possibility, not even the observant James Evans, he must have realized before Bella left the cottage that the journey home could take all the longer for that; yet still he waited.

By Light's own version of events, he and the girl rode on after leaving the cottage, past the turning on their left to the small hamlet of King's Norton, until they came to a second lane on their left, which led then as now to Great Glen, crossing en route the old *Via Devana*, which, because one can also use this lane to reach the village of Burton Overy, is sometimes referred to locally as the Burton Overy Road. At this point Light would claim that he parted from Bella Wright, travelling straight on while she turned off to the left; he would further claim that at that point he had said to Bella that the road straight ahead (which would be referred to later as the top road and was in fact the road along which they had both travelled to Gaulby and from where George believed Bella had collected her armful of gorse) was the shortest and quickest route back to Leicester. The road to which Light referred was indeed the quickest route back to the city, passing through what is now the Leicester East Aerodrome, on through Stoughton village and Evington, until it finally joined the London Road into the city. It must be said at this point that this road also offered Bella her quickest route home to Stoughton from Gaulby, and it is absolutely inconceivable that Bella would not herself have been aware of this fact, having walked and cycled along those lanes between Leicester and Oakham for most of her twenty-one years, and knowing the area like the back of her hand. The route that Light claimed Bella took was not only longer than the more usual route but lay over a much less frequented road. Use of the road which Bella is said to have taken, which was for convenience sake dubbed at court the bottom road (the top road being the more direct route) had one distinct disadvantage. To pass along it and arrive at the point where her body was found it was necessary to negotiate two gates which in those days barred the road. The existence of those gates has often been overlooked when the circumstances of Bella's death have been discussed, probably because they did not appear on the map of the area put forward as an exhibit by the prosecution. The reason for that is that the gates were left off the map in error. When this was discovered it was too late, the map already being an official exhibit, and as was pointed out to the police at the time by the representative in Leicester of the Director of Public Prosecutions, an exhibit simply cannot be altered in any way. The consequence seems to have been that the two gates barring the road have become in the minds of amateur criminologists inextricably mixed up with two field gates which bordered the same lane nearer to the spot where Bella's body was found. Anyone cycling along that lane had to treat those two gates as two separate obstacles, riding or

A photograph of the murder scene taken shortly after Bella had been found. The body of Bella lay near to this field gate on Gartree Road close to Little Stretton. (It is not known who owned the bicycle in this picture, but it is not involved in the case!)

walking the short distance between them. They may have been one reason why the bottom road was less well frequented than the top road. The assumption that Bella took that route seems to have been based almost solely on the position in which she and her bicycle were said to have been found, that assumption being substantiated by Ronald Light's evidence in his own defence. There were no witnesses that could positively place either cyclist on that road at the appropriate time. Let us assume for one moment that the couple did part company exactly as claimed by Light and that, after taking her leave of him, Bella did ride off in the direction that he indicated. In order to get to the place where she was found, Bella would have needed to cycle on to the point where the old Roman road crosses the Great Glen road. When she reached that junction she would have needed to turn to her right along the *Via Devana*, more usually known today as the Gartree Road. There is nowadays no left turning for vehicular traffic at that point, just a footpath which follows the *Via Devana* to the east. Bella is said to have turned to the west, which would have taken her through the two obstructive gates, along a road which in those days was a mere lane with a metalled surface far less firm than tarmacadam. It was a lane frequented mostly by local farmers herding livestock and the occasional vehicle, usually horse-drawn. The body of Bella Wright was found approximately half a mile from the junction with the Great Glen road and eastward about 200 yd from the junction with another even narrower lane that leads north to Little Stretton. The spot was at a distance of approximately $2\frac{1}{2}$ miles from her uncle's cottage at Gaulby. At the point where she was found, the lane passed between hedges that in high summer were reckoned to be, in places, some 8 ft high. Contemporary photographs of the lane would seem to confirm this estimate. Near to the spot where Bella was found those hedges were broken in two places by field gates, one each side of the narrow lane. The body was said to have been found between the two field gates just about 20 yd from the most westerly of the two, though Treasury sketches of the day would seem to indicate that a spot even closer to that most westerly field gate may be more accurate. The body certainly lay within sight of the Little Stretton turning.

Whether or not Bella actually took this route cannot be known for certain. As previously stated, there were no eye witnesses to the couple parting; there were no witnesses to Bella riding alone or indeed for that matter in company on the stretch of road where she was eventually found; nor indeed were the couple seen together at any time after Bella's family waved them off from the cottage at Gaulby, a point that contrasts starkly with the number of sightings before the Gaulby visit.

There has never been the slightest doubt that Bella met her death at the precise spot where her body was found. Heavy bloodstains on the road would seem to confirm that fact, as would gravel from the metalled surface of the road which would later be found embedded in the left side of her face. Certainly a heavy fall from her bicycle on to the road at that point seems to be indicated; that her face was in some way in contact with the surface of the lane to an extent great enough to leave gravel embedded in her skin is certain. How she may have arrived at that spot or how the left side of her face came to be in such damaging contact with the surface of the lane has never been satisfactorily explained. Since there exists no direct evidence which leads us conclusively to know the route taken by Bella on that last ride from Gaulby to Stoughton, it is not implausible that she may have travelled through Little Stretton itself. Although no one came forward to say that they had seen her ride through the village either alone or in company, that in itself does not negate the possibility. The time taken to travel from Gaulby to the spot where she was found would not be appreciably different if the road through the village of Little Stretton had been used in preference to the route that has always been supposed, and which Light claimed that Bella took, given that had she taken the assumed route she would have had those two gates to negotiate. The assumption that Bella took the bottom road seems to have been accepted by and to have satisfied all inquirers both at the time and to date, for not once has it been seriously suggested that Bella may have taken the alternative Little Stretton route.

It ought to be said at this point that the journey by bicycle from Gaulby to the spot where Bella was found would have taken, by either route, perhaps a little over a quarter of an hour given that the ride was taken at no more than a steady pace. Bella was a competent cyclist and would have taken any slight uphill gradients in her stride once that initial walk to Gaulby church had been overcome. It was at approximately 9.20 p.m. that the body was found, her family estimating that she first got up in readiness to leave the Gaulby cottage between 8.30 and 8.45 p.m., while her young cousin Agnes said Bella and the stranger were still at the cottage at 8.45 when she herself returned home. There therefore seem to have been quite a few minutes of conversation outside the cottage, principally between Ronald Light and James Evans but also if Agnes may be believed between Bella and Light. It is also relevant that James found time to have a look at the cycle that Bella was riding, and when Margaret Evans went back into the cottage the stranger found time to follow her to the door and look into the cottage – that much at least is substantiated in her statement to the police. It seems reasonable, especially since George thought the group was outside for about fifteen minutes, to suppose that it may have been getting on for 8.55 to 9 p.m. by the time Bella and her companion left the cottage. Allowing time for them to walk with their cycles up to the church and out of sight of the cottage, it seems that that would leave just time for Bella to reach the spot where she was found if she rode at a steady pace. If for any reason she was delayed en route then she must at some point have pedalled at a rate of knots to arrive where she was found, and for the man who found her to have heard nothing of the circumstances that surrounded her death. In all probability Bella's words to her uncle, that she could easily get in front of the man on the green cycle, may indicate that wherever they parted, either at the place Light pinpointed or at the spot where she met her death, she had given him for whatever reason something of a race.

Joseph Cowell farmed locally at Elms Farm, Stretton Parva. On the evening of 5 July he left his home in order to look over his land and to fetch a herd of cattle nearer to the farmhouse from a more distant field. Shortly after leaving his home, when he was some two or three fields away from the Gartree Road as it bordered his land, forming part of the bottom road, Cowell noticed a couple of cyclists go down the lane in the direction of Leicester. He would recall them later on but at that distance he would not be able to say that the couple were Bella and Ronald Light; indeed he believed that they were not. In the event it would seem unlikely that it was so, because Farmer Cowell put the time as not later than 8.30, and Bella was still at Gaulby, some 2½ miles away, at that time. A little less than an hour later, having rounded up his cattle, Joseph Cowell was driving them along that same lane. As he walked along he saw at a distance of about 400 yd what he first took to be 'something yellow' lying on the road – perhaps a horse rug which had fallen from a passing trap. The time, which again has never been questioned, he put at about 9.20 p.m. He had left his home at about 8.10 p.m. and if Mr Cowell was as much a creature of habit as most men of the land it may be supposed that he knew exactly how long it would have taken him to reach that particular stretch of road. He had probably made that exact journey hundreds of times, and so his timing is probably accurate. As Cowell drew nearer he realized that the shape was a body lying, as he later stated, on the nearside of the road as one headed in the direction of Leicester. The body was lying 'slant wise', partly across a wheel rut in the road and partly on the grass verge. The head lay in the opposite direction to Leicester, and the feet and legs up to the knees were on the grass verge which at that point was 14 in higher than the roadway. The body lay partly on its left side and partly on its back. As he drew closer Joseph Cowell realized that the body was that of a young woman, and he saw that her head lay in a pool of blood. What happened next were the actions of a man finding a young girl lying in the roadway, obviously seriously injured and still bleeding from her wounds, and trying to do his best to put her in a place of safety before obtaining the assistance he believed her to need. In effect the kindliness of Cowell destroyed for ever any precise picture which may have emerged had a more thorough examination of the body been made before the body was moved. Even if such an examination had been possible it seems unlikely that any of those concerned in the case could have done the sort of job which by that time Bernard Spilsbury had gained an enviable reputation in tackling. There would be no 'murder bag' used on the *Via Devana*. As Cowell lifted the body of Bella Wright on to the grass verge her head fell back and he saw that she was dead. It is fair to say that he seems to have been a practical man, for realizing that there was little point in carrying a body any distance, and possibly by that stage sensing that it would be wrong to remove a body from the scene of death, he decided instead to go for assistance. Bella's cycle was lying, according to Cowell's statements on the roadway with the front wheel pointing towards Leicester, handlebars and saddle on the edge of the grass verge, wheels on the road 'only a little way from the body'. Cowell moved it to what he thought to be a sensible place, leaning it against the nearest gate – which happened to be tied up with a piece of string. With the light beginning to fade and both body and cycle safely out of the way of the odd passing vehicle, farmer Cowell set off to summon assistance, totally unaware of the true cause of the girl's death.

Joseph Cowell was the first but not the last to come to the erroneous conclusion that Bella had in some way fallen from her bicycle quite by accident and had thus sustained her fatal injuries. He would later recall that the body was still warm when it was moved, which is hardly surprising since it takes something like eight to twelve hours for the surface of a body to become completely cold. What is surprising is that Cowell had been in that area for some time and yet had heard nothing – but he was, he later explained, 'slightly deaf'. That fact, even though there is no evidence of his having any real difficulty in hearing questions on a number of occasions over the following eleven months, is a point worth consideration.

When she was found Bella was wearing a skirt and blouse under a lightweight raincoat, on the front of which appeared a few drops of blood. She wore no gloves but her hat was, again according to Cowell, still upon her head. She carried very little in the way of possessions and apparently no form of identification, nothing but a torn handkerchief and an empty purse in her left hand skirt pocket and a box of Flag matches in the left-hand pocket of her raincoat. Though not conclusive and probably of little if any significance, these last two facts may indicate that Bella was left handed. Quite why she should carry a box of matches when she had no cigarettes has never been explained. If she had set out with the intention of buying some, in all probability she would have ridden on to the post office and general store in Evington, and not turned back towards Stoughton after handing over her letters to Kathleen Power. Even rural post offices in those days were frequently still open at seven in the evening and Saturday was no exception. Bella would have had a second opportunity to buy cigarettes at the small shop in Gaulby where they were certainly available; in fact one witness purchased tobacco there at the very time that Bella was inside the Gaulby cottage, but that still does not explain why she was carrying the empty purse. Robbery on however paltry a scale as a possible motive must, for a short time at least, have been considered but Mary Wright believed her daughter to be carrying very little money – though she had certainly bought stamps from Mrs Power and it seems highly likely that she had received change. Subsequent enquiries discounted robbery, at least as far as small change received by Bella from Mrs Power was concerned.

When Bella Wright was found, the clothes that she was wearing were said by farmer Cowell to have been in no way disturbed, presumably that is to say no more in disarray than he would expect if indeed the girl had tumbled headlong from her bicycle. Again we have only Cowell's

Joseph Cowell, who found the body of Bella Wright
as dusk began to fall on Saturday 5 July 1919

word for this. Cowell made his way home after moving Bella's body on to the grass verge, and left instructions with his wife to send someone to guard the body. She sent a man by the name of Naylor who was employed on the Cowells' farm, and he was accompanied by another man, named Deacon. Meanwhile Cowell set off on horseback to summon help. He rode to Great Glen, probably calling first at the home of the local constable whom he eventually located on the London Road at Great Glen where he was on duty. Under the instructions of the constable who first went home to collect his bicycle, Cowell then attempted to summon Dr Edward Kynaston Williams of Billesdon by telephone from the nearest post office. Dr Williams, not surprisingly, was a Welshman. His diploma from the Royal College of Physicians dated back to 1904 when he had first practised at Bala in North Wales. He had taken up his duties in Billesdon and the surrounding area in 1906, and there he would stay for the next forty or so years, to be followed into the profession by his son Edward who also practised at Billesdon. Only after summoning Dr Williams did Joseph Cowell and P.C. No. 97 Alfred Hall set out for the Gartree Road. By the time they arrived it was about 10.30 and the daylight even at that time of year had all but gone. Little wonder then that at the time Hall, seeing no reason to suspect that anything other than an accident had occurred, came to the same conclusion as Joseph Cowell.

Dr Williams would say in evidence that, being out of the house when Cowell relayed Hall's message, he did not receive the telephone message from Hall until about ten to eleven, and apparently he first called at the home of Joseph Cowell to get exact directions before proceeding to the scene of fatality. By the time Dr Williams arrived at the spot by car from Elm's Farm those already present (who must have included Hall, Mr Cowell, Naylor and Deacon) were already loading the body of Bella Wright on to a float, later referred to as a milk-float – that is to say a horse-drawn dray normally used for the transportation of milk churns or other heavy loads. The float had no doubt been provided by the practical Mr Cowell and was normally in use around his farm. Since the message that reached Dr Williams probably mentioned that a girl had been found on the road near to her bicycle it is perhaps understandable that he, who like the other men at the scene at that time saw nothing to give cause for suspicion, from the outset treated the death as accidental and made only a cursory examination at the scene. 'Sudden haemorrhage, I think' was Williams's first assessment. By the time he had come to that decision it was dark. Only one man present would ponder those words, and by morning begin to see in them the grains of misunderstanding.

As a result of that brief examination Dr Williams was able to add to his first comment to P.C. Hall that in his opinion the girl may have died from exhaustion or loss of blood. He was hampered to some extent by the darkness but even if he had arrived before the light failed it is unlikely that he could have spotted any sign of the real cause of death at that first examination, given the amount of blood on Bella's face and head and the amount of bruising to the left side of her face. Unfortunately, at his next opportunity the light would again be less than adequate, and Dr Williams was still unable to detect the real cause of death. Had he had any cause to suspect foul play we must assume that he would not have been so easily satisfied.

The body of Bella Wright was taken, along with her bicycle, on the horse-drawn float to what has always been described as an uninhabited or disused cottage. Some versions even refer to it as a shed, and indeed by night it would have looked very like a cottage. The building was situated at Little Stretton and there is a body of opinion in the area today that believes it was not a cottage or shed to which Bella was taken but a small chapel, which at that time being over a hundred years old had fallen into disuse. If that body of opinion is correct that same small chapel, with a plaque displayed on its exterior brickwork, may still be seen and is used today for village meetings. All official sources, however, refer to the building as a cottage, but if an error on this point was made at the outset it has probably been repeated down the years. To distinguish the building from cottages which have already played a part in the story I shall refer to the building as the chapel.

The body of Bella having been placed in the chapel, Dr Williams, who had followed behind the float by car, made a second and again rather cursory examination of the dead girl. The light being as I have indicated hardly better than at the scene of death, came from candles which were apparently to hand. In the poor light the blood which thickly coated the face and hair was visible but little else. Dr Williams, apparently content with his original assessment, left the chapel to return to his home at the White Hall, Billesdon, little thinking that on the following day he would once again be called to examine the body of the dead girl, this time more thoroughly.

P.C. Hall has always received great recognition for his diligent work on the case, and but for him the whole incident might have ended with Bella Wright being listed as just another accidental death of unknown cause, instead of the victim of a killer's bullet fired if not with malice aforethought then certainly with a total disregard for the safety of another human being. Alfred Hall was the one officer engaged on the case who would receive individual approbation, not only from the Coroner for South Leicestershire but also from the Principal Assistant to the Director of Public Prosecutions, a commendation which would be endorsed by the Chief Constable and later promulgated in General Orders to the Leicester Force.

Alfred Hall was born in 1888 at Whatton, Loughborough, and was a carter before joining the force in January 1910. He had enlisted in June 1917 with the Royal Garrison Artillery and saw active service in France, returning to the force in January 1919. Promoted to Sergeant, Alfred Hall was transferred from Great Glen to Earl Shilton in 1922, being later stationed at Moira, Whitwick and finally Croxton Kerrial. He retired on 25 July 1935 after twenty-five years' service. For about ten months he was mine host at the Rutland Arms in Bottesford and then for the next twenty years kept the Rutland Arms Inn (later the Dirty Duck) on the Great North Road, at Great Gonerby, relinquishing the licence for pecuniary reasons in 1955 and moving to Field View, High Street, Bottesford. There he tended his garden and planned to write a complete history of the green bicycle case. He made many notes which he sent to the then Leicestershire force historian Clifford R. Stanley, who would himself, in time, write an account of the case. Sadly it seems that Hall's own account was never completed, and quite why not must remain another mystery. It would surely have made fascinating reading and would have been the only account by someone directly involved in the case.

Hall was quite clearly greatly affected by the events of July 1919 and wrote an account of the case in verse form which stretched to no fewer than eighty-seven stanzas. Simple in style but vividly descriptive, some of the stanzas have survived but to date have not reached a very wide audience.

Alfred Hall died on 11 March 1966, his funeral service being held at Bottesford parish church. He left a son, Roland, at that time a mechanical engineer in Purley, Surrey and two unmarried daughters, Olive and Edna.

By first light on the following morning, Sunday 6 July, Alfred Hall had come to a decision. He had thought long and hard on what he had seen and on what Dr Williams had said on the previous evening, and what he had seen made no sense to him in the light of the medical opinion. He decided that there was more to the case than had at first seemed likely – and it has to be said that the conclusions reached by P.C. Hall ought more properly and promptly to have been reached by a Licentiate of the Royal College of Physicians and a Member of the Royal College of Surgeons. It remains a mystery as to why a constable on the local force could detect what had plainly been overlooked by Dr Williams. Firstly Hall reasoned that if the girl had suffered a sudden and fatal haemorrhage from, as he put it, 'the nose, mouth or chest', there ought to have been more than a few splashes of blood on the front of her raincoat. Secondly, he thought there ought to have been at least some blood clearly visible on her bicycle. It was, he felt, necessary to go over the ground again. Consequently, on Sunday Hall began his day by revisiting the Little Stretton chapel where the body of the dead girl had lain overnight. There he made a close examination of her bicycle. There was some blood on it, but only a few spots on the right pedal, nowhere near the amount he would have expected to find if indeed the girl had died from a sudden haemorrhage. Further examination of the body revealed that beneath the bruising around the girl's left eye there was a small puncture wound, which he thought had been made by a bullet. By that time convinced his hunch had been correct Hall wasted no time in communicating with his superior at Oadby, Sgt. W. Barratt. Clearly a thorough search at the scene of the girl's death was urgently needed; heaven only knew what evidence might already have been destroyed. Hall could see that the exact position in which the body of the girl had been found was now of paramount importance. Accordingly he visited Elms Farm in the hope that Joseph Cowell would accompany him to the scene, but Cowell was not at home and not expected back until about 10.30 a.m. Hall decided not to wait for Cowell but to go over the ground at the scene of the girl's death straight away. Remembering what Cowell had told him of where the body lay in relation to the cycle, Hall was also less than satisfied with the path that the blood had taken as it ran off the road and toward the verge. He felt that in a case of sudden haemorrhage some blood at least ought to have passed beneath the cycle, but he could find no evidence of that having been the case. At this point one more mystery emerges.

Throughout the years that have passed since the death of Bella Wright there have been countless articles and short accounts written reassessing the case, yet this author has been unable to find one that makes any mention of the fact, made evident by Hall's notes on the case, that on the night of Saturday 5 July after the body of Bella Wright had been removed, and before any more investigation or search in the area was carried out, rain fell and in consequence the scene that met P.C. Hall on the Sunday morning had already been irrevocably altered. That rainfall, a relevant and maybe crucial fact of the case, went unreported at the time and in consequence was unconsidered in many later reappraisals of the case. It is certain, however, that Hall took note of the rain, for the only reference to it that can be discovered is extant in the report he made at the time. Certainly the shape and consistency of the pool of blood upon the road was changed, and any footprints that might in the light of day have been apparent on the dusty surface had gone for ever. Not only would the rain of the night have altered the scene considerably, but the very fact that Bella's death had not been recognized as anything other than an accident meant that the road had been left totally open. By the time Hall returned to the scene it is impossible to know what traffic, be it farming vehicles, herds or men on foot, had already passed that way; but Hall was not to be deterred. He set to with a will, but failed to find anything of significance during his first search of the day. He was joined later by Cowell, who confirmed where he had found the body. It lay he said, 'head to the Burton Overy road and feet to Leicester' and 'slant-wise'.

At some stage during his several searches Hall discovered blood stains on the field gate nearest to where the body had lain, and tracks of quite a large bird leading to the gate from the blood on the roadway. Those stains led to an eventual discovery that has provided the green bicycle case with one of its largest red herrings, or as Hall referred to it, a 'black raven'. Quite how soon those blood traces were found we do not know, but it seems likely that they were discovered at some time on that Sunday. They certainly led Hall to extend his search of the area away from the lane and out over adjoining fields, where he discovered the body of a bird. It had apparently fallen dead in a field of corn, having first flown over a field of mowing grass that bordered the lane. The discovery of this bird near the spot where Bella was killed has been a source of constant fascination and varying suggestions over the years. Despite Hall later telling the coroner that it had 'died by gorging itself with blood', a comment which was reported in local newspapers of the day, more than one writer has since chosen to view the finding of the bird as being an indication that Bella Wright was the unfortunate victim of a shooting accident, probably not witnessed by the perpetrator. This theory, and that is all it ever was, persists to this day. The precise facts concerning the dead bird belong to and are recounted in a later chapter, but it is interesting here to look at some of the discussions that the finding of the bird has engendered. Perhaps Hall's words to the coroner may be cited as a possible starting point for the many theories and fancies which stem from the discovery of the bird; the phrase he used almost certainly accounts for the more macabre suggestions surrounding its death. There has been much discussion about what species the bird actually was. It seems quite unlikely that it was indeed a raven, and presumably because the bird was reported at the time to have died from drinking a surfeit of blood it was later said to have been a carrion crow. It has since been pointed out, possibly quite rightly, that even a carrion crow was unlikely to have been brave enough to drink the blood directly from the body of a human being. By the time the body had been removed from the scene it was quite dark, and we may presume even carrion crows would have gone to roost for the night. We might also assume that by first light when the same crows were once again on the wing, the blood left at the scene would have been diluted by the rain which had fallen overnight. It is just possible that a very brave bird might, in the short time between the death of Bella and the finding of her body, have had both the time and the temerity to drink from the pool of blood as it ran and collected near the verge. That is one theory that cannot be proved or indeed disproved. As for the claw marks on the gate and the tracks which Hall said he had found on the roadway (though it is difficult to see how such tracks would show up after the fall of rain), we have no proof that they were indeed made by just one bird; and since crows are usually seen alone it seems more probable that the bird or birds who made those tracks, whenever they were made and if tracks they were, were of the more gregarious rook family.

As we shall see in a later chapter, if the evidence rendered by the finding of the bird had been thought at the time to be anything but misleading, then it would surely have been adduced by defence counsel at the subsequent trial when it could have fitted in quite easily with a suggestion made by counsel on that occasion. The fact that the finding of the bird's carcass was omitted completely from the final speech by counsel for the defence is proof positive that it had no real significance whatever and was thought at best to be a most misleading piece of somewhat dubious evidence. In the event the only reference to the dead bird at the subsequent trial was made in order to explain away the traces of blood found on the nearby gate. Be in no doubt that the bird died a second death in the chambers of defending counsel, and is best left there.

There is perhaps just one significant point in P.C. Hall's report on the finding of the bird. It was found in a field of standing corn and the existence of that corn field might hint why Joseph Cowell who had been nearby for quite some time apparently heard nothing he considered to be of significance. It has always been thought that no bird scarers were in operation as the lane in which the body was found was bordered by fields of mowing grass, but it is possible that bird scarers were in fact in operation in the cornfield, the regular and repetitive sound of them perhaps masking the sound of a gunshot. This may be significant, especially when we consider that Cowell was hard of hearing, and may not have been able to distinguish between the sound of a weapon and the sound of a bird scarer.

It is safe to assume that one of the main objectives of the police in the hours following the finding of Bella's body was to establish the identity of the girl. Hall himself had no idea who the girl was and no one who saw the body on either the Saturday night or early Sunday morning could be of help, so it is apparent that Bella was identified after her mother reported her missing.

Bella Wright was known by her family as a girl who always tried to arrive home by around nine o'clock, unless she was working the late shift. On that particular night she told them of her plans for the evening, and they had no reason to think that she would be late home; after all, they reasoned, she never cycled far from home. When Bella failed to arrive her parents were understandably worried, especially as before that night she had never given them the least cause for concern. Bella's brother Philip was dispatched to the home of relatives in Leicester to inquire if Bella was with them, but we know that she was not and had not been there that evening. From a statement made much later it seems that seventeen-year-old Philip Wright may even have had to walk to Leicester and back, a journey that may have been undertaken late on Saturday night, but could quite possibly not have taken place until the early hours of Sunday morning. It was certainly not until Sunday that Mary Wright made her way to Evington, most probably to the post office, to report Bella missing. There was little then that the family could do but wait and worry.

It cannot be ascertained quite how much assistance was given by Joseph Cowell to P.C. Hall in his search, but since he farmed adjoining fields and knew the area it seems likely that he stayed at the scene for some time. It was in fact Cowell who discovered and pointed out to Hall another forgotten, unreported and relevant piece of what may have been vital evidence. Leading away from the spot where the body was found, and across the adjoining field which was laid down to mowing grass, was a track, obviously man-made. Now it might be argued that anyone, not just Bella's assailant, could have made this, but we have to remember that Cowell farmed that area. He would have known that the track through a crop of some value was freshly made and probably not there when he had passed at around 8.30 p.m. on the previous evening. How thoroughly the track was examined is not known. Certainly Hall seems to have been sure that it was indeed a single track leading away over the fields; sadly there is no indication in which direction it headed, though that may not be vital. There is no mention with the report of the track of any other marks, but we must remember that on the Sunday the police had no idea of the existence of the man on the green bicycle. Indeed, they had barely begun to see the case as one of anything but accidental death. If they had been able to examine the track in the light of information received later, then perhaps that track might have revealed far more and have rated at least a mention at the resultant trial of Ronald Light when the 'dusty' appearance of the defendant later that evening was made evident. The relevance of the track may have been of paramount importance, although we cannot now know for certain if it indicated that the person who made it was also carrying a 'rather heavy machine'; but it does seem significant that those tracks were obvious to the eye even given the overnight rain which had fallen. That Cowell and Hall thought it to be of relevance is borne out by the fact that Hall reported it to his superiors. But Hall's enthusiasm in such matters has never been in doubt, as indicated by his own account of what was described as a most significant discovery at 3 p.m. on that Sunday afternoon – a discovery, according to Hall, made only feet from the spot where Bella Wright had lain. Roughly 17½ ft 'in the rear' (Hall's words), that is to say to the east, in the general direction of Gaulby and away from Leicester, Hall reported finding what has been described as an old pattern .455 calibre spent bullet. Again according to Hall, it had three grooves at the base, and Hall considered that it had been fired from a revolver. Presumably the measurement of 17½ ft was taken from where Cowell had told Hall the head of Bella Wright had rested on the road. The bullet was, said Hall, lying in the middle of the road and was trodden into the metalled surface. Hall reported it to have probably been 'kicked back' to that position by traffic or cattle using the road. It showed marks which Hall thought indicated that it was trodden into the surface by an animal. Having found the small puncture near the left eye of the deceased and now with the .455 bullet in his possession, Hall again contacted his superior, and with Barratt's approval he immediately telephoned Dr Williams to inform him of the latest development and to request his return to re-examine the body. Whether or not the good doctor grasped the full significance of the situation is not clear, but his reaction was less than enthusiastic. He had, he said, to come to Little Stretton on another matter in any case on the following Monday morning, and would drop in then to take another look. It might be imagined what Hall's reaction was, having spent almost his entire Sunday painstakingly quartering the ground near where the body of the girl had lain. 'That is of no use to me', Hall told Williams. 'If you can't come, I shall have to get someone else.' Message understood, Dr Williams said he would come within the hour, just as soon as he could collect his car from Billesdon, which would seem to indicate that Hall had not spoken to Williams by telephone at his home, but after having tracked him down elsewhere. In the meantime Dr Williams asked Hall to obtain some water and wash away the congealed blood from the face, head and neck of the victim so that he might all the more easily see the puncture wound that Hall had discovered earlier in the day. Williams was able to confirm that indeed there was, about an inch behind and half an inch below the level of the left eye, within the bruised and swollen flesh and abrasions caused apparently by the fall from the bicycle, a small hole which may have been caused by a bullet; and upon further investigation what appeared to be another larger hole, the probable exit wound, located at the top right side of the head, the bullet having apparently passed through the brain. This larger wound had originally been obscured by the girl's thick dark hair and hat. The discovery by Williams of the assumed exit hole made a full post-mortem a priority. However, Williams, puzzled by the appearance of the skin around what he took to be the entry wound, which he later described as 'having dark marks around it', cut away the section of skin which included the wound from the left cheek of the victim, in order that he might examine it more closely before he began the full post-mortem examination. That would be carried out by Williams in the presence of a second medical practitioner, Dr Edgar Vaughan Phillips of Kibworth, on the following day, Monday 7 July, most probably in the afternoon.

Apparently the body was not removed from the small chapel even for the post-mortem. Presumably there was finally sufficient light by which Dr Williams and his colleague might work, a definite and rather belated improvement on the candlelight which had been provided for the previous examinations of the body at the chapel.

Sometime late on Sunday or very early on Monday, the discovery of the young girl's body and the report of Mary Wright's missing daughter must have been linked by the police. Bella Wright's parents were most certainly informed of her death during Monday morning, a fact which was revealed in later years by one of Bella's brothers in an interview he gave to a local newspaper reporter – in which he spoke with great affection of his sister and of the distress her death caused his mother. It was at the chapel later that same day that Mary Wright was able to identify the body as that of her eldest daughter. Bella's appearance could not have been improved by the cutting away of a section of facial skin by Dr Williams. Until that point Bella must by all accounts have had the general appearance of a victim of a bicycle accident, but this action must have added considerably to any earlier disfigurement.

Bella's death was not officially recognized as anything other than one of accidental death until after Dr Williams and his colleague had carried out the post mortem on Monday. Further searches at the scene of Bella's death, and presumably over a wider area around the lanes and villages of the area, were carried out, but no weapon of any kind was found, or perhaps it is more correct to say that the police made no claim to have found a weapon. There is no direct evidence that the owner of the weapon that killed Bella Wright ever disposed of it, and no weapon was exhibited when the eventual trial took place. No firearm has since publicly been put forward as that particular weapon.

CHAPTER 4

Inquest

The inquest into the death of Annie Bella Wright opened on the afternoon of Tuesday 8 July. The early proceedings were held at the home of the ever obliging Joseph Cowell. The inquest was conducted by the coroner for the Southern Division of Leicestershire, George Edmund Bouskell. Appointed to the post in 1890, and the son of another Leicester solicitor, James Bouskell, George Bouskell had had the distinction of officiating as coroner in the first case of death by aeronautical accident, that of Lt. Percy Sinclair Pilcher, who was killed at Stanford Hall. At the time of Bella's death he was a partner in the firm of Harris Watts & Bouskell, solicitors of No. 31 Friar Lane, Leicester. He would serve as coroner for South Leicester until his death in 1942, when he was succeeded by his son, James Tempest Bouskell. In 1943 the firm of Harris Watts & Bouskell amalgamated with Freer & Co. of Leicester to become Freer Bouskell & Co. The firm is still in Leicester, now in premises in New Street. There are no longer any Freers or Bouskells involved in the firm, but the link with the office of coroner is still maintained.

Surely the least enviable duty that a coroner is called upon to perform must be the statutory viewing of the body, be it that of victim or in those days convicted murderer. In some cases it falls to the coroner to view the bodies of both the victim and the murderer; such was the case on at least one occasion with George Bouskell and he, in common with many coroners, would not have relished the task. It is said that as far as possible he would avoid looking directly at the body; instead he would remove his bowler hat and put it in front of his face. George Bouskell's dislike of that necessary duty was shared by his son, whose actions are thus described. 'When the body was produced from the refrigerator, he would remove his bowler, look at the bottom of it, courteously thank the mortuary attendant and walk off.' It can be safely assumed that the body of Bella Wright would not have looked particularly horrendous. There was clearly considerable bruising to her face and the specimen of skin surrounding the site of the entry wound had already been removed by Dr Williams, but the larger exit wound was to the back of the head and largely concealed by thick dark hair. It cannot, however, be a pleasant task to look upon the face of a girl cut down so unexpectedly in the spring time of life.

On that Tuesday afternoon there were present besides the jury, as might be expected now that the circumstances surrounding the death of Bella Wright were gradually being realized and a full murder investigation was under way, several high-ranking officers of the Leicester Police Force, among them Superintendent Levi Bowley – a man known in the force for his common sense and quick brain who would in July 1921 accept promotion to Deputy Chief Constable. Also present was the Chief Constable of the Leicestershire Constabulary, Mr Edward Holmes, a colourful character who, it has been said, ruled the force as an autocratic patriarch. Born in Melton Mowbray in October 1847, Edward Holmes's first appointment was with Leicester General Post Office, but he always kept an eye on the local courts and consequently when a vacancy for an inspector at Police Headquarters came up, Edward Holmes made an early application to the then and indeed first Chief Constable of Leicester, Frederick Goodyer. He was duly appointed as Inspector in April 1875. Promotion came quickly: by 1885 he was Deputy Chief Constable and was appointed Chief Constable only four years later. It was a post that he would hold until his death – when, in his eighty-first year, he was one of the oldest Chief Constables in the country. His interests were varied, including, in his younger days, cricket.

Evington post office. Mr Rowe stands outside his joinery shop

He played in a match in 1879 on the Victoria Park ground in Leicester for a Leicestershire twenty-two against a South of England eleven, which included the two Grace brothers. The fall of every wicket was marked by the local band striking up. Throughout his life Holmes rode to hounds, always preferring high-spirited mounts. A freemason from 1883 when he was initiated into St John's Lodge, Leicester, he rose through the ranks of the craft as swiftly as he rose through the ranks of the police, and upon the death of Earl Ferrers in 1913 he was appointed Grand Master of the Province of Leicestershire and Rutland, an office he would hold until his death in May 1928.

On that first day of the inquest there were but two witnesses. The first to take the oath was Bella's mother. She confirmed that her daughter had left home between six and seven on the evening of 5 July, saying that she was going to catch the post at Evington. She had not seen her daughter alive again. Asked about her daughter's intentions concerning marriage, Mary said that Bella was not engaged but was walking out with a young man, a sailor at Portsmouth. The Chief Constable wanted to know if Bella actually had letters to post, to which Mary Wright replied that her daughter had written letters on the Saturday afternoon and that she had been able to see the envelopes sticking out of her daughter's jacket pocket when Bella went out in the evening. It is of significance here that Mary Wright said jacket pocket and not raincoat pocket. When found, Bella was not wearing a jacket, but only a thin raincoat.

Joseph Cowell was the second witness of the afternoon. He spoke of first noticing something on the lane at a distance of around 400 yd, maybe a horse rug or a bag. The spot was about 200 yd from the Little Stretton turning and when he reached her he said the girl was 'bleeding very much from the nose'. He was less sure if there was any blood from the mouth, but there was certainly a 'very large pool of blood close to her body'. Having obtained formal identification of the body, and Cowell having confirmed that it was the body of the young woman he had found on the previous Saturday evening, the coroner then signed the official document releasing the body of Bella Wright into the keeping of her family for burial. The inquest was then adjourned until 25 July.

When the inquest reopened again, now in the Village Hall at Great Glen, the jury was told that police enquiries were continuing and that two Scotland Yard officers, Detective Chief Inspector Albert V. Hawkins and Detective Sergeant William Stephens, had been called in by the Chief Constable. Both Scotland Yard officers were at Great Glen, together with the Chief Constable, Supt. Bowley and Det. Supt. Herbert Chiltern Taylor, of the Leicestershire force who was, with the aid of the two men from the Yard, by that date in charge of the investigations.

The coroner heard both Dr Williams and Dr Phillips give evidence concerning the autopsy that they had jointly carried out some eighteen days earlier, but first Dr Williams gave his version of the events of Saturday 5 July. He said that after being called to the scene by Mr Cowell and while the body was being taken away, he had a look around the road, seeing one large and one very small patch of blood. Later at the 'cottage' he had 'only just looked at the body', and had 'not made any detailed examination'.

Clearly the coroner was disturbed that it had taken so long to arrive at the conclusion that the girl may not after all have died as a result of an accident. He asked Williams if when he had been summoned by telephone anything had been said to him about a bicycle, Williams replied: 'I cannot remember. I would not like to swear if anything was said about a bicycle.' He agreed that someone had said something about a bicycle when he arrived on the scene and saw the body in the milk-float, but he could not remember who had told him that the girl had been found with a bicycle, nor could he remember the exact words; but he imagined that to be before his 'cursory examination' of the body. Williams agreed that, having no reason to suspect foul play, he had treated the injuries as being the likely outcome of a cycling accident. Having been summoned back on the evening of Sunday 6 July, he had probed the wound pointed out to him by Hall, and found that it passed upwards, inwards and backwards. It passed, he said, through the brain to a wound of exit at the right side back of the head. Asked if he could form any opinion as to the position of the girl when she was shot, Williams replied: 'The shot must have been fired in an upwards direction.' Asked if he thought the girl was riding her bicycle at the time that she was shot, he was less sure: 'You cannot say. The girl may have been standing, but there are many possibilities; it is impossible to say.'

The actual cause of death Dr Williams gave as 'shock following a gunshot wound, death being almost instantaneous'. Asked what would have happened to the girl, whether standing or cycling when shot, the doctor replied: 'She would fall like a log.'

Williams was then asked to report on the autopsy. He stated that the body was well nourished, and that the skin was peculiarly fair and white. Speaking of the gunshot wound, Williams described 'a bruise over the left cheek bone, about the size of a two shilling piece in the centre of which was a small puncture wound'. 'The wound would,' said Williams, 'just about admit an ordinary lead pencil.' Shown a bullet produced by the Chief Constable and asked if he thought the wound might have been caused by that particular bullet, Dr Williams said: 'Yes, it might.' Internally, Williams stated that 'the brain substance had been shattered'. He had officially reported the brain to be 'much lacerated'. Describing the exit wound Williams said it 'was an oval shaped hole 1½ in by ½ in.' His official report had been a little more informative and had put the exit wound over the middle and upper third of the right parietal bone.

Other injuries to the face were described by Williams as 'two small contusions below the right angle of the mouth, and a contused cut through the left upper eyelid with discoloration of the eyeball'. There were scratches to the girl's left cheek and also on the left hand and wrist, all of which he considered may have been caused by gravel. Dissection of the portion of skin that he had removed, which included the bruise, revealed gravel and minute particles of metal. He found no evidence of gunpowder but thought the girl to have been shot from a distance of 4 or 5 ft.

There was, agreed the doctor, nothing to show that there been any attempt to assault the girl. Asked if there were signs that she had resisted any such attempt, Williams replied: 'No, her clothes were not disarranged. She wore a bow, like girls do, which was fastened only by a flimsy pin, and it was intact.' Quite how Williams could swear that the girl's clothing was in no way disarranged at the time of her death, when he himself had not arrived on the scene until her body had twice been moved, once on to the grass verge and later on to the milk-float defies understanding. Questioned about the whiteness of the girl's skin, he was asked: 'Would any rough handling of her have left its mark?'

'Certainly it would.'

Dr Edgar Phillips could add little to his colleague's deposition, but he made a point of stressing that in his opinion there had been no struggle. Such was the nature of the deceased's skin that in the event of a struggle there would have been much bruising.

The coroner indicated that he proposed to adjourn for a fortnight, after which more witnesses would be called. This was acceptable to the police, and the inquest was duly adjourned until 8 August.

The Chief Constable then took the opportunity to speak to the press. He pointed out that a man who went away with the girl from Gaulby on the evening when her body was found was now sought by the police, though it could not be said that the man committed the murder. This was the same man who on Wednesday, Thursday and Friday before the tragedy had visited a shop in Leicester to have his bicycle repaired. Edward Holmes then stated that the 'common sense conclusion' that the police had formed was that the man must be living near the cycle shop. He could not, said Holmes, help thinking that someone knew something about him, and he had consequently offered a £20 reward for any information in respect of the bicycle or the man. He added that to date there had been no response.

When the inquest resumed on 8 August, again at Great Glen Village Hall, evidence was taken from the three members of Bella's family who had watched her walk away from Gaulby accompanied by the man on the green bicycle. Bella's uncle described himself as a roadman and deposed that Bella had arrived at his cottage around 7.15 p.m., staying chatting until around 8.30 p.m. Almost immediately after his niece arrived George had noticed a stranger, an unusual occurrence in Gaulby. He had enquired of the carrier Palmer if the man was with him and Palmer had said he was not. The man was of stout build, thirty-five to forty years old and was, in George's words, 'lurking about'. He did 'not altogether like the look of him'. Measures spoke of Bella's previous visit, saying she had brought her 'sailor boy' with her to tea, when they had seemed 'to be on the best of terms, and appeared to be sweethearts'. He had said to his niece: 'There is a strange man up the road, Bella, and the carrier does not know him', his niece replying that the man had overtaken her on the road and had told her that he had come up from Great Glen. He had asked the name of the village (Gaulby) as they came up to it. His niece had got ready to leave and he had said to her: 'Bella, that man is walking up and down the street now.' His niece had replied: 'Well, I will sit down for a few minutes; perhaps he will be gone by then.' When his niece went outside to her bicycle, George said he followed her as far as the doorstep. The man who was 'still in the street wheeling a bicycle' came and stood close to Bella. George had not quite caught all that was said but thought it might have been: 'I thought you had gone the other way, Bella.' He was sure that he had heard the man use the girl's

Christian name. He did not think that his niece had answered. When the man came closer to him, said Measures, his opinion of him was not changed; in fact he liked him still less. He thought that had the man been anyone Bella had known, then she would have asked him in. Asked by the coroner if the man being between thirty-five and forty created any suspicion in his mind, Measures replied: 'Well, I did not think she would want a man of that age.'

The press were at this point asked to leave and for a few minutes the proceedings were held in camera. When the press were readmitted George was still giving evidence. He said that he did not hear the man address his niece as Bella more than once. He agreed that he had told Bella that he did not like the look of the man, and she had replied: 'I'll try to give him the slip.' She had not appeared nervous and had said it 'in a joking sort of way'. His niece was, said George, 'not a girl who would resent being called "Bella" by a stranger'; he was, however, still of the opinion that his niece was a stranger to the man.

Next to take the stand was George Measures' daughter, Margaret Evans. She too had told Bella that the man was still outside, and had added 'He must be waiting for you'. The deceased had replied that she did not know him, but, said Margaret, she had noticed that when the man came up to her cousin and spoke to her, Bella had not replied but 'had blushed a little', and she had gained the impression that her cousin did not want to speak to the man. When she and her cousin had been alone she had said to her: 'Do you really know that man?' Her cousin had replied: 'I do not know him; he is a perfect stranger to me.' Mrs Evans thought: 'He did not look a suitable man to be out with my cousin.' He had spoken, she said, not with a Leicestershire accent but with the voice of a Londoner, and 'had a bit of a Cockney twang'.

Joseph Cowell repeated the evidence he had given at a previous hearing, adding that he did not think that the couple that he saw ride down the lane could have been the deceased and the man, because he put the time of that no later than 8.30 p.m.

Henry Clarke, a gunsmith of Leicester, was handed a bullet by the coroner. He described it as 'an old pattern .455 calibre which might have been used either in a rifle or a revolver'. It had been 'fired with black powder', and if it had been fired from a revolver then that revolver 'had been a large one'. If fired from 50 or 60 yd the bullet would pass through a skull, and he would not expect to see any scorching of the face if the bullet had been fired from 15 yd away. The indentations on the bullet showed, said Henry Clarke, that it must have 'struck the road or something hard when it was practically spent'. It could, he said, have still passed through the head of a person after a first ricochet.

Mary Wright confirmed her evidence given at the first hearing, and for the first time Bella's younger brother Philip told the inquest jury that he had been asked by Bella to accompany her, but had refused.

William Wood was called to give evidence of the events of the evening of 28 June, when he had at the request of Bella's friends escorted her home after their firm's outing to Foxton Locks. His mother's letter had previously appeared in the local press, and Wood's appearance before the coroner marked the end of his involvement in the case.

James Evans corroborated the statement that his wife Margaret had made, to the effect that the man had remained outside the cottage. He further deposed that when the deceased left the cottage he had said: 'I thought you had gone the other way, Bella'. She had not replied. He had 'a look at the man's bicycle' and was 'so struck with the man,' he would 'know him anywhere'. Indeed, when he was later called upon to identify Ronald Light, Evans had no difficulty whatever in doing just that.

Here the Chief Constable told the jury that from what the cycle repairer had said, he was in no doubt that the machine in the possession of the man at Gaulby was the same as the one repaired by Mr Cox 'who had never seen a machine with such a complicated back brake'.

Constable Alfred Hall, the first police officer to reach the scene of Bella Wright's murder

Addressing the jury, the coroner said it was clear that death was due to a gunshot wound, and they would probably come to the conclusion that the wound was caused by the bullet produced. The police, together with officers from Scotland Yard, were doing all in their power. They had discovered that a man had called on four successive days at a Leicester cycle dealer. If the evidence of James Evans was accepted there could be little doubt this was the man at Gaulby, but it was immaterial on this point whether or not the man was known to the girl. Despite publicity it was remarkable, and the jury might find it extraordinary, that no one in Leicester had come forward to say the description of the man fitted someone staying or lodging in their house on those particular nights. It was, said the coroner, inconceivable that the man was sleeping in the open, as his clothes gave no indication of that. Perhaps a closely related person would not give him away, but he would remind them that there was such a thing as being charged as an accessory.

George Bouskell recorded that he thought it regrettable that Dr Williams did not ascertain at his first examination that the unfortunate girl had been shot, but allowance had to be made for the doctor receiving a telephoned message saying that the girl's injuries were the result of an accident and that when the doctor arrived it was already dark. George Bouskell commended Cowell for his actions, which in the light of his comments on the part played by Williams seems somewhat strange. We shall never know if, had the doctor seen the girl as she lay on the lane before being moved by Cowell, he would have come to a different conclusion than that made in the first instance by Cowell and then by Hall. It ought to be remembered that not just Cowell but three men in all had had the opportunity, if only in all innocence, of interfering with the evidence surrounding the body, before the arrival of P.C. Hall himself.

Again the press were asked to withdraw, while some small piece of evidence was taken. The coroner had been displeased by a previous quote in the press and was at pains to ensure that the medical evidence was treated with some discretion. We can safely assume that the evidence taken in camera dealt with the more personal medical facts as revealed by the post-mortem. All the findings on that occasion are still extant; suffice to say that at the time of her death Bella Wright was not pregnant, nor was she technically a virgin – but in a girl who was also an enthusiastic cyclist this will hardly come as a surprise, and is probably of little significance.

A formal verdict of 'Wilful Murder against some person unknown' was returned, and at the same time the jury took the opportunity of adding a rider which commended Alfred Hall for the smart way in which he had performed his duties. The Chief Constable thanked the jury on behalf of Hall, and stated that he agreed wholeheartedly with their opinion.

CHAPTER 5
Brief Life is here our Portion

The afternoon of Friday 11 July brought an extraordinary scene to the normally sleepy village of Stoughton. An estimated nine thousand people gathered, it must be supposed for a variety of reasons, to attend what would, without their presence, have been a simple burial in a quiet country churchyard. It was expected that the burial would attract a large crowd, and in consequence two or three charabanc loads of police officers were drafted in to keep order and to direct those who were entering Stoughton parish church to take part in the funeral service, to be conducted by the Vicar of Stoughton, the Revd W.N. Westmore. Gathered with Bella's own workmates, friends and neighbours were many mill and factory girls, including some from Burley's factory at Oadby, who apparently had the half day off in order to pay their respects to a fellow millworker. One young factory girl later recalled that she particularly remembered Mr Measures, distinguishable by his wooden leg. The thing she remembered most clearly was his bowler hat, which she described as 'so old it was almost turning green'.

The bell of St Mary's and All Saints' church was heard to toll as the cortège set out from Bella's home. The small cottage at the opposite end of Stoughton village had been the scene throughout that sad week of many visits by local villagers, calling to express their sorrow to

Stoughton church. Vast crowds filling the church and churchyard, and overflowing into the surrounding lanes, attended the funeral of Bella Wright

Bella's parents. The simple wooden coffin was made by Mr Rowe who, in addition to being the local carpenter, also ran the post office and general stores at Evington to which Bella had ridden on that fateful evening. It was borne to the church along a route thronged with people, who were standing silently along the grassy banks which border the lanes through the village. Some of those lining the route had known Bella well, but had not been able in that tremendous crowd to secure a place in the church; among them were others who knew no more of her than they had read in their newspapers over the previous four days. To those strangers Bella was just a face, a rather pleasant face, beneath a large brimmed black felt hat. As on all similar occasions there can be little doubt that the local police force scanned the crowd for any signs of the man on the green bicycle. James Evans was particularly charged with keeping an eye open in case the suspect should put in an appearance. No such sighting was reported at the time and it seems now most unlikely that Ronald Light was in Stoughton on that day. Unlikely but not impossible, for had he been more smartly dressed and by then clean shaven he may have escaped recognition by those who had seen him in and around Gaulby on the previous Saturday.

The lucky few who were allowed by the police to enter Stoughton church filled it to capacity. The principal mourners included Bella's parents, her brothers Philip, Tom and Leonard, her uncle George and his wife; and young Archie Ward, up from Portsmouth on compassionate leave from his ship HMS *Diadem*. Among the congregation were representatives of Bate's Rubber Mills and many of Bella's workmates, including Sally and Gertrude Ward who, despite their relationship to Archie, managed only to squeeze in at the back of the church. As the coffin was borne down the aisle to the chancel the strains of the hymn 'Peace, Perfect Peace' could be heard through the doors of the church, left open to let a little air in, for the day was extremely hot.

Many women both within the church and without wept quietly. The vicar's address on that occasion was reported at some length in the local newspapers. He spoke of his hope that the many people who were attending were there to show their sympathy to the family of Bella and not out of a sense of curiosity because the girl had been, in his words, 'so foully murdered'. It would seem therefore that despite the verdict of the coroner's jury being still some weeks away, the local inhabitants or at least their cleric had already made up their minds that Bella had been murdered and had not met her death through accident. Indeed, so had at least one newspaper editor, who on the previous Tuesday allowed Bella's death to be referred to as 'a shocking murder'. Mr Westmore took some pains to stress in his address 'that in the midst of civilization there is a heart of barbarism', but that the reason there were not even more such murders 'was because society in the main was impregnated with the spirit of Christianity'. 'Men may not be regular attenders at their churches but still they live their lives with moral courage.' No doubt the good cleric would not have included in his assessment the man who had killed Bella Wright.

That fine old hymn taken from the Latin by the Revd J.M. Neale, 'Brief Life is here our Portion', was sung; and then, as the body of Bella Wright was gently conveyed to its last resting place, the recessional hymn 'Rest in the Lord' was heard by the crowd who waited, apparently quite quietly, in and around the churchyard and in the lane beyond. The opening verse of that hymn by P.P. Bliss would for one man on that day have held particular significance but it seems improbable that Light was in Stoughton to hear what would in the fullness of time be a very apt comment on his situation: 'What e'er the trials thou may'st see . . . wait patiently.'

The committal of Bella's body to its final resting place completed, many hundreds filed past the graveside and many left floral tributes, including a heart-shaped wreath from Bella's workmates at St Mary's Mill. Both Bella's mother and her father reportedly broke down and wept at the graveside; they were escorted home to their cottage by Archie Ward, walking one on either side of the young seaman with their arms linked through his. Traumatic as it must be to have to bury a daughter so young, the ordeal of Kenus and Mary Wright cannot have been made any easier by the huge crowd that flocked to their daughter's funeral service. It must have been a particularly difficult time for them, for in the twenty-one short years since the birth of Bella, they had already buried three of their children – and now they were burying their eldest child. It must surely have added to their distress to have to walk back to their cottage along the lanes lined with not only the sympathetic eyes of the genuine mourners who had failed to secure a place within the church, but also the less sympathetic prying eyes of the curious, for how can anyone suggest that out of so massive a turnout, even given that the size of the crowd was probably over-estimated, the majority could have been driven to attend by anything but a morbid and ghoulish sense of curiosity and a wish to see for themselves the family of the murdered girl. Notwithstanding that there was in the district great sympathy with the family, out of a crowd of so many thousand, even if we halve the estimate to four or five thousand, many must have been there just for a day out in the countryside and a peep at a quiet family that overnight, or so it must have seemed, had been turned into local celebrities. The fact that the day turned out to be so warm and sunny may have tempted many to attend, while a wet or colder day may have served to keep the numbers down. Another reason for the large turnout may be that the funeral took place on the afternoon of the 11th, a Friday. Perhaps many were tempted to take a trip out to Stoughton rather than return to their places of employment for the few remaining hours of their normal working week. It seems probable that some factories closed early that day, possibly in anticipation of unavoidable large-scale absenteeism. If this was so it would have increased the size of the crowd probably more than any other factor.

Bella's grave in Stoughton churchyard

Kenus and Mary Wright were beside themselves with grief and Bella's youngest brother, Kenus, who was only three at the time of Bella's death, recalled in later years how his father, until his own death in 1954, had forbidden all the Wright children to touch the bicycle that Bella had ridden to her death and how her hairbrush and the last tablet of perfumed soap that she had used were also kept as she had left them. Kenus was around nine years of age before he learned of the manner in which his elder sister had met her death. It took a long time for Mary Wright to recover from the shock of her daughter's death, and in later years she rarely referred to it, preferring to keep her thoughts to herself.

It can only be assumed that the Revd Mr Westmore was so overcome by the multitude that attended Bella's interment that he quite forgot to enter the details of the committal in the Burial Board, and so although Bella's family and friends must have known the exact site of her final resting place, it was lost to the rest of the world for over sixty years. Many had read in contemporary newspapers of the burial service, and so many people at the time must have known that Bella had been interred in Stoughton churchyard, but despite innumerable accounts of the green bicycle case being published over the years, the exact burial spot was lost from public memory. It was not until a local man, A.W.P. Mackintosh, became interested, that the site of the actual grave was once again brought to the attention of an interested public. Mr Mackintosh was able to trace Bella's two youngest brothers, now sadly both themselves deceased. It was one of those brothers, Thomas, who pointed out to Alex Mackintosh the exact position of the grave. At that time completely unmarked, it had from time to time been furnished by the family with a black flower vase; but in the early 1980s when Mackintosh visited the churchyard this was not present. At that time the plot was just a grassy rectangle, dotted with daisies. At the time of writing the grave is now marked by a second vase, this time square and white, affixed to which is a small plaque bearing the simple words: 'In Memory of Annie Bella Wright. Died July 5th. 1919. Aged 21.' That simple plaque can in no way indicate the violent way in which Bella met her death. There is therefore on first sight absolutely nothing to distinguish the grave from many others in the churchyard, and only those who actively seek the grave of Bella Wright will trouble to bend and read the words of the inscription. Bella's last resting place occupies arguably the most peaceful place in the churchyard, and is now one stop on an annual tour of scenes of interest relating to the case. This has been made possible by Bill Richardson, who, in addition to donating the second vase and the small brass plaque, has in the intervening years regularly tended the grave, thus preventing once again nature's relentless course.

CHAPTER 6

Hue and Cry

The first news of Bella Wright's death reached the people of Leicester on the evening of Monday 7 July 1919. A short article of just fifteen lines over one column appeared on page six of the popular *Leicester Daily Mercury*. It was sandwiched between an advertisement for Carr's fever powders and a report of a strike at the Moira Colliery Co., and was printed under the one line headline 'Woman Cyclist's Death', with a sub-heading: 'Found Dead near Stretton Parva'. The report went on to say that the woman (no name was given at this time) was thought by both police and medical opinion to have had a seizure and that she appeared to have fallen from her bicycle; but whether her death was due directly to the seizure or to the fall was uncertain. The article made no mention of the fact that during that very day Dr Williams and his colleague had carried out their post-mortem, or that by the time the *Mercury* went to press, the police knew perfectly well that Bella Wright's death was not an accident, but of a far more sinister nature, and certainly involved at least one other person. They also knew the identity of the young victim, identification by Mary Wright having preceded the post-mortem. On the very same page of the *Mercury* that evening there appeared an account of the level at which Leicester's Victory Loan Stock and Certificates stood at four o'clock that afternoon. It is therefore apparent that the paper was not put to bed until after four o'clock and that had the police wished the news of the manner in which the girl met her death to have been published on that day, they had in all probability time enough to inform the *Mercury* of the latest findings and developments. No doubt it suited their purposes for that first account of the girl's death to be brief and greatly understated. Dr Williams may not have had time to file his official report on the post-mortem findings, but the police would have received at least a verbal interim report from the constable who was present at the post-mortem, and is almost certain to have swiftly told his superiors that the findings of Sunday evening had been confirmed by the autopsy – especially if that police officer was P.C. Hall. That the information concerning the finding of the bullet and the bullet wounds did not reach the public until the following Tuesday is certain. We know that Bella's family were informed of her death sometime during the morning of Monday, though we have no way of knowing exactly how much they were told. It would seem most unlikely that they were told more than was absolutely necessary before the autopsy report reached the Chief Constable's office. News travels fast in small rural communities, and therefore the police may have wished to suppress the find of the bullet and wounds in the hope of discovering quite quickly how Bella had met her death. It is possible that the police may have expected that whoever had fired that fatal shot would be living locally and would get to hear of their enquiry. If as was probably still thought at that stage, her death was the result of an unfortunate shooting accident, it was not inconceivable that the person responsible would come forward of their own volition. The simple report in the evening paper appears to have been designed to encourage anyone involved or with information about the young woman's death to come forward, in the hope that the case would be dealt with quickly. Other than the authorities and possibly the deceased's family, the only person who could have known by the evening of Monday the 7th that a firearm had caused Bella's death was the person who had fired that weapon. At that stage, the police would have listened with some sympathy to anyone who claimed to have shot the girl by accident, or indeed claimed to have been shooting in the vicinity, but if it was thought that the case would be quickly wrapped up the police were to be greatly disappointed and frustrated. Only by a chance discovery, which if used in a novel would be sure to raise an unbelieving eyebrow, was an arrest eventually effected.

On Tuesday 8 July the Chief Constable of Leicestershire Constabulary, Edward Holmes, took the step, usual in those days, of issuing a handbill. As well as being given to the local press, it was circulated to all police forces throughout England, Scotland and Wales. For the first time public attention was drawn to the man who had been seen leaving Gaulby in company with Bella just a short time before she met her death. The descriptions given in the handbill of the man riding the green bicycle and of the bicycle itself are based on the statements given to the police by George Measures and his family, and in particular James Evans. No one reading the brief article of Monday evening could in any way have been alerted to the fact that Bella had been in the company of another person on that fateful Saturday evening. The handbill contrasted markedly with the previous night's article in that it gave clear and graphic detail of the injuries received by Bella Wright, stating that she had been found lying on the Burton Overy road, Stretton Parva, with a bullet wound through her head and with her bicycle lying close by. The description of the wanted man was as complete as these things ever were before the advent of identikit and photofit likenesses; and from the outset, great confidence seems to have been placed in the accuracy of that description. The handbill description of the man that Bella's four relatives had seen in her company as she left Gaulby on that last ride ran to a little over six lines and it is interesting at this point to note that the description of the man's bicycle ran to exactly the same length, but in fact included many more points of reference. The man was described as being thirty-five to forty years of age, 5 ft 7 in to 5 ft 9 in in height, apparently clean shaven but having not shaved for a few days. His hair was described as turning grey, and he was said to be of broad build with a broad full face; he spoke in a low tone with a squeaking voice. He was described as wearing a light rainproof coat with a green plaid lining, a grey mixture jacket suit, grey cap, collar and tie, black boots and cycle clips.

The bicycle was described thus:

'A Gent's B.S.A., having a green enamelled frame, black mudguards, usual plated parts, up-turned handle bar, 3-speed gear, control lever on right of handle bar, lever front brake, back-pedalling brake worked from crank and of unusual pattern, open centre gear case, Brooke's saddle with spiral springs of wire cable.' The handbill added the information that the 3-speed control had recently been repaired with a length of new cable. All personnel of establishments where bicycles were repaired were urged to make thorough enquiries into their past records. The handbill gave further instructions that if met, the man should be detained and any information concerning the man or his bicycle should be wired or telephoned to Chief Constable E. Holmes or to Supt. Bowley at the county police station.

The police could hardly have hoped for a better description of the man. It was as good as most reasonably observant members of the public could come up with in the circumstances, and there was the added bonus that James Evans, having spoken to the man about his bicycle, remembered that the man spoke with what he described as 'a squeaking voice'. The description of the man's bicycle could hardly have been more graphic had James actually owned the machine himself. Perhaps he did, in fact, covet such a bicycle, certainly even for a man so familiar with the intricacies of bicycle design he had stared hard and long at the machine and at its special features, though it is only fair to say that his attention may have been drawn to some of the cycle's features by Light himself. James would later recall that part of their conversation concerned the newly fitted cable. The colour of the cycle may have been slightly unusual but the back pedalling brake worked from the crank, although not unique, was unusual. Put those special features of the bicycle together with the description of its assumed owner with his memorable squeaky voice, with as Margaret Evans could recall a Cockney twang, and the Leicestershire Constabulary could perhaps be forgiven for thinking that with such information

Telephone 357 and 862.

LEICESTERSHIRE CONSTABULARY.

£5 REWARD.

At 9-20 p.m., 5th instant, the body of a woman, since identified as that of ANNIE BELLA WRIGHT, was found lying on the Burton Overy Road, Stretton Parva, with a bullet wound through the head, and her bicycle lying close by.

Shortly before the finding of the body the deceased left an adjacent village in company of a man of the following description :—

Age 35 to 40 years, height 5 ft. 7 in. to 5 ft. 9 in.; apparently usually clean shaven, but had not shaved for a few days, hair turning grey, broad full face, broad build, said to have squeaking voice and to speak in a low tone.

Dressed in light Rainproof Coat with green plaid lining, grey mixture jacket suit, grey cap, collar and tie, black boots, and wearing cycle clips.

Had bicycle of following description, viz. :—Gent's B.S.A., green enamelled frame, black mudguards, usual plated parts, up-turned handle bar, 3-speed gear, control lever on right of handle bar, lever front brake, back-pedalling brake worked from crank and of unusual pattern, open centre gear case, Brooke's saddle with spiral springs of wire cable. The 3-speed control had recently been repaired with length of new cable.

Thorough enquiries are earnestly requested at all places where bicycles are repaired.

If met with the man should be detained, and any information either of the man or the bicycle wired or telephoned to E. HOLMES, ESQ., CHIEF CONSTABLE OF COUNTY, LEICESTER, or to SUPT L BOWLEY, COUNTY POLICE STATION, LEICESTER.

County Constabulary Office,
Leicester, 7th July, 1919.

T H JEAYS & SONS PRINTERS 7 ST MARTINS. LEICESTER

Wanted poster

to go on, the man they sought would not be too difficult to trace, though in the words of the Chief Constable, 'whether the man is a stranger or not cannot at the moment be said'. By the last day of the inquest on 8 August the Chief Constable would, as previously stated, speak to the press with obvious disappointment and perhaps disbelief. Following the release of the police handbill the local Leicester newspaper reports of Bella's death carried on that Tuesday evening bore no resemblance whatever in extent or content to the initial report of the previous day. The *Leicester Daily Mercury*, which at that time claimed to have the largest circulation of any local newspaper, carried the story on the front page of an Extra Special edition. If the local police hierarchy were by that time still debating whether they had a case of accidental death or one of homicide on their hands, there seems to have existed no such reticence within the local journalistic fraternity. The headline read: 'Stretton Murder Mystery . . . Suspected Man Still at Large.' The report went on to reveal 'sensational developments'. For the first time a newspaper named the young victim as Annie Bella Wright (aged twenty-two) of Stoughton. Actually Bella was still six days short of her twenty-second birthday. If the headline had left any of its readers in doubt as to how poor Bella met her death, their doubts would be dispelled by the statement that Bella 'was foully done to death on her way home after a cycle spin round Evington'. The report went on to say: 'It is presumed that she was shot at close range with a large calibre revolver, for there is a small puncture in her cheek and a larger hole at the top of her head, such as would be caused by a bullet passing through the head.' To read more of the tragedy it was necessary to turn to page five where it was reported at some length under the headline 'Murder near Leicester, Police hunt for Unknown Cyclist'. The report commenced with the words: 'A shocking murder was committed on the highway near Stretton Parva, a young woman cyclist being shot in the head on the way to her home at Stoughton.' The man who had been seen in company with Bella was irrevocably linked to her death by the bald sentence: 'the police are searching for a man who was seen in company with the deceased on Saturday evening, and who is suspected of shooting her'. Suspected by whom? Since the handbill issued earlier in the day by the police had made no mention of the man appearing to have any type of weapon in his possession, and indeed no weapon having been found, it can only be supposed that either the editorial staff of the *Leicester Daily Mercury* made that assumption for themselves or that by then the police had somewhat shifted their position and had communicated their suspicions to the newspaper's editorial staff sometime between the issuing of the handbill and the printing of the Extra Special edition. It seems unlikely that in the short space of time between the issuing of the handbill and the printing of the newspaper any new information could have come into the hands of the police, and so we can only assume that the position taken by the newspaper was simply a reasonable reflection of what was being felt and indeed expressed locally and generally after the handbill had been seen earlier in the day.

By Wednesday 9 July newspapers up and down the country were beginning to print their own versions of how Bella Wright may have met her death. One headline in the *Daily Chronicle* read 'Dramatic Race for Life'. The article continued: 'It is believed that the young woman was aware of the danger that was threatening her and was riding her bicycle at its greatest speed in order to escape. The bullet seems to have been fired at close range so that the assailant must have overtaken her.' In time it would become apparent that in all probability the suspected assailant read that report in his regular daily newspaper.

Presumably in consequence of the issuing of the handbill and the subsequent newspaper reports, the police received information from a number of people who believed that they had seen either the man on the green bicycle or a couple answering to the descriptions of the man and Bella in various locations out to the east of Leicester on the relevant day.

It is not certain how the police first acquired the names of two young Leicester High School girls, Muriel Edith Nunney, aged fourteen, and her friend Valeria Cavan, aged just twelve. What is certain is that neither girl gave what may be termed an official statement to the police concerning the man on the green bicycle, until 9 March 1920, and by then Ronald Light was a prisoner in police cells. We cannot be sure, however, that they were not questioned specifically about this case before that date. The date of their statement would be confirmed by Muriel Nunney in her evidence given at police court later the same month, when she said that she and her friend had been riding their own bicycles on the Stretton road out of Leicester at about 5.30 in the early evening of Saturday 5 July when a man riding a green enamelled bicycle approached them from the opposite direction, riding towards Leicester. Both girls said the man wore a light suit and carried a raincoat over his shoulder. Having passed them, the man turned around and began to follow them. Uncertain what to do, they dismounted at the bottom of a hill near to a farmhouse and the man on the green bicycle asked each girl in turn to take the lead and ride on – but the girls in turn refused his request. Finally, feeling somewhat uneasy and frightened about the man's intentions, they climbed back on to their bicycles and rode off, wisely keeping together, back in the direction of their homes at Leicester. The man on the green bicycle, which they described as having 'funny handlebars', rode along with them for a short distance but seemed to the girls to be experiencing some trouble with his own machine, and when he stopped to attend to it they cycled on to Leicester leaving him behind. Quite how early in the enquiry the two girls came forward is not clear but it now seems a possibility that they first saw the police in connection with a completely different enquiry, which was not considered to have any bearing or connection with the green bicycle case. Upon first sight perhaps the police dismissed the girls' statements as adolescent hysteria or perhaps it pointed to a particular type of man who was not thought to be a relevant type of suspect in the case of the death of Bella Wright. Perhaps only in the fullness of time was their information seen as relevant, and only in March 1920 were statements taken from them. It ought to be said, however, that when Bella Wright rode away from Evington it would have brought her out on the road where those two schoolgirls claimed to have met the man on the green bicycle with those 'funny handlebars', and that fact alone ought at an early date to have alerted the police to the possible value of the girls' depositions.

Thomas Edward Nourish, a farmer of Glebe Farm, Little Stretton, was out that evening driving three heifers along the road from Stretton to Gaulby. He told the police that between 7 p.m. and 7.30 he noticed in the distance a man and a girl both on cycles heading in the direction of Gaulby. After safely driving his cattle into a field he called at the village shop in Gaulby to buy tobacco. When he came out and retraced his steps he saw what he took to be the same man waiting on the road where he had first seen him. He described the man as being in need of a shave. This statement tied in with information given earlier by Bella's relatives, and was further supported by the statements of Charles Palmer, the carrier of Illston on the Hill and his wife, Elizabeth. Both man and wife saw the man with the green bicycle but it was Elizabeth who got the better look at him. As they had approached Gaulby, Elizabeth had seen a girl (at that time unknown to her), in the company of a man. They were riding along together towards the village. A little later she noticed the girl go into George Measures' cottage and she saw the man waiting a little way off 'near an elderberry bush'. Among the deliveries on the Palmers' vehicle that day was a box of groceries to be delivered to the Measures' cottage. When she called there Elizabeth recognized the same girl, nursing a baby. George introduced Bella to Elizabeth, saying: 'This is my niece from Stoughton.' Mrs Palmer told the police that she replied: 'I thought so; I recognized her mother's features' to which Bella said: 'Yes, I'm like my mother, aren't I?' Elizabeth further told the police that at the time she thought it strange that the girl should be with a man so much older than herself. She thought it so strange that she almost commented upon it at the time, but decided not to do so. It was as she left the cottage and

George came to the doorway to see her off that he first noticed the man with the bicycle waiting a little way off. Elizabeth was always confident that she would be able to recognize the man again but her husband, rightly as it turned out, was always less sure that he could do so. Driving the delivery van had occupied most of Charles Palmer's time in Gaulby. He had not had his wife's opportunities of noticing who was abroad in the area, and more especially it seems apparent that as the couple passed Bella and Ronald Light they were to the nearside of the vehicle, so Elizabeth Palmer had a far better opportunity to look at them than did her husband. Encouraged by these various sightings of what appeared to be the same man, the police began what has been described as an exhaustive round of enquiry.

In 1920 the relevant male population of Leicester was estimated by Scotland Yard to be something like 280,000 with another 20–30,000, in the surrounding villages. The description of the wanted man, though reasonably complete, gave no hint of any visual peculiarities. Said to be of average height and more or less of average build (only one witness would say broad build) and about thirty-five to forty years of age. One description put the man at around twenty-five years of age but it came from a very young girl who would not in any case be called as a witness, and could safely be discounted. The task of the police was complicated by the influx of men into the town following the end of the First World War, a war that had greatly changed many men: some left as boys and came back looking like old men. It was extremely difficult for the police to know which men were in fact strangers to the town and which were not. In such circumstances we may rightly assume that the police concentrated their attentions on the many cycle dealers and associated repair shops in the Leicester area. A quick glance at a 1919–20 street directory of Leicester will confirm just how many such establishments of that kind there were at the time, and consequently how many visits by the police that might have entailed. The exact size of the Leicestershire force at that time is uncertain, details no longer being available, but in the event those working on the case were saved many hours of legwork – for on the morning of Wednesday 9 July, only hours after the handbill had been distributed, they received early and vital information regarding the bicycle and its owner.

One Harry Cox, whose home was at No. 17 Worthington Street, Leicester, had a couple of months earlier begun to trade as a cycle dealer and repairer from premises at No. 214 Mere Road in the Spinney Hill district of Leicester. On the evening of Tuesday 8 July, Cox was at the opera when he chanced to see a local evening newspaper. As a result of what he read and the information that he was able to give to the police, a report appeared in the *Leicester Mercury* on Thursday the 10th. Cox remembered repairing a green bicycle over a four-day period of the previous week. He told Supt. Levi Bowley that the cycle had been left at his shop for repair between 10 and 11 o'clock on the morning of Wednesday 2 July, after he had been asked to adjust the three speed gear control and to put a John Bull sticky plaster (manufactured at the nearby Evington Valley Mills by the John Bull Rubber Company) on the inner surface of the back tyre. They were simple enough jobs and Cox expected to have the cycle ready for collection on the following day, and the man called a second time on the morning of Thursday 3 July, again between 10 and 11 a.m. The cycle, however, was not ready for collection owing to the fact that in the process of adjusting the three speed gear control, Cox had broken the control cable and was waiting for the owner's instructions. In accordance with those instructions Harry Cox replaced the broken cable with a new one, and when the owner called at the shop for a third time on the morning of Friday 4 July, once again between 10 and 11 a.m., the cycle was ready for him and a figure of 4s 9d was agreed. The owner took the cycle away, but by 4 p.m. that same Friday the man and his machine were back at the premises of Harry Cox. Having tried the bicycle out, the owner asked Cox to 'take an inch off the new cable' so that, as he explained, in future he could adjust it himself. That task was duly carried out and the bicycle was collected for the last time from Harry Cox by the same man at about 2 p.m. on Saturday 5 July. Certainly the cycle that Harry Cox had repaired and described to the police gave every indication of being the actual machine that James Evans had described in such minute detail. The make of the cycle was correct, it was the right colour, and more importantly the repairs carried out by Harry Cox tallied with the new gear control cable that James Evans had seen on the suspect's cycle.

It remained, therefore, to establish if Harry Cox's customer was in fact the same man who had waited for Bella Wright outside George Measures' cottage on the evening of Saturday the 5th, just a few hours after the repaired machine had finally been collected from Harry Cox's shop. On that point Harry Cox could also be helpful, for during his last visit to the shop the owner of the repaired bicycle had told Cox that he was fed up with messing about the town and was going for a run in the country. More to the point, Harry Cox saw the man ride away on the cycle in the direction of Evington village. As to Harry Cox's description of the man, he guessed his height was around the same as that of the wanted man, and he also recalled that when the man had first visited the shop he had worn grey flannel trousers, a sports jacket and a soft hat. According to Cox the man had an unkempt appearance, but perhaps the most significant thing that Harry Cox remembered was that the man spoke in a squeaky voice, and had a Cockney accent. Margaret Evans had said the same of the man she heard speaking outside the Gaulby cottage. Significantly, on two occasions when the man on the green bicycle had been sighted on that fateful Saturday, firstly near to the Gaulby cottage by Thomas Nourish and then by Bella's family as she took her leave of them, he had been described as being badly in need of a shave. Now Harry Cox drew the attention of the police to the same unkempt appearance. One young witness, with typical childlike candour, would later say that she remembered the man because 'he looked dirty'. In addition to his instructions to Harry Cox concerning the repair of the bicycle, the man had also talked of his reasons for being in Leicester and had given Cox what may have been useful information concerning his employment. Perhaps he talked so freely only by way of explaining why he was free to call at the repair shop in Mere Road on three successive weekday mornings. Harry Cox further remembered that the man had given more information on his earlier visits to Mere Road. On his very first visit to the shop he had told Cox that he had just been demobilized, and that he had a month's leave which had not yet expired, but the London firm for which he worked was not very busy and he had been told to take another week or two's leave on full pay – so he had come down to Leicester to visit friends.

Though not unconfuted, in the fullness of time it would become apparent that the man's story and his Cockney accent were partly based on his past experiences. Ronald Light was ever a resourceful character.

The search for the man with the green bicycle proceeded apace, both in Leicester and, as it turned out, at least until early 1920 fruitlessly in London.

On 10 July a detective from the Leicester City Force went up to London to request assistance from Scotland Yard and from that date the Yard was involved, in the persons of Det. Ch. Insp. Albert V. Hawkins and Det. Sgt. William Stephens. That visit pre-empted a suggestion from the office of the D.P.P. that the local force should at an early date call in the Yard and avoid any possible charges of unnecessary delay and mismanagement such as had been levelled at other forces during two recent cases. The Scotland Yard officers would liaise with the man on the ground, Det. Supt. Herbert C. Taylor, who seems to have made quite an impression on the two men from the Yard, and indeed their superiors. When eventually an arrest was made, many months after the two Scotland Yard officers had left Leicester, Trevor Bigham wrote from Scotland Yard to Edward Holmes, saying that he did not think it necessary to take Hawkins from his duties in order to return to Leicester now that an arrest had been effected, as he had every confidence in Taylor's capabilities.

The police in Leicestershire were more than hopeful that an early arrest was on the cards – that the cyclist they sought was a local man and might be spotted moving around the town. With that in mind James Evans was prevented from returning to his work in Rotherham, instead spending some days in Leicester keeping observation at various points around the town, principally near St Mary's Mill as the large workforce at the several factories in the area clocked on and off, but he was unable to pick anyone out. Meantime, and throughout the following months, the police claimed to have interviewed every known friend and relative of Bella Wright. The inference drawn by the police from those interviews was that, apart from Archie Ward who was known to them, Bella at the time of her death had no other regular male associates. The general impression gained from her friends was that she was a most pleasant, sociable and good-hearted girl.

Archie Ward had for obvious reasons been required to come up from Portsmouth to assist the police at the outset of their enquiries, but if he was ever under any suspicion then the police were quick to eliminate him. He was asked to bring with him all the letters that he had received from Bella, so that they might be read and evaluated. When Archie arrived in Leicester by train from Portsmouth he was met by police officers and escorted directly to police headquarters in Horsefair Street, where he was interviewed at some length. His father, who had also met his train, accompanied him to the police station but not surprisingly, despite his request, was not allowed to be present at the interview. Bella Wright's letters to Archie Ward told them very little they did not already know, but perhaps surprisingly there was no mention of any arrangement, albeit unofficial, that the couple had towards marriage. Archie told the police, however, that it had been his intention to return home after the date of his demobilization to marry Bella. Pressed by the police to tell them all he could of his own relationship with Bella, he said: 'before I joined the Navy local gossip scandalized me and Bella and I was said to be going around with lots of girls . . . it was untrue . . . I have only ever been out with two girls'. Encouraged by the police to name any man whom Bella had known and who fitted the description of the wanted man, Archie Ward told them of a former boyfriend of Bella's (I shall call him Terence). A man of twenty-five years, he was described by Archie as dark and 5 ft 7 in tall. Bella had, he said, thrown Terence over to go out with him and as a result of that Terence had goaded him with tales of how he and Bella had been intimate. He had confronted Bella with Terence's accusations and she had denied them. The police were able to trace Terence to Coventry, where by that time he was living with his wife and child. He too was swiftly eliminated from the enquiry.

Archie Ward's intentions to marry Bella Wright seem to have been quite serious; certainly that seems to have been the impression gained at the time by the police, though sadly there is no report extant of the contents of Archie's letters to Bella. Perhaps there is nothing particularly odd or significant in the lack of written communication from Bella to Archie with regard to any arrangement that they may have had for marriage, but it does seem somewhat unusual for a young girl to have made no reference whatever to it however tenuous the arrangement may have been. The police were of the opinion that the parents knew nothing of the arrangement, suggesting that, although Bella had talked to some of her workmates about her arrangement with Archie, perhaps in reality it had gone no further than that. There is no evidence of actual objection by either set of parents but it may be that Archie seems to have had his mind made up, perhaps Bella was less sure. She was, after all, only twenty-one and she and Archie had not been 'sweethearts' for all that long. The couple expected to be parted for quite a long time to come – as at the time of Bella's death Archie's date for demobilization was still some thirteen months away. It is understandable if Bella was waiting to see how she felt when Archie left the Navy, and until that time was wisely taking things rather more slowly than Archie. As will

Bella Wright. A studio portrait, possibly that taken at Gale's Studio a few months before her death, and almost certainly the last photograph taken of Bella

become evident in a later chapter, Bella Wright found some difficulty in discussing just this sort of personal problem with her parents, and in consequence any doubts that she harboured about her relationship with Archie or indeed with any other man, may have been kept very much to herself.

Initially the police enquiry could not have looked more hopeful but by the end of July, despite continuing efforts on the part of the local force, to the newspaper readers of Leicester it seemed that the trail had gone cold. The owner of the green bicycle would remain unknown to the general public for some time to come, yet the inference was that he must have been in Leicester itself or in easy reach of the town on at least the four consecutive days before and including the day of Bella's death, since he would hardly have travelled a vast distance to a cycle repair shop. There again, when the cycle was first taken in for repair it was not ridable, which gave Harry Cox the definite impression that the man had not come far. It was not therefore unreasonable that the police should surmise that he might either be staying in the district with friends as he had indicated, or might very well be a local man, who only wished to give the impression that he hailed from London. The police were, it must be assumed, somewhat hampered on this point as Harry Cox had also been told by the man that he owned a B.S.A. motor cycle in addition to the bicycle. As events would show, Ronald Light never actually owned a motor cycle and the police may have wasted valuable time and effort on that false lead.

The London connection having failed miserably, the local force redoubled their efforts within the Leicester area but to no avail. No one came forward to say that they knew the man on the green bicycle, and no one remembered seeing him in the vicinity of Harry Cox's shop on any of those four days; so for a second time, in an effort to rekindle some dying ember of public memory, the Chief Constable went back to the Standing Joint Committee and received authorization to increase the original reward from £5 to £20. Apart from the usual flood of useless information that always comes in to the police on such occasions it is apparent that nothing of any significance was solicited by the increased reward.

If the police were disappointed by the apparent lack of response to their appeals then so were the people of Leicester, who daily scanned their newspapers for news of the latest developments in the chase for the wanted man. The reports were becoming shorter and more monotonous, and were relieved only by reports of the inquest into the death of Bella Wright, though even the inquest hearings, and the last had closed on 8 August, were not blessed by very large crowds, much to the relief of those who had to attend.

Gradually in certain quarters a feeling of impatience began to creep in, so much so that at least one person in Leicester, totally unconnected with the police of the county, having harboured suspicions from the outset, decided to make an effort alone. It would be many months before the police would share those suspicions, and the route by which they would arrive at that end would be tortuous in the extreme. In ignorance of the earlier investigations by that determined and intrepid person, the local police force did eventually come to share the same suspicions, but only it seems as a direct result of pure chance offering a helping hand. But for that proffered hand, the case of the green bicycle may have been robbed of its controversial ending and of the entrance upon its stage of Ronald Light, a character who has interested, indeed puzzled and fascinated, both amateur and professional criminologists alike throughout the intervening seventy-odd years. It is certain, however, that more than one person in the man's home town were in no way puzzled about his identity and his involvement in the green bicycle case. They already had his measure: his name had passed their lips on previous occasions and now would do so again.

CHAPTER 7

The Hand of Fate

On 23 February 1920 over seven months had elapsed since Joseph Cowell's tragic discovery on the Gartree Road, and the name of Bella Wright was beginning to be less frequently heard upon the lips of the people of Leicestershire. Those closest to the tragedy, however, could not even begin to forget and some, regardless of the happenings of 1920, never did forget or indeed forgive. For the officers of the local police force it was turning out to be the most awkward case that they could remember. The scent, so the public believed, was well and truly cold, and there is little doubt that it would have remained so but for the intervention of a very welcome hand of fate.

Quite how many times horse-drawn barges had threaded their way up and down the canalized section of the Old River Soar since 5 July the previous year we cannot know for sure, but it probably ran into hundreds, for they were used throughout the working day for hauling coal from the nearby railway marshalling yard to the wharfs and factories operating in that industrial area to the west of Leicester. On 23 February Enoch Whitehouse of No. 123A Syston Street, Leicester, was plying his trade as a self-employed canal haulier, owning just two boats. By a strange quirk of fate he was actually in the process of delivering coal to St Mary's Mill, where it will be remembered Bella Wright had last been employed. As Enoch Whitehouse's horse-drawn butty neared the New Lock and the wharf serving St Mary's Mill, the towrope slackened and chanced to dip into the murky waters of the canal. When once again the tension on the rope increased it rose from the water and for a few seconds, no more, Whitehouse saw suspended from the rope what he thought to be part of a bicycle frame. Not perhaps all that unusual a thing to find in any canal, but of significance because Whitehouse believed that he had seen part of a green bicycle. Then, before he could be quite sure, the frame slipped tantalizingly from the tow-rope and disappeared once more into the black and slimy depths of the canal. We must forgive Whitehouse any excitement he may have felt at this point, for were not the local newspapers frequently reminding the public that the police were still offering a £20 reward for information leading to the discovery of the green bicycle or its owner, and did not that amount of money in 1920 represent quite a few days' income to a man in Enoch Whitehouse's position? Whitehouse was not a man given to prevarication, and on the following day, 24 February, he returned to the canal. Presumably using some kind of grappling tool or hook, Whitehouse fished about in the murky water of the canal, his industry eventually being rewarded when he deftly pulled to the surface and succeeded in retrieving not only the frame that he had sighted on the previous day but also the front wheel of a bicycle, a bicycle with a green frame. Enoch Whitehouse was not alone on the towpath that morning. Perhaps by chance, or perhaps because he had heard of the events of the previous day, Archie Ward's father, John who was more usually employed as a farm labourer, was on that particular morning on the towpath when an excited Whitehouse hauled his discovery from the murky water. Whitehouse called Ward over, exclaiming: 'Look what I've got here!' After a short discussion both men agreed that the find was in all probability the elusive machine. For some unexplained reason Whitehouse does not appear to have handed in the cycle frame and wheel at the nearest police office, but rather at Long Eaton. The bicycle parts eventually arrived in Supt. Bowley's office on Friday 27 February. In the fullness of time Whitehouse may have regretted ever making the discovery, as a letter written by him in June of the following year to the office of the D.P.P. reveals. As a result of finding the cycle parts he was, not surprisingly, required to appear as a witness at the eventual police court hearing, and at the subsequent trial of Light. His letter informed the D.P.P. that he was out of pocket, having had his boats laid up during his absence, and claimed £8 10s in lost income. A week later, having received no reply, Whitehouse sent a postcard asking for an acknowledgement of his letter. It transpired that his letter had been passed by the D.P.P's representative on the case to the local Clerk of Assize, who later wrote back informing the office that a payment of 14s a day, plus mileage expenses over a four-day period had been paid to Enoch Whitehouse. He added sympathetically that he knew it to be a case of some hardship, but he regretted that he could not make any additional allowance. Enoch Whitehouse's excitement of February 1919 had somewhat dissipated by June 1920, but that there was excitement at the finding of the bicycle frame and wheel is borne out by a report of many years later. Apparently John Ward went straight from the towpath into Bates's Rubber Mill to give the news of Enoch's find to his daughters Gertrude and Sally. As soon as the news of the discovery spread through the factory, excitement broke out and the mood within the factory was summed up many years later by Gertrude Ward, who said: 'Everyone was talking. I don't think any more work was done that day.' At last it seemed to Gertrude and Sally and the other employees at the factory that the death of their workmate Bella Wright was a step nearer to being explained, and perhaps avenged.

Enoch Whitehouse's find may have been the cause of a slack day at Bates's factory, but for the police it meant the start of a time of fervent activity. That particular stretch of canal was thoroughly dragged over the next few weeks for some distance in either direction from the spot where Whitehouse made his original discovery.

The green bicycle frame and front wheel, recovered separately from the canal by Alfred Whitehouse. They are seen here reassembled before being exhibited at police court, March 1920

Several officers and men of the local force were involved in the cold and messy business of dragging an industrial canal, among them P.C. John W. Bailey who during the First World War had been awarded the Croix de Guerre, and PC 171 (later Sgt.) Tom Steele of Wigston Magna and Oadby, who seems to have led an interesting life. In 1964, when the B.B.C. produced a documentary on the green bicycle case in the 'Call the Gun Expert' series, which was based on Macdonald Hastings' book *The Other Mr Churchill*, a biography of a pioneer of ballistics, Robert Churchill, it was Tom Steele who was called upon to guide the production team around the locality where young Bella Wright met her death. Tom Steele was also the first officer of the Leicestershire force to be granted permission to use his own vehicle, a Sunbeam motorcycle combination, in the course of his police work. During the First World War he had seen service in France with the Royal Flying Corps where he was personal dispatch rider to Major C.L.N. Newell, later Air Marshal Lord Newell. Towards the end of his life (he died in 1974 at the age of eighty-four), Tom Steele remembered that just after the end of the First World War he had caused quite a stir and the local press had dubbed him 'the first policeman to ride a motor cycle through Leicester'. But back in 1920 Steele was stationed at Wigston, and it is not recorded if his acknowledged powers of water divining were of any help to the police in this particular case – although they were certainly utilized on other cases.

Throughout the dragging operations men of the Leicestershire force worked under the supervision of Sgt. W. Healey. The activity along the towpath proved a great attraction to the

Sgt. W. Healey aided by Constables Bailey and Steele are shown together with interested onlookers and an odd assortment of bicycle wheels and other debris, during the dragging of the canal in February and March 1920

townsfolk, particularly, as might be imagined, the children of Leicester. It was well reported in the local newspapers and large groups collected to cheer the police in their every find, however insignificant. Curious onlookers found their way down a flight of steps between iron railings, which led directly to the spot where police began their operations. Photographs of the crowds that collected show a motley assortment of folk, among them many children, some quite ragged but others more warmly dressed, and a fair sprinkling of bowler hats. They watched as a grand assortment of bits and pieces was pulled from the canal. Apart from the green bicycle itself, the police must have been gratified to dredge up an entire bicycle which was of a local make and fitted the description of a machine earlier reported missing and believed stolen. It was eventually returned to its footsore owner.

The police used a variety of instruments to aid their search of the canal. Some of their tools look to be little more than lawn rakes fitted with extended handles, but by far the most impressive and sophisticated piece of equipment used was a tubular metal affair, fitted at one end with a thick and heavily weighted glass aperture. It was designed to give a better view of any sunken object lying on the bed of the canal. We can assume that the use of this equipment was quite successful, since some of the objects eventually retrieved were quite small. The apparatus could only reach out a few feet into the canal if its weighted base was to be near enough to the bottom of the canal for the police to spot anything that had settled in the mud, but it was possible to use the apparatus from a boat. There is a photograph extant which shows this rather cumbersome piece of apparatus being manhandled into position by Sgt. W. Barratt of Oadby and Constable (later Sgt.) R.B. Childs of Evington.

The findings of just one morning resulted in the towpath being littered with all manner of items, some of which would prove to be of importance in the case but mainly just the discarded accumulation that one might expect to find in any town canal, then as now. The police utilized a large handcart to move their findings back to their headquarters in Horsefair Street where each item could be examined.

While dragging for the remainder of the green bicycle continued unabated, the frame section and the front wheel underwent minute examination. It was clear to the police that before the machine was dumped in the canal it had been systematically taken apart. Other finds over the following weeks would indicate that it had been distributed over quite a length of the canal, rather than deposited in only one spot. Assuming that the cycle had been dismantled on the spot and not brought to the canal piecemeal, then the cycle's owner had clearly spent some time on the towpath, not as it turned out completely unobserved. It would be several weeks before the police were satisfied that they had brought to the surface everything of relevance, but they were most fortunate in that the very first section of cycle frame bore the telltale number on which their enquiries would turn. It was clear to the police from examination of that early recovery that before disposal of the cycle a concerted effort had been made to erase any maker's marks or numbers which could result in the bicycle being traced back to its rightful owner, or at least the original purchaser. That very effort must have convinced the police that the purchaser of the cycle and the person who had tossed it into the canal were one and the same. The maker's name, which as usual had been prominently displayed on the front fork of the bicycle, had been erased, as had the maker's number which had been clearly visible on the seat pillar lug. In each instance these identifying marks had been effectively filed away. Given that the cycle had also been systematically dismantled and scattered along a length of the canal the police knew that they were not on the trail of a suspect who had simply panicked and thrown the cycle into the waters of the canal, but had given some thought as to the best method for disposal of the cycle and then set about that task efficiently and effectively – for in doing so he had avoided immediate detection at the time of disposal. It was only after Light's eventual arrest that one

Local inhabitants join in the search for a revolver. Note the two gentlemen on the extreme right of the picture and their sack of coal. Light's cycle gave many a Leicester family an opportunity to indulge in a little recycling

m̃n came forward to say that he may have seen the man in the process of disposing of the bicycle. Samuel Holland told the police in the second week of March 1920 that he could recall either in late November or early December 1919 having seen a man on the towpath near Walnut Street canal bridge. The man had had a bicycle with both lamps lighted. When he saw that Holland was watching him he moved further along the towpath, where he stopped again. When Holland last saw the man he was near to the spot where the green bicycle frame and front wheel were eventually fished out of the canal by Enoch Whitehouse. It was evident from the condition of the more perishable parts of the cycle that it had been in the water for some weeks, and it may well be that Holland did in fact witness Ronald Light, without at the time realizing the significance of what he saw. Holland was a shift worker at one of the factories in the area, and was on his way to work when he saw the man on the towpath, and was apparently able to date the occurrence to one of two weeks, when he worked a night shift and was consequently on his way along the towpath at a particular time of evening when the area was very quiet.

Who the man was and where he was from was still, for the general public at least, a matter for speculation. Enquiries had naturally already been put in hand with the manufacturers, B.S.A. Cycles Ltd of Birmingham, but as the police suspected, to be of any help at all the makers needed the number of the individual machine. Only by that number could they hope to trace a purchaser.

The front fork section of the green bicycle was taken by the police during the last days of February to William East Saunders, who was the manager of the Champion Cycle shop at No. 83

High Street, Leicester (the local agency for B.S.A. cycles) the local expert in the construction of B.S.A. cycles. He examined the cycle frame minutely, and on Monday 1 March was able to detect a second maker's number. Just visible on the inner surface of the front fork of the green enamelled frame, the bicycle carried the number 103648. Saunders' discovery represented the long awaited breakthrough, and if his was the first such examination of the machine then the police were double fortunate; but presumably, the police had inspected the bicycle themselves, and may even have given Harry Cox an opportunity to examine it, as his statement was already to hand. In the event it is Saunders who deserves any credit which may accrue, at least in equal measure with Whitehouse for the discovery of the identity of the green bicycle's owner.

* * *

Armed with the all-important number taken from the front fork of the green bicycle, Det. Supt. Herbert Taylor made his way, probably on the morning of Tuesday 2 March, to the Armoury Road offices of the Birmingham Small Arms Company, so called because their business was centred not on bicycles but on firearms. Birmingham Small Arms Company was the parent company of B.S.A. Cycles Ltd.

It has been intimated on several occasions over the years that the search through the records of the B.S.A. Company was laborious and long. One account written in the 1940s states that Det. Supt. Taylor was told by one B.S.A. official that even with the number to hand it would prove impossible to trace the owner of the green bicycle. It would seem that Det. Supt. Taylor had contacted the firm on a previous occasion, probably when first told by James Evans that the green cycle was a B.S.A. machine with unusual accessories, and had at that time been told of the difficulties of tracing a purchaser without the aid of an exact bicycle number. In actual fact Det. Supt. Taylor's personal approach of that day in March must have been met with courtesy, efficiency and probably enthusiasm, and needed no particular tenacity on the part of the officer, for the timetable of that week which is obvious today allows for nothing else.

While the police had always known that the green bicycle was something a little out of the ordinary, they did not know before their visit to B.S.A. Cycles' head office in Small Heath, Birmingham, that but for the fact that the bicycle had been equipped with just one particular feature it would not have carried that second all-important maker's mark. The colour of the machine and the frequently overlooked fact that the handlebars, rather than being finished in the more usual chrome, were also painted green and somewhat upturned, would not have constituted a special order being placed or indeed an extra number being stamped on the cycle; those attributes were usual on the B.S.A. deluxe model of the day. The only specially ordered feature of the machine which warranted the addition of that tell tale number was the pedal rim brake on the rear wheel. But for that there would have been nothing for the police from Leicester to chase up in Birmingham on that particular day, but such is the luck that often attends such cases.

In 1920, as previously stated, Birmingham Small Arms Company had its head office in Birmingham; the main works, however, was out at Redditch, with other smaller premises at Coventry. It was to the main works at Redditch that Det. Supt. Taylor was directed. A clerk in the sales department of the company, one Albert Davis, was able to point out an entry in an old ledger for 3 May 1910, which clearly showed that order number 103648 related to a special order placed with the company by their agents in Derby, a firm by the name of Orton Bros. A short walk from the sales department to the dispatch department of B.S.A. Cycles was all that was needed for the police to complete their enquiries with the firm. The assistant manager of the department, Sidney Garfield, had been working in that same department in 1910 and was able to show Det. Supt. Taylor an entry in the dispatch book which confirmed that the original order from Orton Bros had indeed been completed and had duly been dispatched to Derby in June of 1910.

Wednesday 3 March found Det. Supt. Taylor and his assistant Sgt. W. Barratt in Derby, where they were able to interview Joseph Orton, a partner in Orton Bros, who had premises in Friargate. Joseph Orton was able to show his visitors a ledger entry relating to a B.S.A. deluxe gent's bicycle, number 103648. The cycle had been ordered from Orton's early in May 1910. The price would have been a special one given the specification required by the buyer. Having ascertained the exact price of the machine the customer, one Mr Light, had paid for the cycle in cash on 18 May, and a date for delivery was supplied. On the day that Mr Light paid for his new machine he gave two addresses, both in Derby, No. 53 Sale Street, and No. 137 St Giles's Road. Enquiries would show that Ronald Light had lodged at both addresses, having removed from the first to the second address sometime during the placement of the bicycle order. From the occupants of that second address it may be supposed that Det. Supt. Taylor found his way to Hartington Street, Derby. There he spoke to Frederick Morris who remembered the owner of the green bicycle very well, for when the family had removed to Hartington Street their lodger Ronald Light had accompanied them. It must be supposed that Mr Morris was able to supply an address in Derby where the elusive cyclist had once been employed, and from there it can have come as little surprise to Taylor that the search was apparently to come to its conclusion on the officer's own stamping ground of Leicester. A few enquiries in Leicester itself finally indicated that Light was resident at a house in the Highfields area of the city. Certainly the police were nearing the end of their search, but they still had a little way to go. One more day and one more trip would bring an end to a chase which had tied up a great part of the Leicestershire force to varying degrees during a period of eight months less just one day.

At this point in the enquiry, the role played by Det. Supt. Taylor seems to have been interrupted. It is apparent that the enquiries made in Leicester on that day were not carried out by Taylor but by Supt. Levi Bowley, for it was he and not Taylor who called at the house in the Highfields district. It was Taylor, however, who made the final journey that would lead to the arrest of the owner of the green bicycle. Possibly Taylor did not in fact return to Leicester but instead waited in Derby to hear the result of Supt. Bowley's visit to the Highfields address. If that is so, whether Taylor or Bowley, having obtained the name of their suspect, had an inkling that the chase had a little more distance to run we cannot be sure, though it does appear likely given recently researched information. It would, however, certainly be Taylor who followed up the information that Supt. Bowley gleaned or verified on that visit to the Highfields house. One more day, one more trip and Taylor would be in a position to make the all-important arrest.

CHAPTER 8

Arrest

Quite what thoughts passed through Supt. Levi Bowley's head as he knocked on the door of No. 54 Highfield Street, Leicester late on that day of Wednesday 3 March, we cannot know. Maybe he welcomed the approaching climax of a long investigation, but maybe he had some idea of the distress that his knock would bring. For the house was home to a mother, her son and their maid, and it may be that Levi Bowley had a good idea of the circumstances which had brought the small family to live in Highfield Street. No doubt the door would have been opened to him by the resident maid Mary Webb, but his questions would undoubtedly have been addressed to the mistress of the house, Catherine Light, mother of the man he sought. If ever a mother had known hope to turn to disappointment it was this mother, and once again she must have known the despair that had gripped her more than once during the previous two decades. The early years had probably been happy enough, full of hopeful anticipation for the future and especially for the future of her young son. Over the past eighteen years, as we shall see, hope had in all probability turned first to disappointment, then later to disillusionment and despair; and to add to her sadness this mother had also known the loss of her husband. Now, when it must have seemed that her son was finally making some small effort to justify all the hopes that she and most especially his father had vested in what must have seemed such a promising child, those dispiriting years culminated in Supt. Bowley's knock on the door. There was but one course of action open to that mother. She gave the police the address they sought, which in any case they would have found when they searched the house over the following two days. Supt. Bowley communicated that last address, that last link in the chain of pursuit, to Det. Supt. Taylor and the next morning, Thursday 4 March, found Taylor in the town of Cheltenham, where he may have noticed 'The Rainbow Trail' was playing at the Winter Gardens Picture House. Taylor's trail had been green all the way, but his visit to Cheltenham brought him within sight of his crock of gold.

Eager to observe protocol and avoid treading on any toes, Taylor began his visit by seeking out the assistance of the local Gloucestershire police force. Having gained that assistance and accordingly accompanied by Det. Sgt. Harold Frank Illes of the Gloucestershire Constabulary who was stationed at Cheltenham, he made his way to Dean Close School, situated then as now in Shelburne Road, Cheltenham. The school was in those days perhaps best described as a suitable establishment for the education of the sons of gentlefolk. Founded in the late 1800s the school was named after the Very Revd Francis Close, one time Dean of Carlisle and former Rector of Cheltenham, who was known as an uncompromising champion of the Evangelical cause. The school's first headmaster was Dr Flecker, father of the poet James Elroy Flecker. The school, small to begin with, grew rapidly through the early years of this century, developing strong traditions of personal faith, mutual respect and integrity, values worthy of the founder's intentions and still prized in the school today, and in 1920 very much expected of the school's masters. However, in those years following the First World War Dean Close, in common with many other schools up and down the country, was experiencing some difficulty. There was a desperate shortage of qualified teaching staff, such had been the carnage among young officers of the British Expeditionary Force. Having presumably advertised for staff, the then headmaster William Flecker had in the first week of December 1919 received an approach from a Leicester man. Flecker interviewed the man that same week and was apparently satisfied that he was a suitable applicant. Accordingly, from the start of the 1920 spring term, Dean Close School had a new assistant mathematics master in the person of Ronald Light, who arrived from Leicester on 20 January to take up his appointment. There is no record of what the principal and tutorial staff of Dean Close School felt as a result of having shared a roof with a suspected murderer, but in response to a late evening newspaper report of that day which erroneously stated that an under-master had been arrested at Cheltenham College, an altogether different establishment, it is quite understandable why the principal of that school was at pains to have a retraction printed in the offending newspaper on the following day.

In the few short weeks that William Flecker had known his new mathematics master he had formed a favourable opinion of him; indeed he gave the police a glowing report. Light had, he said, attended to his duties with zeal and intelligence, he had interested himself in the outdoor pursuits of the boys, and had been put in charge of the school armoury. His conduct was entirely satisfactory.

As Det. Supt. Taylor waited to meet his quarry, what thoughts may have passed through his mind? What manner of man was Ronald Light, this owner of the green bicycle, this man who had seemingly successfully evaded discovery for nigh on eight months despite having been the owner of such a distinctive machine for around ten years and having cycled around his home town on what must have been numerous occasions. Would he accurately fit the descriptions of him given to the police by George Measures and his daughter Olive, James and Margaret Evans, Harry Cox, the Palmers and Thomas Nourish? Would he have that noticeably squeaky voice? The descriptions were, it seems, a reasonably accurate assessment of the man, though it was probably less than accurate to say that he was of broad build, no photographs still extant give that impression, though it is not impossible that he lost weight during the eight months after the death of Bella Wright. There was, not surprisingly, nothing of the unkempt appearance of the suspect remaining, on the contrary the man that stood before Det. Supt. Taylor was smartly dressed, tidy and well groomed, sporting a gold watch and chain. That Light took a pride in his appearance is borne out by the simple fact that a pocket mirror and scissors were later found on him. From the evidence of the man's voice there could be little doubt that the police officer had found his quarry, for Light's answers were given in a voice that was markedly high pitched.

As had been suspected for many months, the owner of that distinctive bicycle and that memorable squeaky voice was a Leicester man born and bred. Born at No. 8 Seymour Street on 19 October 1885, he was at the time of his arrest thirty-four years of age. His confident manner at once conveyed that he was a cultured and well-educated man. He has been described recently to this author as sophisticated; he may have been that, but there was much more to Ronald Light as will become abundantly clear. Light would later deny that when Taylor first interviewed him he already knew of the discovery of part of the green bicycle, and yet the story of that discovery back in Leicester ten days previously had been carried in newspapers countrywide, and it is absolutely inconceivable that Light would not have been keeping his eye on the national and probably the Cheltenham papers too, though he may have considered himself safe in having filed off what he believed to be the only identifying number from which the machine could readily be traced back to his ownership. Finding himself confronted by officers of the Leicester force, he still hoped to be able to bluff himself out of trouble. By indulging in lies and innuendo, something which by that time had perhaps become a habit, Light thought, indeed probably believed, that he could turn the tide of suspicion and escape from the reality that he faced. The position that he took placed him in the greatest jeopardy. Many men have told fewer lies and still felt the pressure of the hangman's rope. Light's attitude at that first interview, indeed his conduct from the evening of Bella Wright's death right up until the time he stepped into the witness box at his subsequent trial, has frequently been described as foolish. For an innocent man, indeed, those actions would have been foolish, but they might in a guilty man equally be described as extremely calculating and resourceful. Light himself would claim that he made no conscious decision, but that he simply drifted into the situation that might so very easily have ended on the scaffold. Such a course of action might point to the fact he was incapable of making a rational judgement, such as might be the case with someone who suffered badly from shell-shock – an argument which in Light's case began in the courtroom in 1920 and continues to be cited today; but it might also indicate a state of mind or self-confidence that is so ingrained, so much a habit, so much a way of life, as to be totally unaffected by even the enormity of the situation that faced Ronald Light in July 1919 and was eventually brought home to him in March 1920. His actions in the summer, indeed in the autumn of 1919 and through to the following year when he was arrested, were simply in keeping with a mode of behaviour which for Light had undoubtedly become the norm and may or may not (I hope to prove may not) have been materially influenced by his time in the trenches of France.

From the very beginning of that interview at Dean Close School, Light denied that he had been anywhere near Gaulby on the evening of 5 July 1919. He said he knew nothing at all of Bella Wright. When asked by Taylor what had become of his green bicycle he said: 'I never had a green bicycle.' Indeed he denied ever having bought any cycle from Orton Bros at Derby. However, when Taylor persisted and it became evident to Light that his purchase of the green bicycle was not only suspected but well documented and consequently well known to the police, he changed his story. Yes, he had once owned a green bicycle but he had sold it seven years previously; he couldn't remember to whom as he had had so many cycles over the years. Det. Supt. Taylor was in no way satisfied with Light's answers, and accordingly he was taken to Cheltenham police station where he was held pending the arrival from Leicester of Harry Cox, who had seen the owner of the green bicycle on no fewer than four consecutive days in July of the previous year. Taylor must have been more than hopeful that Cox, of all the witnesses that had come forward, would be able to successfully identify Light. During the time that he was held at Cheltenham police station, Light again changed his story. Presumably left alone on purpose to consider his position, the door of the room left ajar, Light did just that, for as Taylor made his way past the room in which Light was kept, Light called out: 'What is this stunt?', and went on to add that he had once owned such a bicycle and remembered he had sold it to Charles Henry Bourne of Wilmot Street, Derby. Light also talked of another cycle which he said he had sold to an ex-officer in Leicester, describing that cycle as an All-Weather Raleigh. The truth or otherwise of these statements would need some clarification. Eventually Charles Henry Bourne was traced to Parsons Street, Dudley where he was interviewed by P.C. Salter of the local Dudley force. He had indeed bought a cycle from Light, but, that had been back in December of 1908, almost two years before Light had purchased his green B.S.A. The cycle bought from Light by Bourne was not green at all but black, and Light had told Bourne that it had belonged to his father. Charles Bourne was, however, able to confirm that Light had lodged for two years at No. 9 Wilmot Street, Derby. In point of fact, Light had lodged with the Bourne family from around November 1906, and he did not begin to give his address as No. 53 Sale Street, Derby, until the beginning of 1909, though between leaving the Bournes and settling in Sale Street, he may have had other lodgings. Certainly he seems to have been in the habit of moving frequently. Light later explained his 'confusion' over the cycle that he sold to Charles Bourne by saying that over the years he had owned so many cycles. He seems to have been denied very little through his early years and he may well have owned several cycles, but after all he knew perfectly well that the green bicycle was the one in which the police were interested, and he had not acquired it until two years after he was claiming to have sold it to Bourne. We can only speculate about what his motive was for introducing the name of his former landlord at that point, especially since we do not know the reason for his leaving his lodgings with the Bournes. If there was no bad feeling between Light and his former landlord then any attempt to involve a former friend can only be described as despicable, perhaps all the more so since it does not seem to be an isolated incident. Indeed the ex-officer to whom Light told Taylor that he had sold an All-Weather Raleigh cycle was apparently also a friend. That cycle had been bought from a dealer in Buxton, during Light's time in an Army training camp there. Of the ex-officer, Light said: 'I think he kept a motor cycle at a garage near the Bell,' (a hotel in Leicester which will figure in a later chapter). A witness who resided in the same house as Light would later say at his trial that Light had told her that he was helping a man to build up a business in Leicester. It seems more than likely that the ex-officer was that man, for not only did Light claim in conversation with Harry Cox that he personally owned a motor cycle, and it was shown later that he had on several occasions been seen riding around the Leicester area on such a machine, there is no record that he ever owned any type of motor cycle and the police at the time believed that he had never done so – but they knew of at least one time when he had used one in and around Leicester. There is little doubt that the motor cycle which Light occasionally used was loaned to him by his ex-officer friend. Perhaps as in the case of Charles Bourne this was just one more reprehensible attempt by Light to implicate another totally innocent and uninvolved person who had once befriended him.

Harry Cox arrived at Cheltenham police station sometime during the afternoon of Thursday 4 March and no time was lost in organizing an identity parade, arrangements for which were

Ronald Light at police headquarters, Leicester, while awaiting his turn to be put up for identification. This photograph was retouched before use by the press

entirely in the hands of the local constabulary. Light was put up for identification among nine other men in the reading room of Cheltenham police station. Harry Cox had no trouble in picking out Light who was described at that time in local Cheltenham newspapers as being of dark complexion and smart appearance. As Det. Sgt. Illes escorted Light back to the charge room after Cox had successfully identified him, Light turned to the officer and said: 'My word, that fellow had me spotted all right.' In all fairness to Cox, Light must have looked very different on that day from the unkempt customer he had served some eight months previously and there is no evidence that Cox, before his successful identification, was given an opportunity of hearing the suspect speak, so that noticeably squeaky voice may not have been of any help to him.

Light was detained at the police station at Cheltenham overnight, and was taken back to Leicester on the following morning, Friday 5 March. It is apparent that police forces up and down the country value a certain symmetry in their enquiries. Only the previous month Harold Greenwood had been arrested at Llanelli, near Carmarthen, for the murder of his wife who had died precisely one year before Greenwood's arrest. The green bicycle case would not lack that symmetry. Light was taken back to Leicester to be charged with the wilful murder of Annie Bella Wright eight months to the day from the time that her body was found lying on the *Via Devana* by Joseph Cowell.

Ronald Light was escorted back to his home town in the charge of Det. Supt. Taylor and Det. Sgt. W. Barratt. They arrived at Leicester's Midland railway station at around 11.20 a.m. Alighting from a compartment at the front of the train, they walked briskly along the platform. Light, who was handcuffed to Sgt. Barratt, wore a cloth cap and a dark grey overcoat, and carried in his right hand a small brown attaché case which he transferred to his restrained left hand whenever he needed to remove an habitual cigarette from his lips. The attitude of coolness and unconcern which Light exhibited was remarked upon as he strode smartly along the length of the platform to the waiting taxi cab which would whisk him on to the nearby police station. The party arrived at a minute or so before 11.30 a.m., passers-by taking as little notice as had been apparent at the Midland station, but as the small party stepped from the cab and into the county police office Light, who had probably been warned to expect press attention, turned up the collar of his overcoat in an attempt to hide his identity. Apart from the waiting press corps Light might have expected to see a face or two that he recognized; after all, the police office was just a short walk from his home in Highfield Street.

During Light's time on remand there would be a series of identification parades. The first of these was held on Friday 5 March, prior to Light's first appearance before a local magistrate. While he waited for the identification parade to be held he was photographed, casually leaning against a wall in the yard at the rear of the police office and smoking yet another cigarette. He was dressed in a medium to light suit, a pristine collar and shirt and a dark tie. He also wore a well-worn soft cap and was paraded among seven other men, all somewhat taller than he. Of the other seven, two wore felt homburg-type hats, that is to say hats with the crowns dinted in, three wore bowler hats and two wore caps similar to the one worn by Light. At that first parade in his home town Light was without difficulty identified by George Measures, who picked out Light with the words: 'That's the man I want!' – words that give some insight into what George's reaction might have been when first confronted by Light. In his own words sixty-three-year-old Measures was 'not a very good scholar', though he was at pains to point out that he could read and he seems to have been a man well able to get his opinions across. Measures' conduct as a witness at both the magisterial hearing and at Light's trial later in the year would be proof enough of that. For once, if any newspaper had printed those over-used words 'laughter in court' they would have been entirely accurate.

George's young daughter, Agnes, who had seen the man with the green cycle over a shorter period of time, had more difficulty and was unable to pick Light out. In fact she picked out another man – not, as it turned out, a man so very dissimilar in features to Light himself.

By 10 p.m. on Friday 5 March, Inspector John Hall of the Leicestershire force (no relation of Alfred Hall) was in Rotherham and met James Evans at the pit head as he came off shift at Maltby Main Colliery. He was told to ready himself to travel with his wife Margaret to Leicester early on the following morning, no reason for the trip being given; but it is possible he learned the reason when he reached Leicester, if not before. The late editions of the previous evening had all carried news of Light's arrest, and placards carrying the latest headlines were prominently displayed at the news stands on most Midland stations. James was able to pick out Light without the slightest hesitation; he had after all stood in conversation with the man with the green bicycle and had had a close look at him. Margaret was unable to identify Light, but she realized her mistake immediately and told the police that her nervousness was the reason for her failure. She had in fact picked the man whom young Agnes Measures had pointed out on the previous day. Chief Constable Holmes commented later on both incidents in a letter to Francis Sims of the office of the D.P.P., saying that the man who was wrongly identified bore a striking resemblance to Ronald Light. From a photograph still extant the truth of that remark is evident. Since the man was on hand on two successive days, it seems possible that he was in some way connected with the local force, but Holmes obviously did not name him.

The two young girls Muriel Nunney and Valeria Cavan who said that they had been engaged in conversation, followed and somewhat frightened by a man answering to the description of the man on the green bicycle, were questioned by police on 9 March, and in consequence were given an opportunity to identify Light at another parade held at the Castle, Leicester, on Wednesday 10 March, the day of Light's second appearance at police court. Light was put up between nine other men, who had been, according to one local newspaper account, marshalled amid considerable interest from the waiting crowd. Neither girl had any difficulty in identifying Light: the younger of the two, Valeria, was taken in first, followed by Muriel who picked out Light straight away. She told the police that she remembered Light because 'he looked dirty'; in fact Light would later complain that on the morning of the 10th he had not been allowed to shave.

Little time was wasted in getting Light identified by as many witnesses as possible. Thomas Nourish and Elizabeth and Charles Palmer were all called upon to attend identity parades. Elizabeth Palmer, who had had ample opportunity to take notice of the man on the green bicycle, formally identified Light without difficulty; but Charles Palmer, who always said that he doubted he would be able to identify the man on the green bicycle, failed to do so and would not be called as a witness. Thomas Nourish failed to identify Light but would still be called as a witness, apparently because he had taken a good look at the young girl who was in the company of the man on the green bicycle, and had later been able to identify a photograph of Bella Wright. In that respect his evidence in time was of some value to the prosecution's admittedly circumstantial case against a defendant who, if not a mystery man at the time of his arrest, certainly became one in later years.

CHAPTER 9

Early Days

RONALD LIGHT

Ronald Vivian Light was born with advantages in life that were never to be experienced by Bella Wright. Bella lived in a succession of tied and rented cottages then befitting a not unusually large family of a farm labourer, with little or no prospect of a better or more comfortable life. Light, the only child of George Henry (or Harry) and Catherine Louisa Light knew an easier and if not exactly luxurious, then certainly a softer, gentler way of living. Even though by the year of Ronald Light's birth the average size of families was already falling, albeit working class families more slowly than middle class families, Light as an only child was still slightly unusual. His mother Catherine was the daughter of a Bristol attorney and no doubt she intended that her only son should have all the benefits in life that she had enjoyed as a young child. Her father was John Henry Clifton who, with the aid of various partners, built up a successful solicitor's practice in the centre of Bristol, where over the years he had chambers at various prestigious addresses. Catherine was the fourth child in a family of six. The Cliftons lived in some comfort, employing a cook, a housemaid and a nursemaid to see to the children's needs. When Catherine was born in June 1860 the family resided in a house at Mount Pleasant on Durdham Down, well away from the fumes of Bristol. By the mid-1870s John Henry had removed to Abbey Park, Keynsham where he kept an extensive stud of valuable show horses. Said to have been a man who lived every day to the full, John Clifton seems to have been quite a character. He was a tall handsome man with dark eyes and a moustache, and he kept his well groomed hair unusually long for those times. He was sociable and fond of company, but had little time for the daily routine of a busy solicitor's office, preferring to keep a large staff of clerks in what was probably the largest criminal practice in the West of England. He died at a comparatively early age, having suffered a sudden seizure while appearing in a case at Swindon.

At the time of her marriage to George Light, Catherine Clifton was just twenty-one years old, having reached her majority less than a month before. They married on 28 June 1881 before a large congregation at the parish church of Keynsham. George Light's uncle, the Revd John Light came down from All Saints', Kensington Park to perform the ceremony. The day was blessed by wonderful weather and the village of Keynsham and the surrounding area was described as being *en fête* for the occasion. Neither of George Light's parents attended.

In some contrast, Ronald Light's father, George was not a professional man, his interests lying in quarrying and in the associated manufacture of sanitary ware. Essentially a practical man, by the time of his marriage at the age of twenty-six he was already manager of Ellistown Colliery near Coalville, an appointment which he would hold until his death in 1916. During George Light's time at Ellistown the manufacture of firebricks, boiler seatings and various forms of sanitary ware was undertaken on a large scale, and it was in relation to new ideas in sanitary ware that George Light excelled. In 1890 he took out G.B. Patent No. 3075, which pertained to the improvement of the construction of intercepting traps for drains and the like, and in 1892 came G.B. Patent No. 2146, which referred to improvements in syphon drains and traps. The inventions were commonly known as Light's Patent Back Flush and Light's Patent Quick Flush. In addition to his connection with Ellistown Colliery, George Light was also a partner in the firm of Freeman & Light of No. 39 St Paul's Square, Birmingham. George Freeman was primarily a manufacturer of electroplate. His skill in putting an acceptable finish on an article combined with George Light's obvious flair for innovative ideas came together in their registered designs. In 1896 they created a pen nib extractor, and later a device for fixing scarves and neckties in position. Quite how many syphon lavatories were flushed or neckties fixed in Leicester with the help of George Light's inventions is not recorded, but that some financial reward did accrue seems to have been evident from the houses in which the Light family resided over the years and which clearly reflected their increasing affluence.

From Seymour Street they removed in 1894, albeit to some extent assisted by Catherine's legacy from her father's estate, to a larger house in Leicester at No. 72 London Road. Grosvenor House would be their home until the early 1900s when a family upset forced their removal. By 1904 they were living at another house in London Road, No. 90. In 1914, again under some pressure, they removed to the last house that they would share as a family. This was an even more desirable residence, Park View in Granville Road, Leicester. The house, as its name implies, looked out over Victoria Park with its pavilion and cricket ground. It occupied one of the best positions that Leicester had to offer, situated at the crest of the hill where the London Road leaves the hustle and bustle of the town. In those days, it was a quiet corner of Leicester and a very pleasant place to live. The Lights were used to having the services of a live-in maid, sometimes two, one of whom also acted as companion to Ronald's mother. It seems that she did not enjoy the best of health; her heart was weak, perhaps accounting for the lack of siblings for Ronald, who was born when she was twenty-five and had been married for four years. Catherine's own mother had died at the early age of thirty-nine, her sister Eleanor did not live to see her fourteenth birthday and two brothers died before the age of eight. Catherine's own health was to deteriorate over the years and it is probable that each family upset, and there were several, took its toll. It seems apparent that after the death of George in 1916 she relied to a greater extent on her many friends and on her maids, though she was still able to get out of the house reasonably regularly as late as the early 1920s. On the morning of Bella Wright's death, Catherine Light was preparing for a holiday in Rhyl which commenced on Tuesday 8 July. Ronald would say that he spent part of the previous Saturday running errands in town for his mother in readiness for her holiday.

For as long as his father lived, Light received every benefit that money could buy. His serious education began in 1897 at Stoneygate Preparatory School, Leicester, which he attended until 1899 when he was admitted to Oakham School, one of the two major public schools in the area, the other being Uppingham. In Ronald Light's days at Oakham the school offered a wide curriculum, possibly of a slightly less classical nature than Uppingham, which apparently was eminently suitable to a boy of Light's more practical leanings. Ronald seems to have applied himself to his studies sufficiently well to find eventually a place at university, but that, as we shall see in a later chapter, was not the easy step that it ought to have been for a scholar of his abilities, and a tendency to resist a hard day's work may already have become apparent. He appears to have enjoyed many of the usual schoolboy activities. He had an interest in philately and he collected birds' eggs. Both collections meant enough to him to still be in his possession in his mid-thirties.

Ronald Light was probably always destined to follow his father into a practical rather than a more academic career. Despite his situation at the time of his arrest, in his early years there was certainly nothing to indicate he harboured didactic leanings. His early career would be in railway design, construction and maintenance.

In 1903 Light went up to London to complete his studies, lodging at various addresses in Selhurst and Wandsworth, never staying at any one address for very long. In November 1905 he was admitted as a student member of the Institution of Civil Engineers, the world's oldest professional engineering institution. By the end of 1906 his studies at the City & Guilds (Engineering) College were complete and he was awarded the Diploma of Associateship of the City & Guilds (Engineering) College in Civil and Mechanical Engineering. In effect Ronald now held the necessary qualification to become an associate member of the Institute of Civil Engineers but it would be another six years, not until January 1912, that his name was actually proposed to the council for Associate Membership of the Institution. He was by then twenty-seven years of age, and in the previous year had completed his education at the Central Technical College in Exhibition Road, Kensington where he gained a third class honours degree, which allowed him to add B.Sc. (Engineering) to his name.

Light's necessary practical training from 1906 onwards was gained under the supervision of W.B. Worthington, Engineer in Chief of the Midland Railway at the railway's Northern Divisional Engineer's Office at Derby. Here Light spent two years in the office and one year gaining practical experience in the Midland Railway workshops. When his training was complete he stayed on with the Midland Railway at Derby, employed as an Engineering Assistant. In the years leading up to the First World War Ronald Light's responsibilities gradually increased until he was eventually entrusted with the superintendency of the maintenance and reconstruction of railway bridges, which required an extensive understanding of the work on which the railway's construction gangs were engaged, and which involved among other things the driving of steel piles and the sinking of cylinders under pressure. Gantry work for the electrification of the main line and the design of steel and masonry bridges also fell within Light's remit. That he was in 1912 proposed for full membership of the Institution of Civil Engineers by his superior W.B. Worthington must be some measure of his capabilities and aptitude at that time. Accordingly he was elected as an Associate Member of the Institution on Saint George's Day 1912.

At this time in his career, Light seems to have been well enough liked by his colleagues on the Midland Railway. After his arrest an account written by a Derby contemporary states him to have been quick witted, extremely clever and always smartly dressed. He was said to have been a great favourite with his workmates. It seems likely that around this time he joined a St John's Ambulance Class; a certificate was later found among his possessions. It would seem likely that the classes were organized by his employers, as most railway companies in those days, in common with many factories, organized classes of all descriptions in which their employees might take part. Around this time Light occasionally hired a motor cycle from Orton Bros, a result possibly of having begun to 'walk out' with Ethel Tunnicliffe, who was employed as a tracer in those same Midland Railway offices. They certainly took rides together, though some of these may have been on pedal cycles since it is apparent that Light seems never to have been without a cycle throughout his time at Derby. How serious a relationship this was is not certain, though the police at Leicester in 1920 regarded them as having been 'intimate friends'. Certainly, and at least until 1916, they wrote to each other when parted. Ethel Tunnicliffe kept up her friendship with Catherine Light, and in 1919 was still in the habit of visiting Leicester. During at least one of those visits in 1919 Ronald was present. So it would seem that Ethel made no particular effort to avoid him or, indeed he her; though by all accounts the relationship they had enjoyed while Light was living in Derby had ended in 1916.

In the months leading up to the outbreak of war in August 1914, when Light was not quite twenty-nine years of age, he had lodgings with the Morrises in Hartington Street, which is situated near the Infirmary and had been a conveniently short walk or cycle ride from his work at the Midland Railway Depot. He left his employment with the Midland Railway in October 1914, at which time he told the Morrises that he intended to enlist right away, but in point of fact Ronald Light seems to have been less than keen to join the throng of many of his contemporaries, all eager to get into uniform and do their bit in a war that everyone believed would be over by Christmas. Perhaps at twenty-nine Light was disinclined to join that first flood of youthful enthusiasm but as will become apparent in a later chapter there was little enough to keep him in this country. Finally he donned an Army uniform in February of the following year, having apparently lived at home in Leicester for most if not all of the intervening months. At police court in 1920 it was stated that Light was granted a temporary commission as a Second Lieutenant in the Royal Engineers on 15 February 1915, but Army Lists suggest that in fact the actual date was 27 February that year.

Surely this was a posting for which he ought to have been eminently qualified, and one in which he could have served his country well had he had the will to do so; not only should his engineering background have stood him in good stead but by that time he must have had some experience of handling men, which any newly commissioned officer, even if totally bereft of ambition, would have found quite invaluable.

The home of the Royal Engineers was then, as now, at Chatham but from 14 March Light was at the Royal Engineers' School of Mechanical Engineering at Buxton, during which time he continued his relationship with Ethel Tunnicliffe. It is likely that she visited him on at least one occasion at the camp. Light's training with the Royal Engineers continued from 27 September that year at Newark and on 13 November 1915 he went over to France for the first time on active service. The battle for Loos had ended during the previous month and the offensive on the Somme was yet to begin. Ronald Light served as a Section Commander in the field under Maj. (later Lt. Col.) Rundall, and was assigned a batman/driver by the name of Ambrose. Light's commanding officer Maj. C.F. Rundall enjoyed quite a distinguished career, being awarded the D.S.O. and becoming a Companion of the Order of St Michael and St George. In later years he was C.in C. at the Royal Engineers' establishment on Cannock Chase.

Light's Army career would be short and far less distinguished. He served with his Company during the Army's preparations on the Somme for only ten weeks on that occasion, and missed those awful summer and autumn months of the Somme offensive. Throughout those ten weeks in France Ronald Light supervised his section's work in the construction of all the necessary installations and requirements of an Army deployed in a foreign country. They constructed and maintained trenches which, as was the case in most other areas within that theatre of war, were given strange names like Noodles Avenue, Nobs Walk, Neverending Street and Nuts Lane – names that amused the men and somehow brought a touch of homeliness to a patch of foreign soil. One such trench in Light's sector was known as Stoneygate Street and must have brought many a memory back to him. For the men of the Royal Engineers deployed on the Western Front, a region of Europe known for its inclement weather, there was the endless making and laying of trench boards which gave the men some foothold in the mud along miles of trenches. Since the engineers were also concerned in the constant maintenance of revetments, they would have needed to spend some time in the firing trenches in order to carry out their work, though for obvious reasons any work which had to be carried out within sight of the enemy took place at night, often when things had quietened down. There was also a great deal of time spent in the construction of a rabbit warren of cover and support trenches to the rear of the line. In addition to the constant maintenance of trenches there was the building of concrete gun emplacements for both the British and French armies along the company's own particular stretch of the salient. Perhaps of equal importance there was the building of cookhouses, ovens, ablution blocks and drying rooms. Billets were constructed in nearby towns and villages, often utilizing derelict buildings. Supervision of all these necessary requirements of warfare fell to the officers of the Royal Engineers, commanding their own men and sometimes taking command of men of battalions who, when not actually fighting had been detailed to assist in construction work. Ronald Light, in common with the other section commanders in his company, would have organized the day to day work of the men in his section, in line with orders passed to him from company headquarters.

As an officer Light would have enjoyed many privileges. For instance, officers had their own cooks: what officers ate during their time in France was largely a matter of what they could afford on top of what the Army provided. Food parcels from home arrived regularly, and it was possible to request a particular item and to receive it in a matter of a few days. Catherine Light seems never to have stinted in her care for her only son, and there can be little doubt that throughout at least that first service in France he would have received his fair share of parcels. Again, perhaps particularly as an officer, Light would have had easy access to any home comforts available in the local French village where he was billeted, and as an officer in the Royal Engineers he probably had more chance than most of meeting the local inhabitants.

In those few short weeks Ronald Light's time within the range of the German guns was probably very limited but, to be charitable, any fighting that he may have seen would have had an effect upon him. It is unlikely though, that any effect that it or his subsequent service at the front had upon him was as profound from a psychological standpoint as would be cited as a possible reason for his irresolution immediately after the death of Bella Wright. During those few weeks of Light's first service in France, in fact, his company seems not to have come under either heavy or continuous fire; indeed throughout those weeks in France Light's Company Commander recorded four wounded and two men killed, one by a bullet wound to the head and one by shell fire. Over a three month period this seems a remarkably low casualty rate if set against the reported average figure of thirty men lost each month per battalion.

2nd Lt. Ronald Light's time with the Royal Engineers came to an abrupt end when on 1 July 1916 he was ordered to resign his commission, ironically on the first and worst day of slaughter throughout the Battle of the Somme. Light had already been back home in England for some months when the official reason was given for the Army's decision that he was 'unlikely to make an efficient officer'. Light was duly gazetted out on 21 August 1916. At a later date the grounds for Light being required to leave the Royal Engineers were given as being 'that he showed a lack of initiative'. There can, however, be no doubt that the Army and Light's immediate superiors in particular can have had no serious complaints about Light the engineer; he was more than adequately qualified on that score. It was undoubtedly Light the man who was encouraged to resign his commission so soon after joining the regiment. Had the reason been a genuine lack of initiative it would seem perhaps more appropriate, especially in wartime if his commanding officer had given him a good dressing down and told him to pull his socks up. It is certain that only by his personal conduct as an officer and a gentleman did Light attract the disapprobation and censure of the Army authorities.

By that stage of the war, any ideas that Light may have had of leaving the armed services and returning to civilian life would have been extremely short-lived, for by May 1916 conscription for all men between the ages of eighteen and forty-one had been enacted: at that time Light was a little over thirty years of age. Any fit and healthy man in those days who chose to evade conscription, and indeed many who had a legitimate reason for not being at the front, had to face the wrath of the white feather brigade. Yet after his fall from grace with the Royal Engineers, Light was not quick to re-enlist. He reluctantly returned to army life later that year after spending some weeks in the west of England, during which time his parents had not the slightest idea of where he was or what he was doing.

On 18 September 1916 Light enlisted in the Honourable Artillery Company. The H.A.C. was a territorial regiment which consisted of two artillery batteries and one infantry battalion. It was

Ronald Light wearing the uniform of a Second Lieutenant in the Royal Engineers. Light's entitlement to wear this uniform ceased abruptly on 1 July 1916, but this remains the best-known photograph of him

to a newly formed artillery company that Ronald Light was assigned as a gunner. Initially eighty men were selected to form the new siege battery, the brainchild of Lord Denbigh, the numbers later being made up to around 140 under the command of Major A.J. Edmondson. After enlistment there followed five months of training at various locations including Ewshott, Aldershot, Codford and Lydd. The main force of the siege battery with their equipment, which included four 6 in howitzers, capable of firing at distances in excess of 7,000 yd, arrived in Le Havre on 26 April 1917 where they formed part of the 88th Heavy Artillery Group. They 'went up the line' on 4 May and into action by the 10th of the month, defending a position among the ruins and devastation of Ypres. The position was known to the enemy and consequently heavy casualties were both expected and sustained. Not until June was there a respite; the battery had by then endured five weeks of solid shelling. The battery was again in action in support of the great offensive of 31 July. During this time the battery received several honours, Maj. Edmondson being awarded the Military Cross after going out into the field of fire to carry back a severely wounded man to a place of safety behind the British lines. It is sad to record here that Edmondson was later invalided out, his eyes severely affected by gas. In all, this was a time when the newly formed battery served with courage and distinction.

Ronald Light, meanwhile, together with the rest of his draft, was held in reserve in London and not until November 1917 did he find himself sailing for France to join his battery. During his second period of service in France any fears of injury that Ronald Light may have had were to be realized, though it must be said that the extent of those injuries seem over the years to have been somewhat exaggerated. In 1920 some emphasis on this aspect of Light's war service by his counsel, and by Light himself, was perhaps understandable and only to be expected. During Light's second spell on the Western Front his battery was for some time based at Hannixbeek. With Christmas 1917 approaching the battery handed over their position to 5 Siege Battery on 21 December, and thereafter spent what one member of the battery described as 'a dull Christmas'. On 28 December the battery was moved up to Clifford Camp, near Proven, a few miles to the west of Poperinghe, where they enjoyed what has been described as 'a delightfully easy time'. For the best part of six weeks during February and March the battery was engaged in military exercises and manual work at the Army School of Infantry at Sailly-Flibeaucourt. Exercises complete, the battery headed east into a theatre of war which presented an ever-changing picture as first one side and then the other gained the upper hand. Artillery positions were established, only to be quickly given up again as they came under fire from the enemy. New positions were constantly sought in the villages along the Amien to Albert road, including Lavieville. At this time men of the 88th were killed and wounded almost every day. On 23 May 1918 the battery was withdrawn to a reserve position at Querrieu where they stayed for some three weeks, and the men were able to take advantage of the several small lakes in the area, spending a good deal of time bathing. It would have been even more pleasant if the enemy had not bombed and strafed the village several times. From Querrieu the battery moved forward again, taking up position near the Albert road at Franvillers, but it was a quiet position. In fact the battery fired their howitzers only once during the whole of the next seven weeks.

The Honourable Artillery Company's siege battery, with and without the participation of Ronald Light's draft, was on active service for eighteen months. In all 400 men were at some time assigned to it; of those thirty-two lost their lives, four from sickness, and some seventy were wounded, figures which would seem to reflect the battery's role, to bombard the enemy from the relative safety afforded by the range of their artillery pieces.

Ronald Light was invalided out of France, in his own words 'on a stretcher' and 'wearing pyjamas', via the Corbie casualty clearing station in August 1918. His service in France with the H.A.C. taken with his previous service with the Royal Engineers amounted to less than a year of active service throughout the whole of the conflict. Many a man must have wished himself as fortunate.

Back in England, Light was a patient at Wharncliffe War Hospital at Sheffield from 24 August until 22 October, where he was in the care of Dr Robert Gordon. The hospital dealt with a wide range of injuries, but does not seem to have specialized in the treatment of shell-shock, of significance here.

During his time at Wharncliffe Light was sent to an Army convalescent camp at Worksop and was there from 27 September until 18 October 1918. Four days later he received his discharge from Wharncliffe and spent some time with a reserve unit at Ripon, being finally demobilized early in February 1919.

Leaving aside his active service, those years had been a most eventful period for Light. It would be a time he would not easily forget, and one that without a doubt had great repercussions in his behaviour in 1919. The activities and personal conduct of Ronald Light in those years are necessarily of immense significance in any account of the green bicycle case, conveying as they do so much of the character of the man, but since that conduct has not in any public way been disclosed since 1920, I do not propose to go into further detail at this point. Rather, I will deal with the man on the green bicycle and his subsequent trial for the murder of Bella Wright as it was then offered to the newspaper-reading public of the day and as it has been presented since that time. Any details of Light's conduct other than in direct connection with the green bicycle case, known at that time to just a privileged few, will appear in a later chapter, where it is my hope that they may be seen in better perspective. Ronald Light is presented here as he appeared to the jurors at his trial in 1920.

After his demobilization Light returned to Leicester to live at his mother's new and indeed last, home, in Highfield Street, to which she had removed following the death of her husband. Presumably one reason for the move was that the house in Granville Road held too many sad memories for her; it was also larger than she required and was probably becoming too expensive in what appear to have been her straitened circumstances. It was admitted at his trial that Light had been the cause of great expense to his mother. But if the Highfield Road house was smaller it was just as conveniently placed.

Quite how a widow in Catherine Light's financial circumstances could afford the services of Sir Edward Marshall Hall has always been something of a mystery. The author has been reliably informed that she was aided by a local coal merchant, Farrington Nutt – himself related to the owners of Whitwick Colliery, and whose father was a well-placed freemason who may have been a friend of George Light. When Farrington Nutt's wife asked in later years why he had paid for Light's defence, he replied that Catherine Light had been a good friend to his own mother.

Living in at the Highfield Street house as companion and maid to Catherine Light, who seems to have been experiencing even poorer health, was Mary Webb, who had been a faithful and caring retainer for around eight years. She would remain for some short time yet. Mary had shared in her mistress's traumas throughout those years, but it seems with not quite the same degree of patience.

Light resided in Leicester, at his mother's home, from his demobilization until he took up his appointment as assistant mathematics master at Dean Close School on 20 January 1920.

No. 54 Highfield Street, Leicester (on the right).
Ronald Light shared this house with his mother
and their maid, and he returned here on the night
of Bella Wright's murder

Throughout those months he seems not to have secured full-time employment, though there is some indication that he may have found work on a casual basis.

By July 1919 Light had been living at Highfield Street for around five months, and probably spent in addition some of his leave from the Army at the house. It is not unreasonable, therefore, to suppose that the occupants of neighbouring houses had by July of 1919 enjoyed a chance to notice him and, perhaps more significantly, his rather distinctive green bicycle. Mary Webb would later depose that he rode it regularly, making at least four daily trips along Highfield Street, yet from July 1919 to his eventual arrest in March 1920 not one of those neighbours, whose parlour windows were but a few feet from the pavements of the street, came forward to say they thought they had an idea who the man on the green bicycle might be. It will become apparent in later chapters that this odd fact of the case my be explained by the neighbours' deference to the plight of Catherine Light, whom they may have believed had already borne more than any caring wife and mother ought rightly be asked to bear. Certainly after the trial was over sympathy for Catherine's position was expressed privately if not publicly by a source which to some may have been surprising, and was probably a great surprise to her son who personally received that written expression of sympathy for his mother.

CHAPTER 10

'Damn and Blast that Canal'

Three of the four preliminary police court hearings would be held at Leicester's Castle Court during March 1920. During one lunchtime adjournment Light was held in a room that had a panoramic view of the town to the west of the castle, and in particular the canal, which even as he looked out was being systematically dragged. Quite what thoughts passed through Light's head we can only speculate, but we know of one comment made by him. As he stared through the barred window, he was heard to curse: 'Damn and blast that canal.'

Throughout the time that Light was held in custody, the dragging operations on the canal continued unabated under the directions of Sgt. W. Healey. There were days when nothing of significance was pulled to the surface, although several parts of the green bicycle were still missing and remained so, most notably that distinctive and specially ordered back-pedalling brake mechanism. Since, however, the most important part of the bicycle had already been recovered by Enoch Whitehouse, we might reasonably assume that the chief purpose of continuing the dragging operations was to find the weapon from which the bullet produced by Constable Hall and which the police would claim had killed Bella Wright, may have been fired.

On 19 March, Light's fifteenth day in police cells, Sgt. Healey was personally engaged in dragging a section of the canal opposite St Mary's Wharf. He was fishing about very close to the towpath when he chanced to raise to the surface what was obviously, despite the effects of its immersion, a brown leather Army pattern service revolver holster. Sgt. Healey experienced some difficulty in trying to land the sodden holster and its contents intact, and in fact this proved impossible. As he pulled his catch toward the towpath, part of the contents spilled out and fell back into the dark waters of the canal. Some of the contents were saved, however; there on the towpath lay twelve live and seven blank cartridges. They were of .455 calibre of an old-fashioned type, made for black powder and adapted for use with cordite. The bullets were of a similar type to the one which Constable Hall had handed to his superiors after his search of the *Via Devana*. Sgt. Healey probably thought that the cartridges had been put in the holster for ease of transportation, and in that was probably correct. He also probably thought, with some justification, that he was near to finding the actual weapon which may have been tossed separately into the canal. He was to be disappointed in this, as further dragging at that particular spot and many other places along the canal failed to raise any such weapon to the surface. But Sgt. Healey was rewarded for his further efforts on Friday of the same week, when another ten live cartridges were raised from where they had come to rest after falling from the service revolver holster as it was lifted clear of the water.

The last day of April brought the final recovery, when Joseph Chambers of Highcross Street, Leicester, who was employed as a labourer on the borough dredger brought the left crank and pedal from the green bicycle to the surface.

It seems that the 'missing' parts of the bicycle, most significant of all that braking mechanism, but also its chain and bell and metal guards for the gear case have all been assumed to be lying undetected at the bottom of Leicester's canal, but that was never quite the case.

Not surprisingly, after the arrest of Light both his study at Dean Close School and his bedroom at the house in Highfield Street were thoroughly searched. Among many interesting items the police found at his Leicester home were three metal guards that fitted the gear case of the green bicycle and a Coventry Three Spires chain, which was shown by Constable John

Bailey to be of a 48 x 16 pattern, which perfectly fitted the recovered bicycle. The comparatively insignificant bicycle bell was also found in the house. That chain was proof for those who were still doubtful that the owner of the green cycle had not only resided with Catherine Light at Highfield Road, but had in all probability removed at least some of the parts before leaving the house on his way to the towpath. No cycle lamps were found in Light's room, which would seem to indicate that the cycle was ridden as far as the canal. The chain might easily have been removed and slipped into a pocket, thus finding its way back to Highfield Street. The cyclist whom Samuel Holland had seen on the towpath had two lighted lamps on his cycle. Mary Webb would later state that Ronald Light's green bicycle had two lamps, one of which she could clearly remember him replacing.

Police searches of Light's room at the Highfield address also produced a locked deed box, the key to which was found on Light at the time of his arrest. Among several significant items there were newspaper cuttings relating to his father's death, a silver watch and bundles of letters, and also proof that Light's promising young life had been utterly and wantonly wasted: among the red, white and blue, and blue, white and gold ribbons of Light's 1915 Star and British War medal lay several certificates that he had merited over the years – at the City and Guild College, at London University, his Associateship of the Institution of Civil Engineering and his Army Commission. There could have been no greater proof of the difference in lifestyles of the young Bella Wright and Ronald Light, yet it was because they had been drawn together that the police searched that room in Highfield Street over at least three days. It seems likely that they found all that they sought in connection with the green bicycle case; other items totally unconnected were also of immense interest to them and resulted in the necessary expansion of their enquiries.

Police Court Hearings

On the afternoon of Friday 5 March after his arrest by Det. Supt. Taylor and his mid-morning journey from Cheltenham, Light was brought before a local magistrate at the police office in Leicester's Horsefair Street to be formally charged with the wilful murder of Annie Bella Wright, at Stretton on 5 July. Light was entered on the charge sheet as 'a tutor'. The magistrate on that and indeed the three successive hearings before the local bench was one Alfred Turner J.P., who when he was not occupying Leicester's magisterial bench was conducting his interests in Turner & Jarvis, hosiery manufacturers of Leicester.

Alfred Turner listened to evidence given by Det. Supt. Taylor, who stated that in consequence of investigations into the ownership of the green bicycle he had interviewed the prisoner at Cheltenham and that later Harry Cox had identified Light as the man for whom he had repaired a green bicycle. Taylor had, he said, cautioned Light who, when charged with the murder, had said: 'It is absurd.'

Supt. Levi Bowley then gave evidence to the effect that earlier in the day George Measures had attended an identification parade and had successfully identified Light as the man he had seen at Gaulby on 5 July in possession of a green bicycle. Supt. Bowley went to some pains to point out to the magistrate that the identity parade, which had been held in the yard of the police office, had been conducted in the strictest accordance with the guidelines as laid down by the Home Office. The prisoner had himself, said Bowley, expressed his satisfaction at the way in which the parade had been carried out. Thus began a continuing trend of self-congratulation by those concerned with the investigation into the subsequent prosecution of the green bicycle case. One man on that occasion, however, was not content to sit quietly by and listen without comment to Bowley's words. Throughout the proceedings Light had been sitting with an elbow on a table, with his chin cupped in his hand, closely following all that went on. He spoke only once, and that was in response to Bowley's words regarding his own approval of the way in which the identity parade had been conducted. He said in a voice loud enough for all present to hear: 'Except that I said I didn't have a shave as recently as the other men. I was not allowed to shave today.'

The depositions of Cox and Measures having been read to the court, Light's legal representative, Charles Sale Bigg, interjected for the only time at that first hearing. He wished to be assured that the witnesses named at the hearing would be recalled, which indicated to several present that Bigg would appreciate an opportunity to question or, if it came to it, instruct counsel to question those witnesses. It may be that this first move by Bigg gave rise to the theory that Light's defence would eventually be one of alibi. In later years Bigg would be described by Marshall Hall's legal clerk, Archibald Bowker, who would attend the subsequent trial and must have known him well, as a very able Leicester solicitor. He was recently described as 'a man of tremendous pomposity'. In 1920 Bigg was a partner in the firm Owston, Dickenson, Simpson and Bigg, of No. 23 Friar Lane, Leicester. Bowker ought to have been a shrewd judge for in the course of his eighteen years with Marshall Hall and subsequent work with Lord Birkett he would meet all the notable criminal solicitors of the day, including those two stalwarts of the London scene, Freke Palmer and Sir George Lewis. He had also had the dubious pleasure of doing business with one of London's most talented criminal solicitors at the turn of the century, Arthur J.E. Newton. In 1910 Newton had represented Crippen, a brief which in Marshall Hall's absence Bowker had wisely turned down. By 1913 Newton's cunning, surpassed only by his greed, led him to serve a three-year term of imprisonment and to see his name finally struck from the Roll. The Law Society had warned him about his conduct on previous occasions, his handling of the Crippen case being one example.

Light's first appearance before the magistrate was over in just a few minutes. Supt. Bowley's application for a remand was granted and Light was duly remanded in custody until the following Wednesday, 10 March.

* * *

On Wednesday 10 March, when Light was brought up before the local bench for the second time, the hearing was held for the first time at Leicester's Castle Court. It was five days after his arrest and by then the citizens of Leicester were well aware that proceedings against the man with the green bicycle were at last well under way. A long queue around the building had already formed an hour before the magistrate was due to sit, and half an hour before Ronald Light himself, wearing a smart dark suit, was brought by cab to a side door. The queue had to be parted by his police escort in order that he could enter the building.

The magistrate's clerk, Edward Bennett Fowler, a name that would not have been unknown to Ronald Light as will become evident in a later chapter, ordered the accused to be put up, and as Light was brought into court through the door which leads to the barrister's robing room, some of those assembled noticed that he showed some nervousness for the first time since his arrest. Once or twice he swallowed hard and his throat visibly contracted, but he was, as he would be throughout these and later hearings, quite composed and apparently quite confident. After the charge was read by Alfred Turner, the Chief Constable rose briefly to request that once again Light be remanded for a further week. Addressing Light, Turner quickly replied: 'You will be further remanded until the 17th instant.' Light's solicitor, obviously feeling somewhat resentful that he had not been given a chance to object had he wished to do so, added rather lamely: 'I was going to say, Sir, that I had no objection whatever to that course being taken.' The proceedings were over in five minutes, and Ronald Light had before him another week in custody in which he might contemplate his future and perhaps also his past.

* * *

Ronald Light's third appearance before Alfred Turner J.P. was once again attended by a large crowd. The court was due to sit at 10.30 a.m. and when the doors of the court were opened there was a rush for the few available seats in the public gallery on the first floor. A solitary policeman battled hard to keep control of the men and women who were lucky enough to find places. One reporter filed his article with the sub-heading 'The Castle Besieged'. Once again many had to content themselves with a vantage point outside the court, from where they saw Light once again brought by cab from the nearby jail and quickly escorted inside by police officers. For the brief two minute hearing Light remained standing in front of the dock, near to the benches used by counsel – benches which one eminent advocate of ample proportions who would later in the year be engaged in the defence of Ronald Light would refer to as 'knifeboards'. Again the charge against Light was read, 'that he did feloniously kill and murder Annie Bella Wright at Stretton Parva on July 5 last.'

Many lines of enquiry were still in progress but, explained Supt. Bowley, the Public Prosecutor had been contacted and would be ready to proceed by the following week. Given a chance this time to object, Charles Bigg was happy simply to concur. Light was accordingly remanded until 23 March when for the first time in the case the Public Prosecutor would himself take an active role.

* * *

In March 1920 the office of Director of Public Prosecutions was passing through an interregnum caused by the death in the previous January at the age of seventy of Sir Charles 'Willie' Mathews. His successor Sir Archibald Bodkin, would not be appointed until 31 July. The Department was run in the intervening months under the auspices of the assistant Director, Guy Stephenson, who had held that appointment since 1908. He was the son of a former Director, Sir Augustus Stephenson, and the father of the future Lord Justice Stephenson. The D.P.P., or in this case the acting Director, carried out his statutory duties under the superintendency of the incumbent Attorney-General, a point which in this particular case seems singularly relevant and of some interest, since the then Attorney-General, Sir Gordon Hewart, would himself take a prominent if somewhat truncated role in the forthcoming trial.

It might be apposite to note here that Guy Stephenson, who would be knighted in 1923, and whose knowledge of the law was never in doubt, was not considered to be a strong enough character to take over as D.P.P., but he stayed on in the department as Bodkin's deputy. It was thought that in the turbulent post-war period a man of a more forceful character was needed. This may be the origin of the feeling that men who returned from the Western Front and found themselves charged with capital or violent offences could expect particularly harsh and unsympathetic treatment.

Responsibility for the day to day conduct of the case against Light would be in the hands of the Director's principal assistant, Francis J. Sims, a slim middle-aged, balding man who ranked next in line to Guy Stephenson.

Francis Sims arrived in Leicester on Monday 22 March on the 12.20 p.m. train from London. He was met at the station by the Chief Constable, who drove him to the Royal Hotel, quite near to the castle where a room had been reserved in his name. In addition to the necessary professional contact which Holmes and Sims enjoyed, they seem also to have been socially acquainted. Sims would once again be back in Leicester by Friday 2 April, when he was escorted by Holmes on a visit to the Quorn Hunt kennels.

Sims's interviews with the witnesses began on the day of his arrival in Leicester, when he met Mary Webb, whose evidence would be of great importance to the prosecution's case. Later, possibly as a direct result of that first interview, Sims would express concern for her well being. She was the subject of a letter that Sims wrote to Holmes, in which he enquired about her position in the Light household as a result of the case and her part in it. A reply of 20 April assured him that if Webb's position became untenable she had friends in Leicester to whom she might turn. In fact she was at the time of the trial engaged to be married, and her days at the Light residence were in any event already numbered. There was, however, perhaps understandably, some acrimony on the part of Catherine Light, who considered that Webb need not have become involved in the case at all. Mary Webb's reply to her mistress was that she had had no choice and had simply told the truth.

Tuesday 23 March, Light's fourth and final appearance before the magistrate, would mark the first occasion on which Francis Sims would be seen by the people of Leicester to take an active role in the proceedings, personally conducting the case against Ronald Light at the court on that date.

It is interesting to note here that Sims had risen to be principal assistant to the Director of Public Prosecutions despite the fact that he was not legally qualified, either as a barrister or a solicitor. He was not unique in this, but in 1908 he was one of only two non-professional officers among the Treasury solicitors and the D.P.P.'s department who were allowed to conduct cases before the police courts. There is an obvious and interesting parallel nowadays in the growing lobby to allow solicitors to appear in the higher courts, where hitherto only barristers have acted. Just such an innovation has recently been seen in Scotland.

* * *

Tuesday 23 March saw even larger crowds gathered outside Leicester's Castle Court for the first day of Ronald Light's fourth appearance before the local magistrate. The public had learned of the latest items to be recovered from the canal by Sgt. Healey and for the first time it was expected that the court would hear something of the evidence against Ronald Light and also that witnesses would be called in support of that evidence. The court was scheduled to sit at 10.30 but by 9 a.m. a queue of hopefuls had already formed. By 9.15 the queue already consisted of enough people to fill the public gallery; those who arrived later, and it was thought that there were about a thousand in all, would not secure places in the court and had to be content with watching the arrival of those with a part to play in the proceedings.

There would be two new faces in court that morning, that of Francis Sims and barrister-at-law George Wightman Powers. Powers was a Leicestershire man born and bred. He was born in May 1864 at the Manor House, Barwell, and was educated at Hinckley Grammar School and Highgate School, later attending New College, Oxford, where he gained firsts in the Literary Humanities and Modern History. Married to the daughter of an Essex clergyman, he was called to the bar of Lincoln's Inn in 1896. Never to take silk, that precarious step from junior to leader that many able minds have shunned, Powers joined the Midland Circuit shortly after his call, and in the Midlands he would stay. He was an active cricketer and also played tennis, but his life's interest lay in historical study. In the year following the trial of Ronald Light he was appointed Recorder of Leicester, an appointment that he would hold until November 1932 when he died of pneumonia in a London nursing home. He was in his sixty-ninth year.

As Ronald Light was brought into court he looked around briefly and then stood quietly to listen to the evidence against him outlined by Sims. We cannot know if he was aware of the events that took place earlier that morning in Durham, but it is not unlikely that as he prepared for his appearance in court, some prison officer pointed out that sixty-six-year-old William Hall was at the precise time also preparing himself, not for an appearance in court, but for his execution for the murder of Mary Ann Dixon, a widow with whom he had lived. It would indeed have been a timely and chilling reminder of the possible consequences that Light faced if convicted of the murder of Bella Wright.

Sims's opening words informed the court quite clearly that the prosecution's case would be to a great extent circumstantial. He then reminded the court that they were concerned with the death on 5 July at Stretton Parva of a twenty-one-year-old girl, who was employed by Messrs Bates and Co. and who lived with her parents at Stoughton. She was, he said, quoting the autopsy report made by Dr Williams, 'a well-nourished girl'. She was attractive and enjoyed cycling, and at the time of her death apparently had no troubles in the world.

Turning to the defendant, Sims stated him to be some thirty-three or thirty-four years of age (in actual fact Light was six months short of his thirty-fifth birthday). Summarizing very briefly Light's past life, Sims stated him to have been employed on the Midland Railway at Derby, where he lived in lodgings with a Mrs Morris until just after the outbreak of war. Moving on to Light's Army career, Sims stated that on 15 February 1915 he had been granted a commission as a second lieutenant in the Royal Engineers, and after training had served overseas. It may be of little relevance that the court was not told that Light's commission was a temporary one; many necessarily were in the early years at the outbreak of the war. Referring to the short time that Light held that temporary commission, Sims stated that he 'was not there very long', and that in August 1916 he was ordered back to England and gazetted out of the service. There is an error in dates here which will become apparent in a later chapter. Sims went on to say that in September 1916 Light had joined the Honourable Artillery Company as a private, again receiving training and being sent overseas from where he was ordered back to England, being demobilized in February 1919. From the time of his demobilization Light had lived at home with his mother at No. 54 Highfield Street, until in January of 1920 he had obtained an appointment as master at a school in Cheltenham. It was there that the police had found him.

Returning to the movements of Bella Wright on that fateful day, Sims said that after having a meal and writing some letters she had gone out for a ride on her bicycle and to post her letters at the post office in Evington. She never again returned home. This last statement seems to be somewhat at variance with evidence which is extant today. There is every reason to believe that in fact Bella Wright did return home, albeit only briefly.

From Bella's movements on the day of her death, Francis Sims turned to the movements of the prisoner. During the morning Light had, he said, told the maid that he was going to collect his cycle from the repair shop. Having returned home with the cycle he had had his tea and then left for an evening ride.

It may be remembered that Harry Cox had told police that he saw the man and the newly repaired green bicycle heading towards Evington, but that may not be contradictory to the statement that Mary Webb gave to police; for in fact Light could easily have called in at the Highfield Road house while en route to Evington from Cox's premises in Mere Road.

On that evening, Sims told the court, Mrs Light had arranged a hot supper to be ready by eight. The prisoner did not in fact return until ten. When asked why he was so late he said that his bicycle had broken down and he had had to walk home. The bicycle was put in the back kitchen and afterwards into the box room. Never again did the prisoner ride it, because, suggested Sims, the prisoner had 'the best of reasons' for not riding it again around the Leicester streets.

Sims then outlined Cox's statement to the police concerning his conversations with the owner of the green bicycle, and from that he turned to the statements given to the police by the two young schoolgirls. It had, said Sims, been approximately 5 or 5.30 p.m. when the girls had been riding their bicycles out to the country when, in Stretton Road, they met a man riding a bicycle who spoke to them. He had surprised them by hurriedly coming back and then following and overtaking them. He had got into conversation with them and 'they did not like it'. They dismounted and so did the man; then they remounted and rode back towards Leicester leaving the man behind.

A man called Atkins, said Sims, had seen a girl riding a bicycle about two miles from Gaulby village. She was followed by a man on a bicycle who was said Sims, 'calling out to her'. The two then rode on together. Two miles further on a farmer saw a man and a woman travelling towards Gaulby; later he saw the same man in the village.

Sims continued his opening statement with an account of Bella's visit to her relations at the Gaulby cottage and their sighting of 'a man hanging around as though he were waiting for her'. Before leaving, Bella had found that 'the front wheel of her bicycle required adjustment' and Mr Evans 'did that for her' and the cyclist, who had since been identified by both Measures and Evans, then came up and said to Bella: 'Bella, I thought you had gone the other way home.' The girl had made no reply. The prisoner had got into conversation with Evans and had said that his bicycle was 'a very heavy machine, a B.S.A.' pointing out its extremely complicated braking system. The girl wished her friends goodnight and walked with the prisoner away from the cottage in the direction of Stoughton; they 'walked side by side as though they certainly were not unknown to each other'.

Moving on, Sims spoke of the discovery of the body of Bella Wright at Stretton Parva, and of Dr Williams at first believing it to be 'an ordinary case of sudden death'. He complimented 'the long and laborious search' by Constable Hall, who he said 'acted with great intelligence'. A 'heavy bullet' was found by Hall 17½ ft from where the body had lain, trodden apparently by a horse into the roadway. It lay, he said, 'in the imprint of a horse's hoof'. Dr Williams had then discovered that death had been 'caused by a bullet'. An inquest had followed and Mr Cox had made a statement to the police after reading newspaper reports of the girl's death. Handbills had been posted which offered a reward, and he intended to show that the prisoner had been acquainted with the reports by at least one member of his household. This was undoubtedly a reference to statements made by Mary Webb. The court could, he thought, draw the inference that the prisoner certainly knew of the crime and that enquiries were afoot to trace the owner of the green bicycle; yet he had not come forward. Despite police enquiries the matter rested there until 23 February 1920.

Sims went on to summarize the discovery of the green B.S.A. bicycle parts in the local canal, the identification of those parts by Harry Cox, the filing off of the maker's identifying number and the subsequent discovery of a second manufacturer's number by Mr Saunders, which led to enquiries at the B.S.A. factory. These in turn indicated that the cycle had been ordered by Orton Bros of Derby on 3 May 1910 for their customer 'Mr Light', to whom the cycle was sold on 13 May 1910. Mr Light was, said Sims, an old customer of the firm and was in the habit of hiring motor cycles from them. The cycle had since been identified by Mr Morris, a son of the woman with whom the prisoner had resided while living in Derby. Mr Morris was familiar with the cycle, having on occasions assisted Light in the repair of it.

The police had, said Sims, traced Mr Light to Cheltenham where he had secured a post as master. He was informed by the police that they were making enquiries concerning a green bicycle and that they were also investigating the death of Annie Bella Wright who had been shot at Little Stretton on 5 July, and who had last been seen alive accompanied by a man riding a green bicycle. When asked what had become of his green bicycle the prisoner had replied: 'I never had a green bicycle.' Further, he had denied ever having bought a cycle from Orton Bros., but had later claimed: 'Yes, I sold it years ago, I do not know who I sold it to.' When told a cycle repairer from Leicester could identify him, Light had replied: 'All right, let him come and see me, I shall not run away.' The prisoner later asked the police officer what the 'stunt' was, and then said he had sold a machine before he left Derby and had also given a name, but the prisoner said he was not sure if that bicycle was a B.S.A. The prisoner had also said that he had sold an All-Weather Raleigh to an ex-officer in Leicester in September 1919.

Turning away from the bicycle and Light's arrest, Sims spoke of the bullet found by Hall, which 'could have been fired from a service revolver'. The prisoner, as an officer in the Royal Engineers, would not, said Sims, have been allowed to embark for this country without being armed. 'No revolver had been found among the prisoner's possessions.' That last and unequivocal statement, as we shall see, was not entirely accurate.

Sims continued by stating that a young lady would be called who would say that at Derby she received a letter followed by a large parcel which she was told not to open. The parcel had been brought by her to Leicester, where the prisoner opened it and 'showed her a large revolver'.

Sims then described the recovery from the canal by Sgt. Healey of 'an Army pattern revolver holster' which contained 'some loaded and some unloaded' cartridges; 'the bullets corresponded with that found near the body' and on the inner side of the holster flap there were some marks which indicated that something had been scratched out.

Mary Webb, said Sims, would say that up until the date of the murder Ronald Light rode his bicycle continually. After the murder it was put first in the kitchen and then in 'the lumber room'. In December 1919 'she did not see it' and the prisoner told her that he had sold it. In the light of recent research this date takes on particular importance.

Coming to his peroration, Sims reminded the court that in a case of murder it was no part of the prosecution's responsibility to prove or suggest what the motive might have been. The girl 'was not outraged'; she was left lying on the roadside: 'it was not a question of manslaughter, accidental death or suicide, but of murder and nothing but murder'. Whether or not the prisoner and the girl were acquainted or if they were chance acquaintances was not the question; rather it was the evidence that mattered. It was his view, said Sims, that the prisoner must have known of the police investigations, yet he had not come forward. He was the last person to be seen with the girl 'half an hour before she was found dead', and there was quite sufficient, indeed ample, evidence to justify the prisoner being sent for trial.

It was quite rightly pointed out to the court that Ronald Light could only be sent for trial if the decision of the court was that the evidence before the court was such as to justify that course of action being taken. It would in any event have been difficult, if not impossible, on the evidence before the court, even to address the question of whether or not Light and Bella were 'chance acquaintances' or if indeed they were acquaintances of longer standing. It was not a question to which the police court was required to give an answer, and it was not a question that would be to any extent explored at the subsequent trial. It was nevertheless among the folk of Leicester a burning question, and has remained so for over seventy years.

The first witness to take the stand was Mary Wright. She was, she deposed, the mother of the deceased. Her daughter had been working on the night shift at St Mary's Mills. She had arrived home at 11 p.m. on Friday 4 July and had got up at about 2.30 p.m. on Saturday. After tea she went to Evington on her bicycle to post some letters, and she had not seen her daughter again. In answer to a question by Francis Sims, Mary Wright said that her daughter walked out with a sailor. Rising for only the second time that morning (he had earlier taken exception to the way in which a statement by Light was quoted by Francis Sims) George Wightman Powers put just two questions in cross-examination to Mary Wright. She replied that her daughter would not have spoken to strangers, but agreed with Powers, however, that if spoken to by a stranger her daughter would have answered. This is an interesting point in the light of what Ronald Light himself would say at his subsequent trial, and was a point that Marshall Hall wisely would not care to pursue.

Mary Wright was followed on to the stand by fourteen-year-old Muriel Nunney, who deposed that she and her friend, Valeria Cavan, were riding away from Leicester on the Stretton Road on 5 July. At about 5.30 p.m. they met a man whom she had since identified as the prisoner. He had smiled at them as he passed, and then they saw that he had turned and was following them. They had tried to hurry but the man had caught them up and started to talk to them. He rode along with them until they came to a farmhouse by the side of the road. Then she and her friend had dismounted and he had asked her to take the lead, but she had refused. He had also asked her friend to take the lead; she too had declined. While the man was 'doing something to his gearcase' she and her friend had turned and headed back to Leicester. The prisoner had, said the witness, been wearing a light suit and had a raincoat on his shoulder. In reply to Wightman Powers, Muriel Nunney agreed that she had said nothing of this until questioned by police on 9 March when she had made a statement. Wightman Powers suggested that by that time Light had been arrested and she had seen photographs in the papers. She said she had picked out Light from nine other men. Young Muriel Nunney was not put off by Wightman Power's suggestion that the man she had met had had a moustache, replying that he had not, but did have 'a stubbly growth of hair on his chin'. She added that he was not stout and she could not have told by the way he spoke that he was a Leicester man. In answer to Sims's re-examination, Muriel Nunney said she had been able to pick out the prisoner because she remembered his eyes and his mouth.

Valeria Cavan's evidence varied little from that given by her friend, but she said she had seen no photographs of the prisoner in the newspapers.

In actual fact, two photographs of Light had appeared in the press before he was identified by the two girls. The first, which had been taken at the Midland railway station on his arrival from Cheltenham had appeared in the evening editions that same day. The second photograph appeared on Monday 8 March in the *Leicester Mercury* and showed Light wearing the uniform of a Second Lieutenant in the Royal Engineers; clearly it had been taken some four or five years earlier. The police, as verified in a letter from Holmes to Francis Sims, were confident that as far as identifying Light went the photographs would have been quite useless, and it is difficult not to agree with that assessment, for the first photograph showed Light in half profile at some distance. He wore a soft cap pulled well forward, his coat collar turned up and held tightly by his right hand. With that habitual cigarette between his lips, he left little of his face open to the camera. It seems likely that the photograph to which Powers referred was the one of Light in uniform. Although taken in close-up, even that photograph when compared with others taken at the time of his arrest bore little resemblance, and we are reminded that it was as a man with 'a stubbly growth of hair on his chin' that Muriel Nunney had described, remembered and successfully identified Ronald Light.

John Henry Atkins deposed that he was a farm labourer in the employ of Mr Parker at Stretton. He had been walking along the Stoughton road on 5 July in the direction of Norton. Between 7 and 7.30 p.m. a 'lady and a gentleman' passed him on cycles. The lady was out in front and the gentleman cyclist seemed to overtake her. When they reached the hill they got off and walked up the hill, getting back on at the top and riding away together. He put the man's age at about thirty, but thought the lady to be younger. The point where they passed him by was about two miles from Gaulby.

Thomas Edward Nourish stated that he was driving some beasts between Norton and Gaulby on 5 July, when he too had been passed by a girl and a man riding on cycles towards Gaulby, about half a mile away. Later he had seen the same man standing against a finger post, and noticed that the man badly needed a shave. When showed the photograph of Bella Wright that had appeared in the local press, Nourish stated that it looked like the girl he had seen. There was, Nourish agreed with Powers, nothing in particular about the couple to attract his attention.

Following a request from Wightman Powers, permission had been granted for Ronald Light together with his legal representatives to spend some time during the luncheon adjournment in a side room examining several of the exhibits, including the green bicycle.

The first to take the stand after the luncheon interval was Elizabeth Palmer, who deposed that on 5 July she had called at Mr Measures's cottage in Gaulby at about 7 p.m. As she neared the village in her husband's van, she saw a man and a lady pass them. Later she saw the same lady nursing a baby in Mr Measures's cottage and she noticed the same man standing beside his bicycle. He was, she estimated, between thirty and forty, and had a mackintosh over his shoulder. He was clean shaven but was in need of a shave, and he wore a dark check suit.

Elizabeth Palmer had experienced no difficulty in identifying Light, and when asked by Francis Sims if she could see the man in court she pointed to the prisoner saying: 'That is the man, I am almost sure.' This gave Wightman Powers his opportunity, and when pressed by him to swear that the prisoner was the man she had seen at Gaulby, she answered: 'No, I cannot.'

George Measures took the stand, describing himself as a roadman and the uncle of the deceased. She had visited him on 5 July arriving on her cycle at about 7.30 p.m. His daughter and her husband were staying with him at the time. Mrs Palmer had called, and as she was leaving, he had seen a man standing in the road about 200 yd away, and had asked Bella about him. He had again seen the man walking up and down at a little after 8 p.m. At about 8.30 Bella got ready to go; she had gone outside to the gate and while she was there the prisoner had come down, wheeling his bicycle.

George deposed that he had heard the man say to his niece: 'Bella, you were a long time. I thought you had gone the other way.' She had not answered. It was, said Measures, at about a quarter to nine that Bella went away, wheeling her bicycle uphill, the prisoner, who was wearing a shabby light drab suit, walked alongside her. They had seemed happy together. He took the prisoner to be from twenty-five to forty years of age.

George who himself sported a luxuriant full beard, then told Sims, much to the amusement of many in court that the man he had seen at Gaulby looked 'as though he had not shaved for about ten days'.

At this point Chief Constable Holmes felt constrained to comment on the merriment. It was, he said, a sad thing to hear laughter. A man was being tried for murder, and it was simply horrible. Alfred Turner pointed out that there had been laughter in the reserved gallery, to which Holmes retorted: 'Well, I don't know whether we can expect anything better from anybody else.'

It seems extremely unlikely that anything the Chief Constable had said could have made the slightest impression on Measures, who was obviously a man who responded to an appreciative audience. Continuing his evidence he deposed that he had identified the prisoner from seven other men at the county police station. When asked if he now saw that man in court, he dramatically looked all round the courtroom and then, raising an arm and pointing to the prisoner he said: 'There he is, that's the gentleman I'm after.' When questioned by Powers about the identity parade that he had attended, Measures said that it had taken him about four minutes to pick out the prisoner, and had said: 'Give them a trot round, the same way they do when they are buying horses.' At this point Measures, clearly eager to get his views across was reported to have become rather excited. He was reminded by the magistrate that he must only answer the questions put to him and not make speeches.

Wightman Powers managed to get Measures to say that he had read the newspaper reports and had seen the photographs in them, and had seen the wanted man's age stated in them – all very remarkable for a man who could not read, and as we have seen the police themselves did not think it possible to identify Light from the photographs of him that had already appeared in the press. On each occasion that his age was mentioned it was given as thirty-four or thirty-five. Why, then, if he had been influenced by what he saw in the papers, did Measures put the man's age at twenty-five to forty. George Measures also admitted that he had told the coroner the man he had seen was of stout build. There seems to exist no actual evidence of Light's weight, either in the summer of 1919 or at the time of his arrest in March 1920, but one other witness who identified him had earlier described him as being of broad build. It is not inconceivable, however, that any man spending over seven months waiting for a tap on the shoulder from a member of the local constabulary might lose a little weight, either in worry if he were innocent or even by design if he were guilty. Certainly several photographs taken of Light at the time of his arrest show him with sunken cheeks, and it does seem probable that he had lost a slight amount of weight. It is after all a scientific fact that weight loss shows first of all in the facial features, and only later in the build. Photographs taken of Light around the time of his arrest show him in clothing that was certainly not new but which was still a reasonable fit, so it is extremely unlikely that he had lost a significant amount of weight.

81

Anxious to repair any damage done by the excitable Measures, Sims again asked Measures about his identification of Light, to which Measures stated that he had not seen the portrait of the prisoner in the newspapers until after he had identified him. This was undoubtedly the truth. George Measures had identified Light on 4 March, the day that Light returned to Leicester from Cheltenham before his first appearance before the magistrate. The photograph of Light taken on that day may safely be disregarded; it could have been any man of average height and build being escorted by two plain clothes officers, and the portrait in close up did not appear until Monday 8 March, four days after Measures identified Light.

A waistcoat (which would actually be Exhibit No. 2 at trial) was then produced, and Measures deposed that in his opinion the waistcoat that he said had been worn by the prisoner when he had identified him was the same one he had seen him wearing on 5 July. Here there does seem to be some confusion. At the time of the first police search of Ronald Light's bedroom at the Highfield Street house, the police found and took away a waistcoat. That waistcoat appeared on an official list of items removed either from Highfield Street or Dean Close School, a copy of which was supplied by Holmes to Sims. The significance of that waistcoat to the police is fairly obvious. They believed it to be part of the suit that Light was wearing on the evening of 5 July, the remainder of the suit and the raincoat never being recovered. Light would later say that he got rid of them at the same time that his mother was parting with some old items of her own. If Light thought it necessary to part with the remainder of the suit and the raincoat, would he have been foolish enough to continue to wear the matching waistcoat? It would therefore seem likely that the waistcoat labelled at the subsequent trial as Exhibit No. 2 was the one found at Highfield Street. It seems entirely unlikely, therefore, though not impossible, that Light could have been wearing it at the time of the identity parade attended by Measures. If, however, Measures was correct and Light, at that parade on the afternoon of 4 March, was wearing the very waistcoat that had been removed from his bedroom at Highfield Street earlier in the day, the implications are obvious. It must have been handed to him by the police. It is of some interest to note that it was to that same identity parade that Supt. Levi Bowley was referring when he told the magistrate at that first hearing on 4 March that it 'was arranged and carried out strictly in accordance with the orders of the Home Office'. Light, readers may recall, responded by saying that he had not had a shave as recently as the other men in the parade. In the absence of further information it is impossible to comment further on this incident.

James Evans was next to be called. He told the magistrate that at the time of the visit by the deceased he had seen a man standing some distance away. Some time later he had gone to the front gate and, with Bella, had attended to the plate on the free-wheel of her bicycle. The man had come up behind them and said: 'You have been a long time, Bella. I thought you had gone the other way.' He had not heard Bella make any reply to the man. The man had said that his bicycle was a B.S.A. machine, at which point James Evans had, he deposed, fetched his own B.S.A. cycle out of the house, and there had been a conversation concerning the condition of it. (Here it appears that James Evans was referring to the stranger's cycle and not to his own machine.) The prisoner, who had 'a squeaky voice and spoke with a cockney accent', had told him that his cycle had just been repaired with a 'new three-speed cable'. The cycle was, said Evans, a green B.S.A. machine, with a three-speed gear control operated from the right side of the handlebars. It had a right front lever brake and a back pedal brake of an unusual pattern which worked from cranks to rim. The gear case had an open centre, and the cycle was fitted with black mudguards. It appeared that the cable was of new material and was silver-plated. James Evans further deposed that he had told the prisoner he had never seen a cycle brake which operated in that way, and the prisoner had told him that he had had it (the cycle) for some time. Thoughout this conversation, Evans stated that Bella was present. The prisoner and Bella then walked away. They were pushing their cycles, it was about 8.30 and they were, James Evans deposed, 'speaking in friendly terms'. The man looked as though he had not shaved for some days, had worn a shabby grey suit, and was carrying a raincoat. He had, he said, later identified the prisoner at the county police office.

Parts of the green bicycle recovered from the canal were shown to Evans who identified them as being from the bicycle that he had seen at Gaulby on 5 July. He pointed out that several parts of the cycle were missing – the back pedal brake, three-speed cable control, the mudguards, the chain and the gear case.

Questioned by Wightman Powers as to the extent of his evidence given to the coroner about the conversation he had had with the prisoner, James Evans said that he thought he had mentioned his conversation with the man. In actual fact there was quite a lot that James Evans had told the police at the time of his first interview which has never since been properly addressed, not being revealed by his evidence to the coroner, before the magistrate or indeed at the subsequent trial. There was one portion of his statement to the police upon which he was at no time questioned further. It was and is still an important part of his deposition, and in light of information that subsequently came into the hands of the police it ought not to have been overlooked or ignored.

Joseph Cowell deposed that he found the deceased at about 9.20 p.m., about 2 miles from Gaulby, not on the direct road to Stoughton. The body was lying on the left side of the road within a few yards of a gate. There was a lot of blood beneath the head and there was a cycle lying by her side. The girl's clothes had not been disturbed in any way. After summoning P.C. Hall and telephoning Dr Williams, he had placed the body on a float. Dr Williams arrived before the float was moved, and he examined the body.

At that point the hearing was adjourned until the following day, when William Keay, a partner in the firm of Pick, Everard & Keay in his capacity as county architect and engineer produced a plan showing the roads around Gaulby, which gave indications of the various distances between Gaulby, Stoughton and the spot where the body had been discovered. What the plan did not indicate, as previously stated, was the existence of the two gates across the route which was later termed the bottom road, a route which Ronald Light would later say Bella Wright had taken. As we have seen this was one of two possible routes, but one which the police seemingly readily endorsed and which has since, rightly or wrongly, never been queried.

Alfred Hall was the next to take the stand. On 5 July he had been on duty in the London Road at Great Glen when he had been approached by Joseph Cowell at about 10.30 p.m. The body was lying near the gate on the left hand side of the road, the whole of the left side of the girl's face and her hair was 'clotted with blood', but there was no blood on her hands or on the right side of her face. There was no blood on her clothing except for a few splashes of blood on the front of the raincoat. Her clothing was not disordered and her hat was upon her head. A bicycle was leaning against the gate, but by that time it was too late for him to examine it. There were no identification marks upon the girl's clothing. There was no reason to suspect foul play. On the following morning he had returned to the spot and searched about, also examining the bicycle, and had found a few spots of blood on the right pedal. He had gone back to the scene twice more, and at about 7.30 p.m. he found a bullet. It had been, he said, lying in the centre of the road about $17\frac{1}{2}$ ft from the pool of blood. There was a mark upon the bullet and it was lying in what he took to be a horse's footmark. It appeared to have been trodden on. The bullet had, deposed Hall, 'evidently been fired from a pistol or revolver'. Dr Williams had then been informed. When the blood had been washed from the face of the girl he had found a bullet hole about 1 in behind and $\frac{1}{2}$ in below the left eye. Dr Williams had returned at about 8.40 p.m. and

Hall had shown Williams his discovery. As a result an inquest had been opened on Tuesday 8 July and adjourned. Hall stated that on 12 March he had been on the canal towpath near St Mary's Mill, and had seen a man called Chambers fish up the rear wheel of a bicycle. The wheel was shown to him and he duly identified it.

For a description of the bullet said to have been found by Hall, the court would rely upon the evidence of a local gunsmith, Henry Clarke. In actual fact, Hall's own statement to his superiors gives a detailed description of the bullet. That description, which includes none of the jargon associated with ballistics, is based purely on Hall's own powers of observation and is probably all the more valuable for that – but the evidence presented over the months of the investigation and trial by Henry Clarke, even given the dearth of knowledge in those days, seems to have been somewhat confused and confusing. Possibly that evidence suffered in the reporting, but had that gunsmith taken a certain and positive line and felt able to adhere to it, then surely that would have been evident in the reports. That at the time his evidence was considered a very necessary part of the prosecution's case is apparent. Nowadays his evidence, in all its inconsistencies, seems to be of less importance than Hall's own description of the bullet he claimed to have found embedded in the *Via Devana*.

Henry Clarke was a partner in the firm H. Clarke & Sons of Gallowtree Gate, Leicester. Notepaper of 1920 states the firm to be 'Practical Gun & Cartridge Makers . . . by authority Military Contractors'. First established in 1832, the firm was listed as 'High Class Gunmakers' before the First World War; any military connection seems to have been a result of the outbreak of war. Throughout the war years many small gunmakers and indeed engineering firms of all descriptions that had previously had no dealings whatever with the military turned their hand to what was undoubtedly a very lucrative market. So it appears to have been with H. Clarke & Sons.

At the inquest Clarke stated that the bullet found by Hall had been fired with black powder. By the time of the police court hearing on 24 March, some seven months later, he seemed to be less sure. He deposed that it was a bullet 'adapted for firing with black powder'.

In the years before the war the Army had begun to see the advantages of cordite over black powder as a propellant. Not only was it far less susceptible to deterioration, but even more importantly it greatly increased muzzle velocity. It was something like three times as efficient as black powder. Black powder is still available today for a variety of purposes, but the black powder cartridge was, in service terms, declared obsolete in 1912.

In referring to the bullet found by Hall, Henry Clarke was able to tell the magistrate that since early in 1915 such bullets were made up with cordite. Given an envelope containing both loaded and blank cartridges said to be those fished up out of the canal, Clarke said that he had compared the bullet found by Hall with those in the envelope and they were 'identical'. He had examined one of the cartridges found in the canal and it had been 'charged with cordite'. He said it was an E.C.11, made by Eley. Yet he had already stated at the inquest that the bullet found by Hall 'had been fired with black powder', and in his evidence before the magistrate given only moments earlier he had said that 'it was a bullet adapted for firing *with* black powder'. Some of the cartridges from the canal, stated Clarke, bore the capital R and broad arrow that was the Government's mark. Such cartridges under D.O.R.A. (Defence of the Realm Act) regulations could only be obtained by those connected with the Services, and were issued for use with the service revolver. Henry Clarke was not explicit but we can only assume that he was referring to the .455 calibre Webley & Scott Mk VI service revolver which had been introduced in 1915. As suppliers of revolvers to the British Government Webley & Scott enjoyed virtually a monopoly. The Mk VI was the last of a long line of revolvers and it was not abandoned by the authorities until 1932, when it was replaced by a similar but smaller calibre (.38) arm, which many officers considered to be inferior in stopping power.

In Henry Clarke's original statement to the police, before the inquest, he stated the bullet found by Hall was 'a rim fire No. 44 bullet', a 'foreign bullet' and 'fired with black powder'. By the time of the inquest he had decided that it was 'not a rim fire bullet', though how he could possibly judge whether a bullet had been rim or centre fire after firing is beyond comment. This writer is assured by a present-day expert in ballistics that even now that would be a tall order.

In respect of the weapon that Clarke thought may have been used to fire the bullet found by Hall, he seems no less confused than he was about the bullet and its propellant. In his original statement to the police he had been loath to commit himself at all; it must, he said, have been a large revolver, 'almost service size', whatever that may have meant. By the time he gave evidence at the inquest his thoughts had hardly crystallized. If a revolver had been used, he said, then it would have been a large one, but the bullet could have been fired from either a revolver or a rifle. That the police too were labouring, quite possibly correctly, under the impression that the bullet found by Hall had been fired with black powder seems to be borne out by Holmes's interjection at the inquest to say that it was possible that the bullet had been fired from a rifle of an old pattern.

It is curious that given the presence of an 'expert witness' Holmes had felt constrained to interject at all, until we consider that Henry Clarke was never paid as an expert witness for his appearances at police court or at the subsequent trial. He questioned the correctness of that in a letter of 23 June to Francis Sims and was told that 'all allowances possible had been paid'.

As to what type of weapon fired the bullet produced by Hall, Clarke's mind was still not made up by the time Wightman Powers rose to question him. Clarke is reported as once again saying that the bullet found by Hall 'might have been fired either from a rifle or a revolver'. Clarke agreed with Powers that the velocity of any bullet when fired depended upon the quality of the rifling of the weapon used, be it rifle or revolver. Clarke agreed with Wightman Powers that assuming it had been fired from a weapon with good rifling then it might pass through the head of a person at a considerable distance, and it might still pass through after a ricochet. He could not explain all the marks on the bullet found by Hall, but it was possible that 'some of them' might have been caused by a ricochet. On this last point there would be a little guidance for the police, albeit unsought, from another source.

Even by the standards of the day the depositions from Clarke were confused and misleading, sadly indicative of the level of 'expert witnesses' to be utilized by the authorities throughout the investigation of what was stated by Holmes to be 'one of the most important cases to have occurred in years'.

Dr Williams of Billesdon was next to give evidence. It had been about eleven o'clock when he had first seen the body; he estimated that death had occurred within the previous two hours. After the body had been removed from the lane he had made what he admitted was a second 'very casual' examination. He was then of the opinion that 'it was just an ordinary bicycle accident'. It was not until the following evening at about 7 p.m. that he had re-examined the body and had found 'a small puncture wound under the left eye' which 'would admit an ordinary lead pencil'. There was said Williams, an exit wound in the upper middle parietal bone 'which might have been caused by the bullet produced'. At the inquest Williams had said that the entry wound 'would *just about* admit an ordinary lead pencil'. In answer to Wightman Powers Williams stated that the bullet found by Hall was 'bigger than a pencil' and that the bullet was 'thicker than an ordinary pencil', yet he had little hesitation in confirming that he thought the wound sustained by Bella Wright had been made by that bullet.

Dr Williams, as at the earlier inquest, still made no mention of the size of the entry hole through the skull itself, an omission of considerable importance which had fortunately been remedied at the inquest by the evidence given by his colleague at the autopsy, Dr Phillips. Dr Williams did tell the court, however, that he had cut away a section of skin from around the entry wound which showed a darkening, so that he might better examine it with the aid of a glass. He had he said 'found no powder' but he had found 'some minute pieces of metal'. Questioned by Wightman Powers, Dr Williams said he did not know the composition of the minute pieces of metal. Williams would say on a separate occasion that he thought the metal fragments had been stripped from the bullet. When asked if he had told the coroner that the shot could not have been fired from more than 4 or 5 ft away, Dr Williams replied that he could not remember what he had told the coroner. Despite his later admittance that he was no expert on gunshot wounds, it does seem probable that Dr Williams may have had something of an intuitive feeling concerning the wound and Hall's bullet – a feeling that confuted his statement that he believed the bullet to have caused that wound.

Credit must go to Dr Williams in that he did suggest to the authorities that an expert forensic pathologist be called in. That suggestion, which Williams took seriously enough to put in writing to Holmes, was rejected and the glimmer of, albeit unreasoned, enlightenment which Dr Williams clearly felt, was never explored or addressed. For his part Dr Williams retained the section of skin taken from the left cheek of Bella Wright; he preserved it in formalin and when he next appeared in court at the subsequent trial, his production of it caused something of a stir.

There was in Leicester at least one man besides Dr Williams who was more than ready to offer his opinion on the metal fragments which had been found embedded in the skin surrounding the entry wound.

A.E. Timperley, of No. 11 Latimer Street went to considerable trouble to put his feelings on the case before the police. He too, like Williams, wrote to Holmes. He included drawings and detailed explanations, but there is no evidence that anything that Timperley said, and some if not all of it was more than worthy of consideration, influenced any decision made by the police about the bullet found by Hall and its part in the death of Bella Wright. Timperley had written to Holmes on 24 March, the day after Light's final appearance at police court, but it was not until 12 April that a cursory report of Timperley's letters being received was included in a letter from Holmes to Francis Sims.

Thirty-five-year-old Timperley was a former police officer, who in earlier years had been attached to the Rotherham force. He had spent some time in Canada but had returned to Leicester where he was working as a journeyman bricklayer. Timperley's hobby was the study of and experimentation in the action of bullets. He claimed to have invented an anti-Zeppelin bullet but considered himself to have been badly treated by the Board of Trade in respect of his invention. That invention may have resulted from his knowledge of the Zeppelin raid over Leicestershire on 31 January 1916, when enemy action caused serious loss of life at Loughborough.

In Timperley's opinion the metal fragments found by Williams were the result 'of stripping of swages on the bullet' and would be present at a bullet's 'highest velocity', as it exits the muzzle. Timperley also pointed out that a bullet which had suffered a ricochet would carry what he referred to as 'a facet' or 'flat surface'. In the case of the bullet found by Hall it would have been extremely difficult to say whether or not it had suffered a ricochet, since it had been kicked along and trodden on. Timperley, who seems to have been at least as well informed as Clarke, was never given the chance to put his findings before the court.

Ronald Light's former girlfriend, Ethel Mary Tunnicliffe of St Thomas Road, Derby, then stepped into the witness box. She had, she said, made Light's acquaintance in 1910 or 1911 when they were employed by the Midland Railway in the same offices at Derby. She also knew the prisoner's mother and had visited her. Correspondence that she had had with the prisoner

Ethel Tunnicliffe and Mary Webb photographed before giving evidence at Leicester Castle court, probably at the time of the police court hearings

had ceased in 1916. Ethel Tunnicliffe agreed that at Derby the prisoner had lodged with a Mrs Morris, among other places, and she told the court that she remembered Light having a green bicycle at Derby. It had a three-speed gear and he had told her it was a B.S.A. machine. She knew of no other machine in his possession. She had last seen the bicycle at the time when Light had left Derby to take up his commission. They had corresponded during the time the prisoner was in the Army, and she had written to him at Buxton, Newark and in France. Until just a few months before she had kept a letter sent to her by the prisoner from either Buxton or Newark. The letter had informed her that the prisoner was sending her a parcel which she was not to open, but to take to Leicester. The parcel had arrived in the summer of 1915, before the prisoner went to France. She had taken the parcel a few days later to Mrs Light's house in Leicester; there she had given it to Light and had watched him open it. The parcel contained 'a large revolver'. He had explained to her that at Buxton he did revolver practice. Later, about the middle of July 1919, she had again been at Mrs Light's house when the murder at Stretton had been discussed. Mrs Light had asked her son if he did not think it was a terrible thing and he had replied that he did.

In her statement to the police Ethel Tunnicliffe said that had she known the parcel to have contained a revolver she would not have taken it to Leicester, but it seems from records still extant that in fact Tunnicliffe's statement was, although useful to their case, distrusted by the police for reasons which will become evident. Readers may best be able to judge Tunnicliffe's part in the case after reading later chapters.

Sgt. W. Healey gave evidence of his recovery from the canal of the revolver holster some four days earlier, on 19 March. On the inner surface of the flap of the holster there were, he said, marks which suggested something had been scratched out. He had found the holster about 20 yd from the spot where the back wheel of the bicycle had been recovered.

Enoch Whitehouse then stepped up for the first of his unprofitable appearances in court. He testified to having found the green bicycle frame on 23 February when he was working his boats and carrying coal to St Mary's Mill.

As the luncheon interval approached, William East Saunders deposed that he had examined the green bicycle frame and had not at first been able to find a maker's number, as it was not in the usual place, the seat pillar lug. After further examination and after removing the fork from the frame he had found a second maker's number, 103648.

The two B.S.A. clerks, Albert Davis and Sidney Garfield, then attested to their roles in the handling of the order for the green bicycle number 103648, to the order having been placed with the firm in May 1910 by Messrs Orton Bros of Derby and to the cycle having been duly dispatched to Orton's premises in Friar Gate on 12 May 1910.

Joseph Orton, carrying his ledger, followed Sidney Garfield into the witness box to testify that he had ordered such a bicycle from the B.S.A. Cycle Co. in May 1910. The ledger showed the additional entry for bicycle 103648 which Joseph Orton had entered when he received the cycle; the ledger further recorded the sale of the cycle to a Mr Light at a cost of £13 13s cash. Orton was able to recognize the prisoner as his customer and stated that he had been a customer for 'some time'. In answer to a question by defence counsel, Joseph Orton said that he had never sold another cycle to the prisoner, a statement of more value to the prosecution than to the defence, and one can only wonder at the risk taken by Wightman Powers in posing the question in the first place.

The last witness of the morning was Frederick Morris, who described himself as a metal pattern-maker of Byron Street, Derby. It was with his mother that the prisoner had lodged in St Giles Road, Derby, in 1911. At the time the prisoner owned a green bicycle which he still had when the family moved to another house in 1914. He believed the machine to have been a B.S.A. and he thought the frame of the green bicycle shown to him to be similar, but he could not swear that it was the same machine.

Following the luncheon adjournment Harry Cox, the Leicester cycle dealer and repairer, took the stand. Having given evidence in line and indeed hardly at variance with his original statement to the police taken some eight months earlier, Cox was questioned by Wightman Powers. Asked how many cycles had passed through his hands, Cox said something around three hundred. He had made no note of his transactions with the prisoner, whom he had never seen before and whom he thought was a Londoner.

Had the man who came to the shop 'a squeaky Cockney voice?' asked Wightman Powers.

'I should say he had a feminine voice' was Cox's reply. Was the man clean shaven, asked Wightman Powers? 'Usually he was, but he had not been shaved for two or three days.'

Francis Sims asked how long Cox had been in business at the time the man called at the shop, and how many bicycles had passed through his hands at that time. He had been, said Cox, in business for about two months and he had handled about forty cycles. He was asked by Sims if at Cheltenham when he had picked out the prisoner, he had known who he was. 'No' said Cox, and no, he had not known he was a Leicester man.

Det. Sgt. Frank Illes of the Gloucestershire Constabulary deposed that he had been present when Harry Cox had identified the prisoner at Cheltenham police station on 4 March. Afterwards, as he was escorting the prisoner back to the charge-room, the prisoner had remarked to him: 'My word, that fellow had me spotted all right.'

Walter Francks, a cycle dealer and repairer of No. 43 St Stephen's Road, Leicester, deposed that he had known the prisoner for eight years during which he had done repair work to the prisoner's green bicycle, a B.S.A. deluxe model. During the previous spring he had fitted a pair of black mudguards and had repaired the tyres. He identified the green cycle exhibited as the same machine on which he had worked. He was able to identify patches which he had personally applied to the inner tubes.

Mary Webb, maid to Catherine Light, then took the stand. She identified the prisoner as Ronald Light, whom she described as an engineer. She remembered that for some time the prisoner lived at Derby but returned to Leicester each weekend. He was living in Derby at the time war broke out. About October 1914 he came home until he took up a commission which he gained in April 1915. He had brought with him from Derby his luggage and a green bicycle. It had a three-speed gear 'controlled by a little black disc on the handlebars'. In 1914 they were living at Park View in Granville Road, but had moved later to Highfield Street. At the time Light went to take up his commission, he left the bicycle at home and it was placed in the box-room at Highfield Street after the move from Granville Road. The prisoner took the bicycle from the box-room and started to ride it after he was demobilized in January 1919. From that time he was at home until January 1920, during which time he helped a man work up a business. He used to leave the house at 9.30 in the morning and return for lunch, leave again at about 2 p.m. and come back for tea. He would go out again after tea sometimes, and he rode the bicycle every day. Mrs Light had gone to Rhyl on 8 July 1919, after which date Mary Webb recalled, the prisoner no longer went out 'to business'. He told her that the man he had been helping was not doing well. She could also remember that just before her mistress went away, the prisoner had told her that he was taking his bicycle to a 'fresh man' to be repaired. She remembered the prisoner bringing his bicycle in again on a Saturday evening before Mrs Light went to Rhyl. He had had his tea at home around 4 p.m. and he should have returned home for a hot supper at about 8 p.m. It was about 10 that evening when he returned, looking 'tired and dusty'. She had let him in through the back gate and when she asked why he was late he said he had had to walk because the bicycle 'had broken down again'. The bicycle was left in the kitchen for several days, then it was put in the box-room. One night the prisoner took the bicycle out and did not bring it back; a week or two later, she thought 'just before Christmas' 1919, he told her he had sold it. It was while Mrs Light was in Rhyl that Mary had exercised Mrs Light's little dog in Victoria Park, and had heard talk of the Little Stretton murder. On returning she had asked Light if he had seen the papers and told him of 'the dreadful murder'. He had simply replied 'Oh.' Mary Webb explained that a London morning newspaper was delivered daily to the house, and sometimes they had an evening paper. She described Light's usual clothing as grey and said that he owned several raincoats, but since her mistress's return from Rhyl some of the prisoner's clothing had been sold.

When handed the waistcoat which had earlier been shown to George Measures, Mary Webb simply said: 'Mr Ronald wore a suit like this last summer.' He was, she said, in the habit of shaving every day; if he missed a day he looked very dark around the chin. To her knowledge he had never owned a motor cycle, but he had once come home on one when he was an officer. She agreed that during a visit to the county police station on 8 March she had been shown a bicycle. She said the colour of the bicycle and the shape of the handlebars was exactly the same as the bicycle owned by the prisoner, but she could not remember what colour the handlebars had been. She was also able to identify a rear lamp which the prisoner had newly fitted to his machine during the previous summer.

Wightman Powers had few questions for Mary Webb. She agreed that she had not been able to recognize the saddle of the bicycle produced, but she remembered that the prisoner had had only one bicycle, and that was the green one.

The evidence being concluded, Wightman Powers rose to ask the magistrate if he believed there was a prima facie case to go before a jury. The magistrate Alfred Turner said he thought there was.

Formally cautioned and asked if he wished to make a statement, Light answered in a quiet but steady voice: 'I am innocent, and by the advice of my legal advisers I reserve my defence.'

Thereupon, Alfred Turner stated that Light would be committed to stand his trial at the next assize. Light stepped smartly from the dock, looking around the court and throwing a glance up to the gallery. We cannot know whether or not he noticed Margaret Evans, who although not a witness herself had accompanied her husband and father to court, but she certainly saw him and more importantly she heard the short statement that he had made. Immediately she turned to a police officer and said she had no doubt that the voice was that of the man who had stood outside her father's cottage at Gaulby on the evening of her cousin's death. Her nervousness had let her down at the identity parade when she had mistakenly picked out a man very similar in appearance to Light, but her ears had not been deceived. Her nervousness may have been a secondary factor in the decision not to call Margaret Evans as a witness; obviously her failure to identify Light was the primary reason, but her nervousness which she seemed unable to master had already let her down once. Had Margaret Evans been able to overcome her qualms, she would have made an interesting witness, and her instincts concerning the man she saw with Bella at Gaulby in retrospect proved to be entirely correct. A woman's intuition is not always a bad thing!

In leaving the court that day, it must be assumed that Francis Sims was reasonably well satisfied with the outcome. Light had been committed to stand trial, and that had after all been the purpose of his visit to Leicester. Despite the formality of Wightman Powers's questioning the strength of the case, there was a very strong and patently a prima facie case to be answered. There is no doubt that with the possible exception of Elizabeth Palmer, the witnesses had all taken a very positive stand in confirming their identification of Light, and it is hard to see how any alibi conjured up at the last hour, for that is what would have been required, could have moved any of those witnesses. They had stood firm for over eight months and had not been noticeably shaken by questioning from an experienced barrister of the day. Were they then likely to falter in the next few weeks?

It begs the question, just how many witnesses and what strength of evidence would the defence have needed to produce in order to present a feasible alibi? Yet it is said to this day that an alibi was expected by many, despite the fact that at the close of that final two-day police court hearing there was no clear indication of exactly what Light's defence at trial would be.

By the time of the trial the prosecution, while recognizing that the evidence was plainly circumstantial, believed that it pointed to one person only. They also believed that questioning of the witnesses in the lower court may indicate that the defence could be one of mistaken identity or may point to the death of Bella Wright being the result of an accidental shot by someone standing a considerable distance away, the bullet hitting the ground first. It is here that Timperley's advice would have been of value and where clearly Henry Clarke's was not. The conclusion of the prosecution team was that unless the defence was prepared with something very surprising in the shape of an alibi, despite the obviously circumstantial nature of the evidence the case was still unanswerable.

It must be assumed that at least Charles Bigg and Wightman Powers had some idea of what might succeed and how leading counsel might be instructed, but in the event the defence that was put forward by Light's counsel at the subsequent trial bore all the hallmarks of its presenter. It was bold, it was risky, but in its sheer simplicity it was brilliant. It addressed the one obvious, perhaps for many at the time, too obvious flaw in the prosecution's case, given that there was undoubtedly another but lesser weakness in the case, that of lack of motive.

If the prosecution's eventual case lacked some detail, it may not have been in all instances the fault of the police, who in one particular instance had experienced great difficulty in obtaining evidence of Ronald Light's activities during the time he had been in the Army. From the time that Light's rooms were searched, it was obvious to the police that he was an ex-Army officer as they found his Army Commission documents. Accordingly letters were written by the Chief Constable to the secretary of state at the War Office asking for some indication of the weapons served out to Light, and for confirmation that he had actually been in possession of a service revolver in 1916 when he was gazetted out of the Royal Engineers. Letters still extant show the growing frustration of a senior police officer unable to instil some sense of urgency into a government department, in spite of making it clear to that department that a murder enquiry was in progress. A letter to the War Office dated 17 March 1920 reveals that the police had no idea where Light got his revolver, and that they were anxious to trace someone who was in the Royal Engineers with Light and could say if he and his fellow officers were supplied with revolvers before proceeding overseas. The letter concludes that it was of vital importance that information be found. Later the same month, with the same questions still unanswered, Holmes tried again, pointing out to the secretary that the matter was 'very pressing'. The War Office eventually provided the police at Leicester with some useful information and it was followed up in interviews, but it seems doubtful, given the lack of witnesses in this aspect of the case, that the police were ever satisfied that the line of enquiry had been as fruitful as it might have been in more favourable circumstances. Certainly it seems that more information could, indeed should, have been gathered. Light's batman during his time with the Royal Engineers ought surely to have been traced.

As the prosecution admitted, the evidence adduced and used against Light was purely circumstantial, a fact that would be fully appreciated and mercilessly exploited by his counsel at the next assize. But it would be on that perhaps too obvious flaw in the case that counsel for the defence would gratefully pounce in a sensational performance, which he would acknowledge to have been his best.

CHAPTER 12

The Stage is Set

With abolition of the death penalty still some forty years away any man charged in the twenties with a capital offence, regardless of guilt or innocence, ought to have felt more than a little apprehension. Leaving aside the very real threat of a guilty verdict, the ordeal in itself would have been anathema to most men.

What then might not happen at Leicester's Castle court? What might Ronald Light have imagined his reception and fate to be? Certainly he had walked along Leicester's streets in the custody of police officers and had been recognized by very few people, but his trial was another matter. People had had time to make up their own minds, and many had already decided whether he was guilty or innocent. It might therefore be imagined that Light would have been sick at heart, not only the centre of attraction but also with the added fear that he could have the rest of his natural life snatched from him by a publicly appointed executioner.

No signs of insanity had been observed in Ronald Light. During his confinement in Leicester Prison, in keeping with the usual practice in those days, he had been watched carefully. The prison medical officer, Dr C. Moore, filed a report which stated that Light was kept under observation over two periods during the day of 24 March 1920 (having been then in custody for almost three weeks) and that he did not exhibit any indication of insanity. Therefore, in Dr Moore's opinion he was fit to plead.

If not insane, might we not expect to find evidence of Light's apprehension, of his fear for the future? Strangely, though most of the photographs taken of Light at this time, and there are an extraordinarily high number of them still extant, show him looking relaxed, unconcerned, yet not (as might be expected in a man suffering from shell-shock) uninterested. Some show him smoking his usual cigarette, while others show what can only be described as a contemptuous sneer upon his unshaven face. One might believe that he was enjoying the notoriety, the feeling perhaps of standing centre stage, of being the focus of attention. Looking at those photographs one can almost believe that he was certain of the outcome of his trial, for in none of them does Light bear even the remotest resemblance to a man who fears for his life. Maybe it was just bravado, or perhaps one might argue that he was a man of unusually strong nerve, a possibility that stands in sharp contrast to his eventual defence, which invoked consideration for a man who had returned from and had been mentally affected by war, whose determination, judgement and nerve had been completely and utterly destroyed. Archibald Bowker would later say: 'He was the calmest of us all.'

* * *

Wednesday 9 June 1920, to the relief of the vast majority who would not secure places within the cramped Castle courtroom, dawned bright and sunny. As some consolation they would watch the comings and goings from their vantage points on the nearby grassy hillock. Inside the courtroom just twenty people were allowed at first into the public gallery to sit in one row at the front; later several more were allowed in, but found there was standing room only. Some press men found themselves relegated to the public gallery.

Those left out in the sunshine eagerly awaited any movement which might herald the approach of either the defendant or counsel. An early arrival was the main exhibit, the frame of

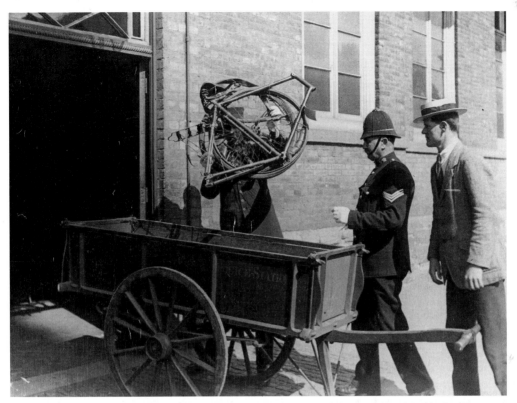

The green bicycle is taken into Leicester's Castle court. The main exhibit is accompanied by Det. Supt. Herbert Taylor, seen on the extreme right of the picture wearing a blazer and straw hat

the green bicycle which as it might be imagined, was carried into the building with some pride, for upon proof of ownership of that particular item rested quite a sizeable portion of the prosecution's case. As time would show, however, proof of ownership of the machine would be far from the crucial and vital evidence that the police believed it would be.

Next to arrive, just before 10 a.m. was a black maria. It was of the usual wooden construction, equipped to carry some six men, each housed in a narrow individual cell with no window and only a small roof ventilator to supply air. A narrow passage from front to back of the vehicle allowed access to the individual cells. This particular black maria appeared especially spick and span, possibly freshly painted for the occasion, and was pulled into the castle courtyard by well-groomed horses supplied under contract by a firm in the town. P.C. W. Gibson stood in readiness as the vehicle drew to a halt before a crowd which included small boys wearing flat caps, and one lady who, rather incongruously considering the sunshine, sported a large fur stole over a tweed costume. The only occupant of the vehicle on that morning, Ronald Light, was quickly taken out by two prison warders and ushered into the court building by a side door. The waiting crowd caught but a fleeting glimpse of him as he passed out of the sunshine and into the comparative coolness of the ancient building. Those with sharp eyes might have noticed that he was wearing a blue serge suit and light waistcoat, together with a tie and soft collar. His hair was neatly combed with a side parting on the left. Hardly surprisingly, he could not on that occasion have been described as being 'in need of a shave'. Once inside the castle, Light was taken to a small room situated under the staircase, which led from the mayor's parlour to the Grand Jury Room on the first floor, there to await his call to the dock.

Those waiting outside were now kept occupied in a continuous game of spot the well-known face as counsel for the prosecution and defence hurried into court, keen to take up their places before the arrival of the judge, a man of punctilious habit, which was scheduled for 10.30. To a man, counsel and clerks had made their way over from the usual watering place favoured by members of the Bar on visits to Leicester, the old Bell Hotel on Humberstone Gate, pulled down in the 1970s to make way for the Haymarket shopping centre.

Counsel for the prosecution was led by the fifty-year-old short, and decidedly rotund, Attorney-General Sir Gordon Hewart, at that time undoubtedly at the peak of his forensic powers. A much admired prosecutor, he had earned a reputation for that cool and clear marshalling and presentation of evidence which so aided a jury in the early stages of any trial.

Born in Bury in 1870, the delicate son of a draper, Gordon Hewart swotted while other boys played. In three years at Bury Grammar School he showed particular promise and in the autumn of 1885 Hewart entered Manchester Grammar School. A lover of the classics, Oxford beckoned him, and in 1887 he won an open scholarship to University College. There he gained a Second in Classical Moderations and the Literary Humanities. Many would have been content with that, but for Hewart, who would have liked to stay on with a Fellowship at Oxford to live the life of an academic it spelt failure. After some time as a freelance journalist, much of it in the press gallery of the House of Commons, Hewart was finally called to the Bar of the Inner Temple in 1902. Just ten years later he took silk and for the first time contested a parliamentary seat, unsuccessfully, at Manchester. He eventually entered parliament in 1913.

Hewart's rise through the minefield of the law was steady. Regularly briefed for the Treasury he was appointed Solicitor-General by Lloyd George in 1916 after turning down the Home Office. He was knighted in the same year. Three years later he became Attorney-General.

Finally, in 1922, Hewart achieved his lifelong ambition and what he would undoubtedly himself have thought of as the peak of his career when he was appointed Lord Chief Justice, but there were those who would say that he had passed that peak. From the moment he was appointed to the bench his ability to display impartiality that had so marked his conduct as a leading Treasury counsel seemed to desert him. Perhaps to say that he was corrupted by power is too strong a phrase, but it is no exaggeration to say that many who had previously been proud to claim him as a friend were frequently embarrassed and often angered by his displays of arrogance and hostility toward many defendants and, indeed, counsel. Hewart's partiality during his final years became legend, and he was frequently in trouble with the Bar Council for it. A tireless committee man, Hewart also found time for membership of many freemasonry lodges; for some time he was Grand Warden of England.

Always something of a workaholic, (he considered that he could master more than one complicated brief in the time it took his train to travel from London to Manchester), Gordon Hewart in his early days at the Bar would have drawn nothing but praise for the determined way in which he climbed the legal ladder of preferment from a humble beginning.

Quite why the Attorney-General of the day was at Leicester to prosecute Ronald Light has never been questioned. At the time, and for many years previously, it was traditional for the Attorney-General of the day to prosecute in all cases of wilful murder by the administering of poison, probably because it was thought of as so heinous a crime. Clearly poison was not a factor at Leicester in 1920. It has been suggested, though it seems never satisfactorily substantiated, that in the years following the end of the war, there was a conscious decision by the authorities to prosecute strenuously any indictment of murder against an ex-serviceman in the hope of instilling a belief that any violent feelings engendered by trench warfare and made manifest in later crimes would be treated with the utmost severity.

If anyone found the presence of the Attorney-General in any way unusual they might also have considered it relevant that by 1920 Sir Gordon Hewart was known to dislike having to travel to courtrooms out of London, though he was from time to time tempted back by high fees to his own Northern Circuit. Generally speaking there was more than enough casework to keep him permanently occupied in London, and little reason for him to go off circuit to appear in the Midlands or elsewhere.

If Gordon Hewart's position as chief prosecutor at the castle court was unusual it was made more so by his position in Leicester. When Gordon Hewart was elected as a successful Liberal Candidate in 1913, the news of his victory, with a greatly reduced majority of just 1,584 votes, was flashed on a gigantic screen to the waiting electorate in their local market-place. That market-place was in Leicester and Ronald Light, living as he did in the Highfields district, was at the time of his trial a constituent of one of the members for Leicester East, Sir Gordon Hewart K.C.

Escorting the Attorney-General into court was his clerk and friend Edward 'Teddy' Hall, who had served Hewart faithfully for many years. Hewart had been so impressed by Hall's services in the Law Officer's department during the war that he had secured the M.B.E. for his clerk, who he described as charming, gentle and of high ability.

Briefed for the Crown along with Hewart and destined to take a rather more prominent role than his junior brief would have indicated, or he himself expected, was a member of the Midland Circuit, Henry Maddocks K.C. Harry Maddocks (to his friends) had first practised in Coventry as a solicitor, where he quickly established a considerable commercial reputation. Later called to the Bar he was known to his friends as a fine sportsman with a good sense of humour, but he was never known to crack a joke in court. Maddocks's presence at Light's trial was probably attributable to the fact that a large part of his career had revolved around the early days of the bicycle and motor car industry in Coventry, when he had inevitably gained a good working knowledge of such machines. Since proof of ownership of the green bicycle was seen to be of paramount importance, Maddocks's help in working up the brief in relation to the peculiarities of the green bicycle would have been of particular benefit to the Treasury. In 1922 Maddocks would be elected Member of Parliament for Nuneaton. He was knighted in 1923 and was later appointed Recorder of Birmingham.

The second junior Treasury brief went to Norman Birkett, later Lord Birkett of Ulverston and a much respected judge of the High Court. Born in 1883 in the Lancashire town of Ulverston, now in Cumbria, Norman Birkett was educated at Barrow-in-Furness and at Emmanuel College, Cambridge. It was as President of the Cambridge Union that one of Birkett's most distinctive assets as a barrister was first noticed; he possessed a wonderfully soft and melodious speaking voice. Having abandoned his first love, the Church, Norman Birkett spent a time as private secretary to George Cadbury, son of the Bournville chocolate manufacturer, who made a gift to Birkett in 1911 of a brand new B.S.A. three-speed gear bicycle, which cost £10 13s 6d. Obviously it cannot have been the deluxe model and it did not sport that distinctive braking system – Light paid more for his B.S.A. machine one year earlier – but at least the intricacies of the green bicycle would not have been entirely lost on the most junior member of the prosecution's team.

Norman Birkett was called to the Bar of the Inner Temple in 1913. At the time of the Light trial he was a member of the Midland Circuit, in the chambers of John Hurst in Temple Row, Birmingham. If before the Light trial Birkett was considering a change of scene, then perhaps his experience at Leicester made up his mind. It was the first murder case in which he was briefed, and not surprisingly he remembered it throughout the rest of his life. One of his most vivid memories of the trial was Marshall Hall's entrance into the courtroom on that first morning. He came, in Birkett's own words 'with all the prestige of the greatest criminal defender of the day . . . who brought with him a strange magnetic quality that made itself felt in every part of the court'. Within a year of the Light trial, Birkett was installed in Marshall Hall's London Chambers.

Given that Light had already been ushered inside, the man whom the crowd now waited excitedly to see was that 'greatest of criminal defenders' Sir Edward Marshall Hall K.C.; of all counsel present he was the one man they were most likely to recognize. Almost daily it seems throughout the 1920s his name appeared in the legal columns of the national newspapers, often accompanied by a photograph of him entering or leaving a court building. Those photographs showing his arrival, immaculately attired with pristine linen cuffs peeping from an habitual overcoat, and an ebony and silver cane swinging jauntily, gave an impression of fitness and eagerness to get on with the job at hand. They gave not a hint of the nervousness that all his life plagued him, a nervousness that only dissipated as he stood to address the court. In striking contrast those photographs taken of him as he left the courtroom at the end of a trial give a very different impression. Then he was totally spent, often in great pain from varicose veins which were exacerbated by long hours spent on his feet. The misery of the pain in his legs and the attendant complications of the ailment and the necessary wearing of tightly bound heavy bandages from toes to groin frequently left him drained of energy. Yet, as that Leicester crowd

Mr. Justice Horridge.

Crowds gather on Castle Green, only a tiny minority managing to secure places in the cramped courtroom. Inset is Sir Thomas Gardner Horridge

96

would have appreciated, if one briefed Marshall Hall one briefed the whole man; he knew nothing of half measures and gave one hundred per cent – a jury advocate to his fingertips.

Once he had embarked on a case Marshall Hall's own reputation meant little more to him than his discomfort. Many times in his early years he put his own career in jeopardy. If during the course of a case he so much as sniffed injustice for his client, his hackles rose and he would worry away in his client's cause until he felt that he had achieved his aim, often at great professional pecuniary loss to himself. Those who briefed Marshall Hall may not have secured the services of the greatest lawyer in the land (he would have been the first to own to that) but they certainly secured the services of the greatest fighter of his day.

Born at Brighton in 1858, the son of a physician, Marshall Hall had in his youth harboured an intention to enter the Ministry, a calling for which he had his mother's blessing and encouragement. His father, however, had other ideas and when his son reached the tender age of twelve he was taken along to the local police court to witness the prosecution of a local 'gentlewoman' Christiana Edmunds for the wilful murder of a young boy.

The young Marshall Hall may have been struck even at that age by the obvious pathos surrounding the case, but his most striking memory was the way in which the evidence was marshalled into order by Douglas Straight. It would be several years before Marshall Hall made up his mind to go into the Law, and then apparently only because he saw a need to make money and support a wife. In the meantime he went to public school and later to St John's College, Cambridge. Called to the Bar in 1884, he was already a married man, but not happily so. He and his first wife Grace were entirely incompatible. He loved her too much, while she loved him not at all. He tried all he could to keep her but after six years of misery they separated. Within two years she was dead, the victim of a botched abortion. The abortionist was tried at the Old Bailey, and received fifteen years' penal servitude. For Marshall Hall as a practising barrister-at-law, the situation in which he found himself was very difficult. To add to the grief he felt at the death of the woman he still loved, there was the inevitable loss of income, a result of solicitors not really wishing to bring business to a young barrister tainted by an affair in which his wife had been bound up and of which he had in all probability known nothing. Not for the last time he fought back to build up a practice, and his eventual reputation as the great defender. He was and is frequently ridiculed for the occasions on which, particularly when speaking of the plight of some poor woman in the dock, he would be quite overcome by his own emotions. The tears would pour from his eyes, but he would seem totally unaware of them and would do nothing to wipe them away.

By 1920 Marshall Hall was at the peak of his career. He had taken silk as early as 1898, the year in which for the first time a defendant was allowed to speak in court on his behalf. His spirited defence of Robert Wood in 1907 would be notable for the fact that Wood was the first man charged with murder to give evidence in his own defence and live to tell the tale.

With a view to possible preferment Marshall Hall had twice successfully contested parliamentary seats on behalf of the Conservative party. In 1916, when he retired from politics, he was appointed Recorder of Guildford, a position that he held until his death in 1927 at the age of sixty-eight. Knighted in 1917, for forty-four years he served the Bar to the utmost of his ability, striving to uphold what he perceived as the honour of the Bar, a factor which in the trial of Ronald Light in particular would have presented exceptional difficulties.

Marshall Hall was never to know the preferment that he would have valued, and the comparative ease of the Bench which might have served to lengthen his life was never to be his. In 1922 he would withdraw his application to become Recorder of London in favour of Henry Dickens. Eventually the position went in controversial circumstances to Sir Ernest Wild, who was no stranger to Ronald Light. Perhaps in the end, though, Marshall Hall knew happiness. He married again, and there was a long-awaited daughter to cherish. There were innumerable friends, many of whom would in 1927 pack the Temple Church for the memorial service to a man who in the words of F.E. Smith, first Earl of Birkenhead, had by then 'not an enemy in the world'.

How much of this was known to the crowd that waited on the Castle green in Leicester we can only speculate, but there would certainly have been a buzz of excitement as Marshall Hall walked across the courtyard accompanied by his legal clerk of some eleven years standing, Edgar Bowker, who had first joined Marshall Hall in 1909 at the time of the Lawrence case. When Marshall Hall died in 1927 Bowker would say that he had lost a great friend and the boyhood inspiration of his own career. He would thereafter serve as clerk and later judge's clerk to Norman Birkett.

As advocate and clerk strode towards the Castle court they made a striking pair. Edgar Bowker, some inches shorter than Marshall Hall, sported a lightweight suit and, in common with many in the crowd, a straw boater. This stood out in sharp contrast to his chief who was as ever on such occasions attired in a black jacket and pin-striped trousers worn, even in the warmth of June, beneath an habitual dark overcoat, a precaution against chills and bronchial trouble – ever a threat to the health of the defender after 1895, when at the age of thirty-seven he had contracted and almost died of double pneumonia. His outfit on that day, perhaps a slight concession to the brightness of the day, was topped off with a light grey homburg.

The familiar face of George Wightman Powers, at fifty-six just six years Marshall Hall's junior would have been recognizable to the crowd as he made his way into the building where just over two months earlier he had stood to conduct Light's case before the local magistrate. He would in fact be appointed Recorder of Leicester in the following year, but on that day held a junior brief and completed the complement of arriving counsel.

The final event to stir the crowd on that Wednesday morning was the arrival of the judge. Sir Thomas Gardner Horridge was a Bolton man, born in 1857. He began his legal career as a solicitor in Manchester, and was called to the Bar in 1884, the same year as Marshall Hall. He rapidly established a prosperous junior practice on the Northern Circuit. Taking silk in 1901, he stood for the Liberals at Manchester East in the 1906 general election, where he had perhaps a rather surprising win over Arthur Balfour. Thomas Horridge had been appointed to the King's Bench Division of the High Court in 1910, a position he would hold until illness forced his retirement in 1938. It was an appointment which attracted some criticism, but he seems to have been a conscientious if not a flamboyant holder of that office. It was his invariable practice to write down in longhand every answer given by each witness, which had the effect of drawing out the proceedings somewhat. He had also one rather odd mannerism, the twisting of his features into a sort of half smile which gave a false sense of geniality. It was said that he had no sense of humour whatever and those who found themselves before his court either as defendants or as counsel and made the mistake of thinking that he had, did so at their peril. His way with witnesses was hardly polite, as he could be quite brusque, some have said downright rude, though there would seem to be no evidence of that during the trial of Light.

Punctual as ever, the judge's procession made its way from the judge's lodgings in the Old Assembly Rooms, which were always given over for that purpose during assize sittings. Sir Thomas Horridge's carriage was given a mounted police escort, led by Supt. Levi Bowley who remained on horseback to oversee the safe arrival of the judge who, as he entered the building, was met by the clerk of assize, George Pleydell Bancroft, who would within a few minutes read aloud the indictment against Ronald Light. George Bancroft came from a theatrical background; his father was Sir Squire Bancroft and at first the stage beckoned him to follow the family tradition. After Eton came Oxford, where together with Harry Irving, the son of another famous

The judge, Sir Thomas Horridge, arrives at Leicester's Castle court for the trial of Ronald Light

actor, he wrote plays. The diplomatic service followed and then came the Law. When his predecessor, Arthur Duke Coleridge, a descendant of the poet, died in 1913, the choice of a new clerk of assize to the Midland Circuit fell to Sir Horace Avory, the right of ancient title being virtually in the gift of the judge on Circuit at the time. Avory had no hesitation in selecting Bancroft who was at the time Avory's own marshal and had previously been marshal to Charles Russell, Lord Killowen. George Bancroft filled the post of Clerk of Assize for the Midland Circuit for thirty-three years. He has been described by Arthur Ward K.C., who knew him well, as urbane, dignified and courtly, a friend to both Bench and Bar. It was said that the conduct of the courts was always safe in his keeping, but it is probable that at the trial of Ronald Light, Bancroft would more than once have been a little surprised by what he heard, or failed to hear, and by what he saw in that Castle courtroom, which he himself described as an odd and uncomfortable court, with a table for counsel so narrow that nothing would stay on it. He recalled that Marshall Hall came well prepared with an air cushion to pad the narrow seat. It would be needed, for of the twenty-odd murder trials in which he was involved, this one would stand out as the one in which, despite the discomfort of counsel benches, he spent comparatively the shortest time on his feet. There would be little in the way of cross-examination and no witnesses would be called by the defence, and as Marshall Hall walked into that Castle courtroom he had still to meet for the first time the man he was about to defend.

The Castle court was filled to a comfortable capacity. Seating for members of the press in the well of the court being somewhat limited some reporters found themselves with those lucky few, for so they must have considered themselves, who were accommodated in the public gallery. Among the press corps were several reporters from the London papers. *The Times* reports would, as might be expected, be brief, to the point and clinical in the extreme, and in line with the paper's policy, no photographs were included. In complete contrast, over the three days that the case ran and during the following weekend, some London papers carried lavishly illustrated accounts of the case which in the number of photographs used almost rivalled the accounts in local Leicester papers. Some local photographers seem to have managed to find space for themselves and their equipment in that crowded courtroom. Some of the best-known photographs were taken by Robert Buchanan, a noted local journalist who conducted a newspaper column under the name of 'Mr Leicester'; others were taken by an amateur photographer, John Lumbers, who was better known as a jeweller and watchmaker. Not surprisingly the *Illustrated Leicester Chronicle* on the following Saturday carried a front page pictorial spread. It included no fewer than sixteen photographs of the scene in court, of the defendant, and of witnesses and counsel.

In a trial for which apparently no transcript has survived, it is something of an irony that so many who attended made their own notes of the proceedings, from the judge's longhand down to the more usual shorthand notes made by the press corps. The local *Leicester Mail* reporter, Tommy Mannock, later to be editor of the *Rugby Advertiser*, managed to find a seat close to the witness box and therefore featured in several of the photographs taken in the courtroom. Mr Mannock had taught himself shorthand and increased his speed by taking down the sermons he heard preached in church. On at least one occasion during the course of the trial the prosecution, led by Sir Gordon Hewart, actually asked to see Mannock's own shorthand notes, which really does beg the question whether anyone in that court was taking down an official note of the proceedings? And if not, why not?

Press and public watched silently as junior counsel took their places, followed by their leaders and their legal clerks. The short rotund blunt-faced figure of the Attorney-General contrasted noticeably with the taller, hawklike and almost ascetic figure of Marshall Hall who would be seated a few feet further along directly below the prisoner in the dock. Edgar Bowker, in accordance with his usual practice, had already arranged upon the narrow table his chief's spectacle case and several coloured pencils habitually used by Marshall Hall to mark the brief. A nasal spray to be used should catarrh strike during the proceedings and the indispensable air cushion were placed in readiness.

As Marshall Hall entered the court and slowly walked to his place every eye was fixed upon him. Some forty years later Lord Birkett would write that the spectators were stirred with excitement, a murmur running through the court from floor to gallery. All eyes then turned to the Bench as the judge, whose presence had been heralded by a fanfare of trumpets, took his place precisely at 10.30 a.m. Once again attention was diverted as in the company of two prison warders Ronald Light was brought up into the dock. He appeared quite calm and self possessed, several people in court noting no more than the odd swallow, which may or may not have indicated nervousness. He stood with his hands lightly resting on the edge of the dock as the clerk of assize addressed him. To the reading out of the charge and in answer to Bancroft's inevitable question, Light replied in his high pitched, 'feminine' voice: 'Not Guilty'.

The names of the jurors in waiting were then read out and Light was given the then statutory right of objection before they were sworn in. In 1920 Light would have been allowed to object, without any reason being required, to the swearing of up to seven men as jurors, a figure that was in later years reduced to three. Since 1988 there has been no such automatic right, and objections may now only be made in very exceptional and specific circumstances. The jury that woud try Ronald Light was an all male jury. Less than three weeks later six women in Bristol would be the first to share the responsibilities of jury with their male counterparts.

Light looked across and scanned the faces of all twelve men, but made no objections. The jury was then duly sworn in by the judge's clerk. Then in keeping with tradition the clerk of assize once again rose, this time to address the jury. The exact form of the words used by clerks of assize varied to some extent, the words used (with obvious amendments) on that and every occasion it was Bancroft's lot to remind a jury in a case of murder exactly where their responsibility lay, are given here. 'Members of the jury, the prisoner at the Bar, Ronald Vivian Light, stands charged upon this indictment with the murder of Annie Bella Wright on the fifth of July of last year. To this indictment he has pleaded not guilty and puts himself upon his country which country you are. It is your duty to hearken to the evidence and to determine whether he be guilty or not guilty.'

As the court settled down in readiness for what it was estimated would be a three- or four-day trial, there was a brief lull in the proceedings during which Marshall Hall took his opportunity to speak for the first time to the man he was to defend. For a short time Marshall Hall stood leaning against the dock and spoke quietly and confidentially to Light, who leaned forward to catch what counsel had to say. Light would claim to have been affected, even at that time, with deafness, yet as keen as all those in the immediate vicinity must have been to hear what was said between counsel and prisoner, not one account of that conversation exists.

For many years, indeed since 1898 when for the first time a defendant was allowed to speak in his own defence, it had been Marshall Hall's invariable practice in such a case to obtain a signed slip from the defendant before the opening of the trial stating quite clearly whether or not the defendant wished to avail himself of that privilege. Since it was not open to Marshall Hall, by tradition and by his own personal standards, to propose any particular line of defence, and incumbent upon him, he believed, simply to follow his instructions, it was imperative (he asserted) that the defendant and not counsel took full responsibility should it be decided that the defendant would give evidence in his own defence. On occasions Marshall Hall himself wrote out two slips, one stating that the defendant wished to give evidence, one stating that he did not. The defendant merely signed whichever he chose and returned it to Marshall Hall. Since it is certain that there was no meeting between Marshall Hall and Ronald Light before that brief and hurried conversation as Light waited in the dock, it is entirely unlikely that Marshall Hall had by the time the trial opened received a slip stating Light's decision, though he had almost certainly told Bigg that he must receive that unequivocal statement of intent and may already have handed his usual slips to Bigg so that they could be passed to Light. If that were the case it is certain that neither slip had been returned, for had Light done so he would have taken the opportunity to add the instructions which in the course of the day's proceedings would be handed to Marshall Hall. Edgar Bowker was of the opinion, and it was no more than that since Marshall Hall did not confide in his clerk on this occasion, that the line of defence eventually taken was totally in keeping with the instructions given to Marshall Hall by Charles Sale Bigg at his first visit to Marshall Hall's chambers in the Temple, and yet he remembered that after that meeting Marshall Hall, who was ever prone to moodiness, withdrew into himself, his mind fully occupied with what was clearly a difficult case. It was a mood which frequently affected the 'great defender' when he thought his chances of success were slim.

Clearly the instructions that he received at that first meeting with Bigg left Marshall Hall in something of a dilemma. He found himself defending a man against whom the evidence of identification was virtually complete. Wightman Powers had not been able to shake the witnesses' resolve at the police hearing, so there can have been little doubt in Marshall Hall's mind that his client was the man who had walked away from Measures' cottage with Bella Wright; and he cannot have doubted for one moment that Ronald Light was indeed the owner of the green bicycle. If nothing else, the police had brought that much at least home to Light. Yet Marshall Hall was asked to stand in court and defend this man who had constantly and over many weeks in interviews with the police, consistently denied any knowledge of Bella Wright, and had not admitted to ownership of the green bicycle. It was an onerous task. Clearly Marshall Hall could not have agreed to Light going into the witness box knowing that he had every intention of denying what was patently undeniable. Regardless of what the jury may have chosen to think, the honour of the Bar would have been uppermost in his mind. That honour together with his own personal beliefs would not have allowed him to encourage Ronald Light to take such action. Though it seems clear that Marshall Hall had not discussed the case with Bowker and even Wightman Powers may have been following his leader into court without the slightest idea of what was on Marshall Hall's mind, undoubtedly Marshall Hall would have discussed all this with Bigg, and the position had therefore, presumably, been explained to Light himself. That proceedings had progressed as far as the day of the trial itself without Marshall Hall being completely satisfied with the situation seems obvious, his moodiness after reading the brief speaks volumes for that. He could not suggest a line of defence and he could not knowingly go along with any defence which would result in his client committing perjury, so he could only point out the pitfalls if things progressed along the lines suggested to him by Bigg on behalf of Light. Quite what Marshall Hall said to Light during those few minutes of conversation must be a matter of speculation. Ronald Light was an extremely intelligent man and his maternal grandfather had been a lawyer, so he must have known that to continue along the path of total denial could, if the jury chose not to believe him, have but one end. Yet even as the court sat we cannot know that he had been convinced of the error and the dangers of following that course. If he were indeed still thinking along those lines, then those few words spoken by his counsel must have had the desired effect, for had Ronald Light insisted on stepping into the witness box still convinced that he could persist in his denials of ownership of that green bicycle, and deny before a jury that he was the man standing outside the Gaulby cottage even in the face of the weight of evidence against him, he would undoubtedly have appeared to the jury as a not very convincing liar – and in such circumstances there was little his counsel could have done to save him. Marshall Hall probably left Light in no doubt that if he persisted in his denials against all advice then the responsibility was entirely his own, and nothing Marshall Hall could say to the jury would make the slightest difference. He would in all probability be found guilty.

In the event Light was persuaded of the only course open to him, but still he seems to have taken time to think it over. It would not be until much later in the day that a note was passed from Light to Marshall Hall which indicated exactly what he would say in the witness box. That note must have come as some small relief to Light's counsel who, in the meantime, conducted the defence along the only lines possible.

CHAPTER 13

Rex v. Light

THE CASE FOR THE PROSECUTION

The Attorney-General's opening speech has frequently been praised for the lucid and cohesive account of events it surely was. Speaking in a clear voice, audible throughout the crowded courtroom but rarely rising above a conversational tone, Sir Gordon Hewart, without so much as removing the white tape from his brief, began to relate by heart and at least in the early stages of the speech in chronological order, the events which culminated in the indictment of Ronald Light for wilful murder.

After Sir Gordon had related the events leading to Bella's death, and stated that there were no signs of violence or outrage upon her body, Marshall Hall rose to his feet. In keeping with the usual practice, and having no desire to let the defence rest throughout an opening speech from the prosecution which might be of considerable length, Marshall Hall took an early opportunity of stamping his own personality on the court and allowing those present to listen to one of the greatest assets that any advocate can possess, a beautifully modulated speaking voice. Many of the great advocates have had such voices. The young Norman Birkett, hearing Marshall Hall for

Sir Gordon Hewart K.C., the Attorney-General who came down to Leicester to prosecute Ronald Light, but returned to London leaving his juniors to finish the case

103

the first time on that day, would be no exception. Might his client, asked counsel for the defence, be allowed to sit? The judge readily agreed and Ronald Light, in a voice that was clearly audible to attendant reporters, said: 'Thank you, my lord.'

Marshall Hall nodded his thanks to the judge and retook his seat. Gordon Hewart picked up the threads of his speech and continued in the same steady tone. It was the interruption he had expected, and one he may well have made himself had the roles of counsel been reversed. That interruption may not at the time have been seen in all its significance by those who were in court that day. Clearly it had the desired effect of bringing counsel for the defence to the notice of the court, but probably the primary reason for the interruption at that precise moment was that it undoubtedly succeeded in diverting the jury's attention from the last few words spoken by Gordon Hewart. He had been using the parlance of the times to state that the girl had been found fully clothed and showed no signs of sexual interference, but in the mind of the jury a small seed of suspicion that perhaps the girl's assailant had been making unwelcome sexual overtures to her may have been planted. Marshall Hall's polite request on behalf of his client had been designed to dislodge that seed; perhaps now it would not take root. He would be at some pains to reinforce the point later in the course of the trial.

Returning to the day of Bella's death, the Attorney-General stated that at about 5.30 p.m. two little girls cycling away from Leicester were passed by a man travelling in the opposite direction. At about six o'clock Miss Wright left home and went on her bicycle to the post office, purchased stamps and set off again. The road which she took easily connected with the road upon which the two little girls had parted from the man with the green bicycle.

Turning to the arrival of Bella Wright at her uncle's cottage Hewart told the jury that both Bella's uncle and her cousin (it seems evident here that he was referring to James Evans, since only he and Measures were called to give evidence of Light's presence outside the cottage) saw the man with the cycle who appeared to be waiting about. Evidence would be brought to the effect that the man had been heard to say: 'Bella, I thought you had gone the other way home', indicating that the man knew the girl's Christian name. The man and Miss Wright, he said, set off from the cottage at about 8.45 p.m. appearing to be on perfectly friendly terms. And so, asked the Attorney-General, who was the man in whose company Miss Wright was last seen alive? 'The evidence I have to submit to you is that that man was the prisoner, Ronald Vivian Light and that his was the hand that fired the revolver that took her life.'

For the first time the Attorney-General had referred to the prisoner by name. It must have been an electric moment for those in court; once again all eyes were diverted fleetingly to the dock where Light sat quite impassively, listening to the Attorney-General's words. After outlining Light's career Hewart moved on to 1910, stating that on 13 May that year Light bought a cycle from Orton Bros, Derby. On the day of Saturday 5 July the prisoner had not returned home from a ride in the country until 10.30 p.m., explaining his lateness by saying that his cycle had gone wrong. The cycle remained in the kitchen of the house for three or four days, after which it was put in the box room.

In the light of comments that I shall make in a later chapter the next sentence spoken by the Attorney-General is of great importance, bearing in mind that he was speaking from memory and not from notes. His brief still lay unopened before him on the narrow table. What he actually said would not be substantiated in evidence by the domestic servant Mary Webb to whom Hewart obviously attributed the words. She was asked no question at any of the preliminary hearings or at trial to which she could have given that answer. The inference, therefore, that she had at some time actually spoken those words to someone in authority is unmistakable, and when seen in conjunction with statements that would repeatedly be made in future years, of tremendous significance. Hewart's own exact words were reported as being:

'Later, when the servant asked him about it [the cycle] he said he had sold it.' The significance of this point, as will be seen later, is that Light did not volunteer this information, but gave it after a short time in reply to a question previously put to him by Mary Webb. The interest lies in what prompted Mary Webb's question.

Leaving this crucial but apparently unappreciated point, Hewart continued. He did not think, he said, that it was of small moment in the case that up to 5 July the prisoner rode his green enamelled cycle not merely often but regularly, and after 5 July 'never' rode it. He, Hewart, would not anticipate why; neither would he anticipate what defence might be put forward on the prisoner's behalf. But he would say that a man owning such a green bicycle might have heard the talk concerning the case and have been nervous, taking steps to conceal his possession of such a machine. The Attorney-General continued: 'Why then did he begin on this line so early?' He came home when nobody knew that the murder had been committed, and not until P.C. Hall made his search on the following Sunday was foul play suspected. The prisoner continued to reside in Leicester throughout the seven months, and the case remained a mystery until part of a bicycle was fished out of the canal. With rather uncharacteristic colourfulness Sir Gordon then referred to the coincidences of truth being innumerable, but it would seem that he did not include in this the words that he had apparently so correctly attributed to Catherine Light's domestic servant only moments previously, words that would never be given in evidence.

One of the most significant pieces of evidence in the case, continued Hewart, had been that while one identifying number on the bicycle had been filed off, there was another concealed on the inner part of the front fork. The evidence of ownership of the bicycle was described as wholly and perfectly complete. If the jury accepted that evidence, then he submitted there could not be a moment's doubt that the bicycle part fished from the canal was from the bicycle purchased by the prisoner in 1910, and since that time regularly ridden by him until 5 July 1919.

Moving on to the eventual arrest, once again Hewart drew the jury's attention to false statements by the prisoner. Why, he asked, were these false statements made? Continued dragging of the canal had resulted in a police sergeant finding on 19 March a revolver holster containing both live and blank cartridges. The jury would be told that those bullets were compared with 'those' found by Hall and that the wound could be produced by one of that type.

If this is exactly what the Attorney-General said, and it is reported in two places, it directly contradicts what has always been reported about Hall's discovery on the *Via Devana*. It was also in contradiction of the evidence given by Hall himself – that he found 'a bullet', not bullets – as those two independent reports of the Attorney-General's speech indicate. Hewart pressed on: 'Did the prisoner have a service revolver? He did not seem to have one now, but if the jury accepted the evidence that would be put before them, he certainly had once possessed one.

Sir Gordon Hewart then moved on to what is usually seen as the most important aspect of any murder case, that of motive. It was difficult, he said, but not necessary to prove any motive. He pointed out, as he was bound to do, that lack of motive need not negate guilt if all the rest of the evidence pointed clearly in that direction. Hewart went on to hint at what that motive may have been: 'there might have been a motive of a pretty obvious kind'; 'suppose the prisoner had made certain overtures'; 'suppose that in anger or in a desire to conceal that which had been attempted . . .'. It was not for the jury to speculate on the motive if they were satisfied that the deed had been done. Hewart went on to indicate that the jury should not think of circumstantial evidence as being in some way second-class evidence or, as he put it, 'of a low degree of force'. He pointed out that, unlike eye witness reports, circumstantial evidence (which might be corroboration of unanticipated incidents and as such point unmistakably toward guilt) was of great value.

Coming to the end of his opening speech, the Attorney-General once more drew the jury's attention to the throwing away of the bicycle and holster. It was, he said, manifestly done for reasons of concealment. Once again he reminded the jury of the several false statements given to the police by Light. If after hearing the evidence they had reasonable doubt they should act accordingly, but if they were satisfied that this was the man whose hand fired that shot then they should not flinch from their undertaking, which was to bring in a true verdict in accordance with the evidence.

The Attorney-General's marshalling of the facts had been splendidly placed before the twelve men of the jury, who could not have failed to be impressed. To many in court that day the case against Light at that point appeared damning in the extreme. It was almost but not quite perfect in its completeness, for it lacked, as Hewart himself had been forced to admit, a credible motive. All the evidence that the prosecution would utilize would be circumstantial, but many people had been executed as a result of circumstantial evidence far less strong than would be brought against Light.

Those with experience in such cases who heard Gordon Hewart's speech were convinced of the difficulty of the defence's position. Lord Birkett stated in later years that at the time he thought the charge to be quite unanswerable. For Ronald Light it looked grim indeed, yet he himself showed no particular emotion as he watched the Attorney-General retake his seat. No apparent worry showed on the face of Marshall Hall, yet he had walked to court on that morning in almost total silence and had made no mention whatever of the case to his clerk Bowker. He had, with the exception of that one brief interruption, sat impassively throughout the Attorney-General's speech, occasionally using his nasal spray, but otherwise outwardly unmoved and deep in thought. Upon accepting the brief, he had undoubtedly told Light's solicitor, Charles Bigg, of the difficulty he saw in pursuing a line of defence based on Light's total denial, information that must have been communicated to Light at the time. He had had that short conference with Light as he was brought into the dock; now everything hinged on Light himself as one by one the prosecution witnesses were brought before the court.

Perhaps more than once during the trial of Ronald Light, Marshall Hall would recall his own words, spoken after an earlier capital case: 'In any case it's not the speeches that matter but the witnesses.' In this case several witnesses would not be troubled at all by Marshall Hall; he was content to let them go without a question, and it may be supposed that more than one of them was thankful for that.

William Keay was the first witness to take the stand, in his capacity as county architect and engineer. He was a partner in the firm of Pick, Everard & Keay of No. 6 Millstone Lane, Leicester, and was in court to attest to the accuracy of plans showing the area to the east of Leicester which was relevant to the case. All the roads and lanes in the area, and the main points of reference, were marked on the plan. The plan also showed what would be referred to as the top road (the most direct route from Gaulby back to Stoughton and Leicester) and the bottom road on which Bella Wright's body was found, which again led back to Stoughton and Leicester, albeit by a longer route. The plan included a series of distances from point to point, including the mileage from Gaulby to the spot where Bella was found and the distance back to Light's home in Leicester from the same spot. After giving formal evidence of the accuracy of the plans and distances, though as previously indicated they were clearly inaccurate as those two obstructive gates across the bottom road were not shown, William Keay faced just one question from Marshall Hall, who asked which was the shortest way to the defendant's home in Leicester from Gaulby. In reply William Keay stated, and the truth of what he said was borne out by the plan, that the straight way home from Gaulby to Leicester was by the top road through Stoughton and Evington.

Here Sir Thomas Horridge took an early opportunity to check that the jury, and perhaps he himself, understood the plan thoroughly before the trial proceeded any further, laboriously reading aloud his own longhand notes of all that William Keay had said. To further aid the jury several photographs of the scene of the crime, supplied by S.W.A. Newton, a local Leicester photographer, and a plan of the relevant stretch of the local canal showing the precise spots at which the various exhibits had been recovered were made available.

Next to step into the witness box was the sad and rather slight figure of Mary Wright. She again wore her mourning coat of dark grey with a black bound edging and a matching dark felt hat with upturned brim. After taking the oath she stood with her hands clasped before her. Her evidence was simple and straightforward, and there were no questions for Mary Wright from Marshall Hall after she had stated plainly what she knew of Bella's last day alive. This included the fact that Bella had left the house wearing a light raincoat and carrying an oilskin (which had been handed to Supt. Taylor only a few weeks before the trial) when she had last seen her alive.

Following Mary Wright into the witness box came the tall and moustached figure of Joseph Cowell, his dark homburg style hat hung on a peg at the rear of the box. In answer to Hewart, Cowell stated that he farmed at Elm Farm, Stretton Parva, and related his finding of the body, and his further actions before Bella's body was taken to the empty cottage. Marshall Hall had just one question for Cowell. How close, he asked, was the nearest cottage in Little Stretton to the point at which the woman's dead body lay? Joseph Cowell estimated the distance to be about 220 yd. Clearly Marshall Hall's intention was to implant in the minds of the jury that there were on that night people in the area, even residing in the area; that it was not the isolated spot some may have thought it to be. Yet no witness would be brought forward to say he had

A recent photograph of the chapel at Little Stretton, where the body of Bella Wright was taken

heard a shot in the vicinity around the time in question. Marshall Hall was careful not to ask any question that might have given the prosecution a reason to re-examine any of the witnesses. He knew perfectly well that the fewer words spoken by any witness, the shorter the time in which they could impress the truth of their evidence on the jury. If Light failed to see the only course open to him, then the less the jury remembered of the witnesses the easier it would be for Marshall Hall to speak in Light's defence, though quite what even Marshall Hall could have found to say in such circumstances defies speculation.

P.C. No. 97 Alfred Hall then stepped smartly into the witness box, looking every inch the reliable officer. Tall, good looking and sporting a handle-bar moustache, he gave his evidence in a confident voice. He had, he said, arrived at about 10.50 on the Gartree road, where the woman's body lay. Her clothes were not torn and her hat was upon her head. At that time there seemed no reason to suspect that a crime had been committed, and it was not until he was performing a second examination that Dr Williams found a small puncture under the girl's left eye. The only possessions on the body had been an empty purse, a handkerchief and a box of matches. Hall went on to relate that at six on the following morning he found a few drops of blood on the bicycle's right pedal, and at about 7.30 p.m. he found a bullet lying in the centre of the road about 17½ ft from the pool of blood. He stated that he had had some experience of firearms and in his opinion the bullet had been fired from a pistol or a revolver. Hall went on to say that it was he who washed the blood from the girl's face and discovered a bullet hole about 1 in behind and ½ in below the left eye; at that time no other wound was found. These words seem to completely contradict those already spoken by Hall only minutes before, when he stated that it was Dr Williams who found the bullet hole near Bella's eye. It must be assumed that he was trying to say that it was he who found what he thought was a bullet hole, but only when Dr Williams returned was the puncture confirmed as a bullet wound. The truth of this sequence of events seems to be substantiated by Hall's next sentence, when he says that at about 8.30 p.m. he pointed out the wound to Dr Williams. The Attorney-General's questions then moved to 12 March 1920. Hall stated that on that day he was travelling along the tow-path of the Leicester canal in the vicinity of St Mary's Wharf when he saw the back wheel of a bicycle fished out of the canal; he identified the wheel exhibited.

For the first time Marshall Hall had more than the odd question to put in cross-examination. In answering, Hall said he was led to believe that Dr Williams had first formed the impression that the girl had fallen from her bicycle. When asked in what position the bullet was found in relation to the body, Hall stated that it was found nearer to Gaulby than the place where the body had lain. When asked how big the puncture was that he had found in the girl's cheek, he said that a lead pencil could easily be inserted into it. In answer to a question concerning the police handbill which Marshall Hall pointed out was dated 7 July 1919 and offered a £5 reward, Hall told the court that it was circulated throughout the district on the Tuesday after the tragedy and was affixed at police stations. Marshall Hall clearly made no reference to the description of the man whom the police wished to trace, but Hall agreed that the handbill contained a description of a green enamelled bicycle, thereby smoothing the path should Light even at this late hour see the sense of Marshall Hall's words to his solicitor, which in all probability had once again been emphasized in that courtroom just a couple of hours earlier.

Then Marshall Hall made his only direct reference to a statement that Hall had given to the coroner at the time of the inquest. In that statement Hall had referred to blood found on an adjoining gate. Hall explained to counsel for the defence that that point was cleared up later, when a raven which had died by gorging blood had been found in a field. He said he had traced the marks of its claws on the gate.

The testimony of Hall would seem to indicate that the bird was not found before the opening of the inquest into Bella's death which was on the afternoon of Tuesday 8 July 1919. It is easy to see why counsel for the defence left out all mention of the bird from this point onwards, as clearly the bird could have found its way into the field on any of at least three days following the discovery of the dead girl.

Gordon Hewart rose to re-examine, and in answer to him Hall stated that no notices were posted in his district before the evening of 7 July.

P.C. Hall, his evidence completed, was not allowed to leave the stand before the judge had added his own words of congratulations on the constable's efforts – in which he entirely agreed with what the Attorney-General had said concerning Hall's intelligence.

Any adult called upon to give evidence in a murder trial must find it a disquieting prospect, but for a fourteen-year-old girl to face not only examination by the Attorney-General or one of his lieutenants but then cross-examination by perhaps the country's leading defence advocate must be a particularly daunting task. Young Muriel Nunney dressed in her school boater and belted coat stepped into the witness box, and in minutes the whole atmosphere within the courtroom would change, although it would in no way be attributable to anything Miss Nunney had to say. In answer to Norman Birkett's first question, Muriel, a daughter of Albert Nunney, managing director of Keite's, a local coach and car building company, stated that she lived at No. 28 Evington Drive, Leicester. 'Had she' Birkett asked, 'cycled with her friend Valeria Cavan on 5 July [1919]?' Before she could answer, Marshall Hall was on his feet, justifiably protesting that Birkett was leading the witness. At this stage it seems more than probable that Marshall Hall had strongly advised Light of his position and of the value of giving evidence on his own behalf; he may also have received some information that Light was considering doing just that. But Marshall Hall still had a little time to wait before he would receive written notice of that decision. It seems evident that it would not have been before the luncheon adjournment that Light (reported as taking a keen interest in the morning's proceedings) would find the time to write a note containing his own specific instructions, which would be handed somewhat belatedly to his counsel.

Meanwhile, Marshall Hall's somewhat dramatic statement took the whole courtroom by surprise. He intended to cross-examine this particular witness and if necessary the next one, Muriel's friend Valeria Cavan, and he had no intention of anything upsetting his plans for what he knew to be a crucially important cross-examination. Having seen the two girls' earlier depositions he had a very good idea of what they would say. If the implications of their statements were allowed to stand unchallenged it could be most damaging for his client's case, whatever Light's eventual decision regarding his own evidence might be. Any suggestion that Light had in any way threatened the two young girls or was indeed capable of such an act had to be dealt with at the very first opportunity.

The words that Marshall Hall spoke on that occasion rang through the court as they have rung through forensic history ever since. It was the first hint that those in the Castle court had of exactly what the chosen line of defence might be. Possibly those few words spoken before Ronald Light's instructions were received by his counsel may have galvanized Light, probably with the assistance of Bigg, into taking action during the approaching luncheon adjournment.

Marshall Hall's words were directed to the judge but hardly a person present failed to grasp the significance of them: 'I might tell your Lordship that these two young ladies will be the only witnesses to fact for whom there will be any cross-examination. There will be no cross-examination as to identity or ownership. The girls' part of the story will be denied entirely; I of course admit to nothing. I would point out that the two girls were not called upon to give statements to the police until March 9 1920, statements of something said to have occurred on July 5 1919.'

The two schoolgirls, Muriel Nunney and Valeria Cavan, who identified Ronald Light as the man who tried to engage them in conversation near Evington shortly before he rode into Gaulby with Bella

The point was well made, and the judge felt constrained to instruct the jury about the evidence of the next witness, Valeria Cavan. Turning to the jury, the judge charged them that they must remember Mr Birkett had suggested the date to the last witness; they must be sure that a date was not mentioned to the next witness. It was clear to those in court that whatever the exact line of defence may turn out to be, it would not be one of alibi as many who had attended the preliminary hearings thought likely.

Muriel Nunney's examination continued and she went on to say that the man whom she and her companion saw on the road on that day (5 July) had later been identified by her from twelve men. He had a green bicycle with 'funny handlebars'. The man wore a light suit and carried a raincoat over his shoulder. She was asked by Norman Birkett if the man had spoken to her and her friend; she said he had and then in a tense courtroom, a witness was asked for the first time if the man they described was in court that day. Muriel Nunney had no hesitation in pointing to the dock and saying clearly: 'There, Sir.' Marshall Hall rose to cross-examine: 'Did you hear about what was called the green cycle case?'

'Yes, Sir.'

'And I think you saw the photographs?'

'Yes, Sir.'

'You knew about this poor girl being found dead in the road?'

'Yes, Sir.'

'You read it in the papers, I suppose?'

'Yes, Sir.'

'You were asked if you had seen this particular man on the 5th of July?'

'Yes.'

'They [meaning the local police] gave you a date?'

'Yes, Sir.'

Further questions from Marshall Hall resulted in Muriel Nunney telling the court that she and Valeria Cavan had talked it over and quite made up their minds that it was on 5 July that they had met the man on the green cycle; but any impact that her evidence might have had on the jury was largely destroyed by the prosecution's own goal in the opening moments of her appearance. The remainder of her evidence had been partially if not entirely demolished by cross-examination. The intention of counsel for the defence to cross-examine both girls and show the jury that they had discussed the case after reading about it and only at that point thought that they had met the man, and had in fact had the actual date of the meeting suggested to them by the police, was obvious, but the full impact of counsel's intention was to an extent thwarted by the luncheon adjournment, which divided the evidence given by Muriel Nunney and Valeria Cavan.

By the luncheon interval the case for the prosecution was not nearly complete, and it became evident that, as previously suspected, the jury would have to spend at least one night if not a second in seclusion. Sir Thomas Horridge informed the jury that they should take the opportunity to send home for anything that they might need for the night, adding the usual warning that they should not communicate in any way anything connected with the trial. They would, he said, be lodged overnight at a Leicester hotel, the Royal, which had previously been home to Francis Sims during his time in Leicester for the police court hearing.

It was under the roof of the Bell Hotel, readers will recall, that throughout the trial counsel both for the prosecution and defence and their respective retinues would be housed. The atmosphere at the Bell within what was commonly referred to as the Bar Mess, was as ever congenial. Convivial dinners, carefully laid down stocks of wine and a never-ending stream of anecdotes ensured that the members of the Midland Circuit enjoyed their stay in the town. On that very first night at the Bell, the 'off circuit' Attorney-General found himself climbing into an apple pie bed. Not known for his sense of fun, Gordon Hewart was less than pleased and insisted that his own clerk find out who was responsible. The culprit was apparently never discovered, or perhaps Teddy Hall chose not to reveal his identity, but in later years Edgar Bowker gave the impression that he at least was certain who had given the clerks and moreover, counsel for the defence a good laugh at the expense of the Attorney-General.

The luncheon interval being over, twelve-year-old Valeria Cavan stepped into the witness box. As might be expected she appeared even more nervous than Muriel, and she was certainly more hesitant. She told the court that she had been out cycling with her friend Muriel Nunney one Saturday in the summer. She was confused about which summer, but did not think it was the previous summer. She seemed, however, quite sure of where they had cycled. It was on the Stretton Road, and it was there they met the prisoner. He was riding towards Leicester, but later caught them up and rode along with them. Valeria described how she and her friend dismounted at the foot of a hill. The prisoner spoke to them, first asking Muriel to take the lead, and when she would not asking Valeria herself. She too had refused, and the friends had then turned their cycles around to head back towards Leicester. The prisoner, Valeria said, seemed to have something wrong with his cycle because he stopped to attend to it. It was a green cycle and he was wearing a light suit and carried a mackintosh. She had later identified the prisoner at the castle. In reply to a question apparently put to allay any fear that the jury might have had about when the girls first gave their evidence to the police, Valeria Cavan agreed with prosecuting counsel that the incident she had just described had taken place before she heard of the green bicycle murder case.

Next to take the oath was Dr E.K. Williams. He stated that on the evening of Saturday 5 July he received a telephone message from Joseph Cowell at about 10.50 p.m. as a result of which he had gone to the Gartree Road. There he saw P.C. Hall, and had made a casual examination of the dead girl, sufficient to satisfy himself that death had occurred. It was his opinion that death had taken place within the previous hour and a half. Dr Williams further stated he thought at that time that death was due to an accident. On the following day he again met Hall and, the face of the girl having been washed, made a detailed examination, finding a puncture wound on the left cheek and a larger wound on the top of the head. The small puncture wound on the cheek would 'admit an ordinary lead pencil, which passed upwards, inwards and backwards' to another oval wound which was $1\frac{1}{2}$ in long and $\frac{1}{2}$ in wide, over the middle and upper right parietal bone. By way of explaining why he had not previously noticed the two wounds, Dr Williams said that the exit wound was in the hair and that there was dark discoloration around the face wound. This discoloration he at first thought (presumably after the discovery of the exit wound) to be due to burning, but when he had later examined it under a magnifying glass he had seen the natural down around the wound. He had taken the skin away and extracted some tiny pieces of metal. He had performed a post-mortem examination together with another doctor on 7 July. He had found that the body was well nourished and showed no signs of bruising on the arms or body. There were scratches on the left cheek and on the left hand and wrist, probably caused by gravel. He further found two small contusions near the right angle of the mouth, and the left eyelid and eyeball were injured. At this point Dr Williams was asked to examine Exhibit 6, the bullet produced by Hall after his search of the *Via Devana*. Dr Williams agreed with prosecuting counsel that the wound to the head might have been caused by the exhibited bullet. He thought the other wounds might have been caused by a fall from a bicycle.

As might be expected, in cross-examination Marshall Hall concentrated on the actual wound and on the damage that the bullet might have been expected to inflict. After an initial and apparently innocuous question concerning the time at which Dr Williams arrived at Cowell's house, to which the doctor replied that it had been about 10.45 or 11.15 p.m., Marshall Hall asked perhaps the most significant question put to the doctor so far. Dr Williams had been a little thrown by the first question – 'What time did you arrive at Mr Cowell's house?' – thinking, no doubt, that counsel was asking what time he had arrived at the scene of Bella's death. A little taken aback, he was a little hesitant in his answer; but in an effort to recover his composure he answered the second and far more important question with undoubted accuracy. He had, he said, not much experience of gunshot wounds.

Then, almost as though he could in some way mitigate his lack of knowledge Dr Williams did a remarkable thing. There and then he produced, from the black bag which he carried with him, a bottle of formalin which contained the actual piece of skin he had removed from the face of the victim, and which encompassed the small puncture wound where the bullet had made its entry. Never an official exhibit, though left on display in the courtroom throughout the rest of the trial, the specimen had apparently been in Dr Williams's sole possession for the whole of the previous eleven months. The production of this specimen gave an opportunity of which Marshall Hall was quick to make capital. Using his slim silver propelling pencil he carefully lifted the specimen out of its protective fluid and proceeded to demonstrate to the jury that the pencil could hardly pass through the small puncture made by the bullet that had killed the deceased, the bullet that the prosecution claimed to be the one that Hall had found. It was certainly one of the most gruesome of all Marshall Hall's many and varied demonstrations in court over the years, and undoubtedly one which throughout their deliberations would remain, as counsel for the defence intended, in the minds of the jurors.

In answer to further questions put to him by Marshall Hall, Dr Williams said that he thought that the bullet that had killed the girl had been fired at a distance of not more than 6 or 7 ft. In reply to what must have been a question put with some incredulity by Marshall Hall, he did not think that with a bullet of this size, travelling at a tremendous velocity, there was likely to be a larger exit hole. He did not know what distance a Service revolver would throw a bullet; no, he was not surprised that it was more than half a mile. Dr Williams apparently agreed with Marshall Hall that the clean cut hole in the skull and the small exit hole indicated high velocity. To a question framed to lead on to Dr William's depositions of some months earlier, he stated that in Leicestershire there was both hard and soft ground with stones in it against which a bullet could be arrested; he thought the bullet may meet the soil and hit the hard underlying ground, which would give it sufficient momentum to carry it into the road. That theory, countered Marshall Hall, was only tenable on the assumption that the woman was on the ground, or that her head was between the revolver and the ground. Did not the witness remember that he had previously told the coroner he could not form an opinion as to the position of the woman when she was shot? Dr Williams agreed that this was so, but added rather lamely, and giving no supportive reason for his apparent change of heart, that he had thought about it a good deal since. He was bound to agree with counsel, albeit somewhat reluctantly, that it was absurd to suppose that if a bullet (and here presumably Marshall Hall meant of the type produced) was fired without any further resistance than the head of the girl it would be found only 6 yd away.

The prosecution team apparently felt themselves to be on rather shaky ground with Dr Williams; they chose to leave well alone and not re-examine. If either the Attorney-General or his juniors at that point thought of the name of that most eminent forensic pathologist Bernard Spilsbury, 'that incomparable witness', they might be forgiven. There can, however, be little doubt that throughout the eleven months that Dr Williams had held that specimen, he had often himself thought of Spilsbury and of Wilcox and wondered what they might have concluded if given an opportunity to handle the specimen which he so carefully retained.

If the prosecution felt that they had failed so far to make the most of their 'expert' witness, perhaps they hoped that any lost ground might be made up when the local gunsmith gave his evidence. They would have been only too well aware that Marshall Hall would, as with Williams, again be in his element during that particular encounter. It turned out that this was listened to with particular interest by Light, who from time to time throughout the prosecution case was seen to make notes. In actual fact he would, rather distractedly, carry his pen into the witness box where he would toy with it throughout his testimony.

Mrs Kathleen Power then took the stand. On 5 July 1919 she had been employed at Evington post office, and while on her round she had met the deceased who had bought some stamps from her and had given her some letters to post. The deceased had then ridden towards her home. There was nothing for Marshall Hall to gain from cross-examination and Kathleen Power stepped down, with perhaps a sigh of relief.

Her place was taken by farmer Thomas Nourish of Glebe Farm, Little Stretton, who told the court that he was driving his beasts along the Little Stretton to Gaulby road, he believed on 5 July, when a man and a girl riding cycles passed him. They were going towards Gaulby and were about a quarter of a mile distant from him. It was between 7 and 7.30 p.m. Nourish went on to say that after putting his beasts in a field he came back along the same road where he saw a man whom he described as 'a gentleman' waiting there. He thought the gentleman to be the same as passed him with the young lady. The gentleman was dressed in a grey suit, aged about thirty-five and was 'in need of a shave'. Thomas Nourish was then shown what became the best-known photograph of Bella Wright, which had appeared in the *Leicester Daily Post*. The photograph showed Bella wearing a large brimmed hat. Nourish said it was very like the girl that he had seen.

Once again there was no cross-examination, but conscious that those in court who were frequently present on such occasions would be wondering what precise strategy was uppermost in Marshall Hall's mind he leaned over and passed a pencilled note to George Pleydell Bancroft, clerk to the Midland Assize. The note in Marshall Hall's usual scrawling hand brought a smile to the face of Bancroft. It reminded him of a mutual friend of the Bar in earlier years, saying simply: 'Wasn't dear old Montagu Williams right when he said to me, "My boy, remember the real art of cross-examination is not to cross-examine."'

Bancroft may have realized that in that piece of humour Marshall Hall exhibited some relief, for if in doubt he was the most reclusive of men, but his naturally ebullient personality would surface the moment those doubts dissipated and he could see his course straight and clear before him. There can be little doubt that by this point in the proceedings the long-awaited written instructions from Light had finally passed into his hands.

Several more witnesses would leave the witness box, grateful for not having had to face cross-examination, and it is a fact that in none of his capital defences before or after would Marshall Hall so vividly recall Montagu Williams's advice, and allow so many prosecution witnesses to leave the box untroubled.

Mrs Elizabeth Palmer of Illston-on-the-Hill gave evidence to the effect that a man and a woman riding cycles passed her near Gaulby on the evening of 5 July. She had seen the girl dismount and go to Mr Measures's gate. In response to Henry Maddocks's request she turned and looked at Light as he sat in the dock. 'Is that the man?' asked Maddocks.

'Yes, Sir.'

Now into the witness box stepped George Measures. He stated that he was a roadman and that the dead girl was his niece. He said she had visited him on 5 July, when his daughter and son-in-law, James Evans, were also on a visit. He saw a man with a cycle standing near to his house and when Bella was about to leave the man had said to her: 'Bella, you were a long time, I thought you were gone the other way.' The man had, said George, accompanied the girl when she set off on her cycle. He had noticed that the man had not had a shave. Prosecution counsel retook his seat, and George, keen to ensure that the court knew exactly of which man he had spoken, before Marshall Hall could get to his feet and in a scene reminiscent of the earlier hearing, raised his arm and pointed directly at Light, speaking out in a voice that was audible right across the courtroom: 'That's the man who was outside my house.' For his sins George received a rebuke from Mr Justice Horridge, but it was too late. No one in that courtroom was in any doubt that at least George Measures had no difficulty in recognizing Ronald Light as the man who had been in company with his niece Bella Wright on the evening of her death.

With George's accusation ringing in his ears, Marshall Hall rose to cross-examine. It was not the identity of Light that interested him but to whether or not Light and the girl were known to one another; he hoped to take this early opportunity to indicate to the jury that they were not.

'Did not you ask your niece if she knew the man, and did not she say, "I do not know the man, he is a perfect stranger to me?"'

'Yes, Sir.'

'Did not your niece tell you the man had overtaken her?'

'Yes, Sir.'

'And that he said he had come from Great Glen?'

'Yes.'

'And that he had asked her the name of the village?'

'Yes.'

Marshall Hall had established as well as he might that Bella had told her uncle that the man who waited outside the cottage was a stranger to her. With that he decided to let George go; he

George Measures, Bella's uncle, an excitable witness

recognized a man who was likely to speak out beyond the expectations of counsel. He had already done so once in the previous few moments, and no doubt Marshall Hall had been warned by Wightman Powers of Measures's enthusiasm in the lower court. There was clearly more to be lost than gained in risking more questions. Marshall Hall, perhaps a little unusually for him, decided to take the path of caution. Henry Maddocks had just one question on re-examining Measures; in reply, George Measures told the court that Bella also passed the remark: 'I'll sit down a little while, and he will perhaps be gone.'

George Measures's place in the witness box was taken by his son-in-law James Evans, who repeated the man's words spoken to Bella as she left the cottage almost word for word as they had been given to the court by his father-in-law: 'Bella, you have been a long time. I thought you had gone the other way.' Evans then went on to say that he had had some conversation with the man about his bicycle, the man saying that he had had the bicycle for some time. He said that he noticed the bicycle was, as he called it, pea-green, that it had a three-speed gear and a back-pedalling brake. He also noticed that the man needed a shave. When asked by Henry Maddocks who the man was, James Evans replied: 'The prisoner.'

For the first time the main exhibits, namely the green bicycle frame and other parts of the cycle including the back wheel and handlebars, were produced. James Evans stated that they were similar to the bicycle that the prisoner had, except that he thought the carrier was not the same and the disc for the three-speed gear was missing from the handlebars.

Again Marshall Hall had no questions for the witness, but the judge Sir Thomas Horridge was at pains to be certain of what the witness believed the man on the green bicycle said to Bella outside the cottage. Had the man said 'Hello', or had he said 'Bella' to the deceased. James Evans was emphatic: the word was 'Bella'.

Ethel Tunnicliffe then took the stand. Examined by Norman Birkett she told the court that she had taken cycle rides with the prisoner. She could remember a green bicycle and that the prisoner had told her it was a B.S.A. machine. She could also remember receiving a letter from the prisoner who was either at Buxton or Newark in about 1916, in which he told her that he was sending her a parcel which she was not to open but to take to his Leicester home. When it arrived she had taken it to Leicester and seen it opened: it contained a revolver.

'Who opened it?'

'Ronald opened it.'

Ethel said that she visited the prisoner's home soon after the murder, and it had been discussed. The prisoner's mother had said that it was a terrible thing, and when asked if he did not agree the prisoner had said 'Yes'.

Cross-examined by Marshall Hall as to whether or not the prisoner had actually asked her to keep the parcel for him, Ethel Tunnicliffe replied that she did not know. She seemed also to be unsure of the date that the parcel had arrived. Marshall Hall noted that during Birkett's examination she had said 'about 1916', when on her police court deposition he clearly read '1915'. Pressed by Marshall Hall she said she thought the revolver arrived in 1915, but she could not remember the exact date.

At police court Ethel Tunnicliffe had seemed more certain, and her words of qualification at that time 'sometime in the summer of 1915, before he went to France' would seem to have more of the ring of truth than her evidence at trial. Any confusion over the date may have been a measure of her nervousness, and probably was in no way significant.

Following Ethel Tunnicliffe on to the stand was another Derby resident, Frederick Charles Morris, who described himself as a metal pattern-maker. He told the court that the prisoner lodged at his mother's house in St Giles Road, Derby, in 1911, while he was employed at the offices of the Midland Railway. In 1914 the Morrises moved to Hartington Street and the prisoner moved with them, staying until he left for Leicester either just before or just following the start of the war. Throughout the time he lodged with them he had owned a green bicycle, which he took when he left. Morris could remember seeing it almost daily. Offered Exhibit 3, the cycle frame which Enoch Whitehouse had raised from the bed of the canal, the witness said it was exactly the same except that the three-speed control was missing from the handlebars.

Frederick Morris having left the stand, the first day of the trial came to a close. The proceedings ended with a short discussion between the judge and Marshall Hall which indicated that in all probability the case would not be concluded on the following day, which would mean a second night of enforced seclusion for the twelve men of the jury. Apparently at that point Marshall Hall apprised the judge of his intention to call Ronald Light.

* * *

THURSDAY 10 JUNE 1920

At the opening of the second day of the trial, Mr Justice Horridge indicated that he wished to put another question to Dr Williams. No one, he said, had thought fit to ask the doctor what the actual cause of death had been. It was, Marshall Hall assured him, just an oversight, but Horridge was insistent. It was, he said, imperative in such a case that everything be properly proved. Williams was not in court to answer the judge, for whom that seems to have been the first of a series of minor irritations that he would comment on throughout the day. Very much the master in his own court, it has been said that he was a man who was apt to stand severely on his dignity. This was probably simply because he liked to see the due process of law enacted with some degree of efficiency.

Joseph Orton of Orton Bros for a second time produced his ledgers in court, his evidence under examination varying not at all from that given at the police court hearing. Cross-examined by Marshall Hall he explained that a standard B.S.A. cycle in 1910 would have been black, but the only thing about the green bicycle which made it a special order was its back pedal rim brake.

The two B.S.A. clerks, Albert Davis and Sidney Garfield, who had travelled over from their homes in Redditch, reiterated the evidence that they had given at police court and were not cross-examined by Marshall Hall.

John Henry Atkins, who had been expected to give evidence on the first day, now stepped into the witness box. He had been, he told the court, on the top road from Stoughton to Gaulby between 7 and 7.30 p.m. on 5 July. He had seen a man and a woman riding bicycles and had noticed that the man spoke 'in a highish tone'. He had not been able to hear what was said.

Mary Elizabeth Webb, maid and companion to Catherine Light, was next to step on to the stand. Her evidence, hence Francis Sims's earlier concern for her well-being would be of the greatest import. She was a pleasant looking woman in her early to mid-thirties. She came to court wearing a wide brimmed straw hat and a high collar. She had, she said, been in Mrs Light's employ for almost eight years. The prisoner was a civil engineer and had worked and lived at Derby, coming home at weekends by train. In about October of 1914 he had returned, bringing a green bicycle and his luggage with him. The green cycle had a three-speed gear which was controlled by a black disc on the upturned handlebars. The prisoner stayed with them at the Granville Road house until April 1915 when he took up an Army Commission. The bicycle had at that time been put in the box room. By the time the prisoner returned home after his demobilization at the end of January 1919 they had removed to the Highfield Street house. The prisoner then used the cycle each day. In answer to a question from the judge Mary Webb said that at that time the cycle was kept in the back kitchen.

117

The prisoner had not used the bicycle since July 1919. Before that time, Light had told her that he was helping a man with a business, and he used then to go out around 9.30 in the morning, return home for lunch, go out again about two and be back home for his tea at 4 p.m., occasionally going out again after tea. Supper was usually between 7 and 8 p.m. He normally went out on his bicycle in the morning and afternoon.

Mary Webb recalled that her mistress went to Rhyl in the previous July, but she could not quite remember Saturday 5 July. She recalled, though, the green bicycle being taken for repair just before Mrs Light left for Rhyl. The prisoner had told her that the cycle was being taken by him to 'a fresh repair man'. She could remember the prisoner bringing the cycle back from having it repaired; he had had his tea and then gone out with his cycle. There was to have been 'a particular supper at 8', but the prisoner did not return until about 10 p.m. She had let him into the house through the back gate with his cycle. He had looked tired and dusty and when asked why he was late he explained that his cycle 'had broken down' and he had had to walk. He had had his supper and gone to bed. The cycle had remained in the kitchen for some days, after which the prisoner, during the time that Mrs Light was at Rhyl, took it up to the box room.

Mary Webb's answers to Maddocks's questions concerning just when the bicycle was brought down again from the boxroom are of particular interest in the light of recent research, and when compared with Light's own version of the timetable of events. She replied: 'As well as I can remember, it was brought down just before Christmas.'

Some time afterwards the prisoner told her, unprompted, that he had sold the bicycle. She identified the exhibited cycle as being 'the same shade of green'. She thought that she had first heard of the Stretton murder on the evening of the day that her mistress left for Rhyl. She had asked the prisoner if he had seen the papers as there had been a dreadful murder. He had only said: 'Oh.' The prisoner usually wore grey and he had several raincoats. Some clothes had been sold in December. Normally the prisoner shaved regularly; if he missed a day he looked very dark on the upper lip and around the chin. There was really nothing different here from her evidence at police court, and very little for Marshall Hall to query without risk to his case.

In cross-examination Mary Webb agreed that she had said before the magistrate that the cycle was in the back kitchen for several days.

'Was that where it was usually kept?'

'Yes.'

'From the time the prisoner joined up in 1915 until January 1919 the cycle was kept in the box room?'

'Yes, he brought it down once while he was on leave.'

In answer to a question by the judge Mary Webb said that to her knowledge after 5 July the bicycle was never taken out again, until the prisoner took it out on the evening 'shortly before Christmas'. She had been told by the prisoner that the man he was helping had given up his business and left town.

Having been summoned back to court, Dr E.K. Williams then retook the stand to inform the court formally that Bella Wright had died as a result of the gunshot wound.

Enoch Whitehouse then stepped into the box to repeat almost word for word his evidence about his finding of the bicycle frame and front wheel on 23 February.

The next witness to be called was Joseph Chambers, which immediately had Sir Thomas Horridge complaining once again, as the name did not appear on the original list of depositions as it should have done. He was not calmed by Henry Maddocks saying that the name was included on his own list.

'The way in which these books have been sent to the judge is a scandal. I have had to complain at Maidstone and I seem to recollect that I have also had to complain here of the same thing.' It was not a good day for Horridge.

Then came what has always been seen as the first hint of Sir Gordon Hewart's curtailment of his own role in the case. In reply to the judge, Henry Maddocks said that he would convey his Lordship's comments to the Attorney-General who, clearly, could not have been in court at that point. In actual fact Gordon Hewart did return to court later that day, and his absence during Sir Thomas Horridge's comments may or may not have had any connection with the real reason for his premature departure from Leicester.

Joseph Chambers' evidence was just as it had been at police court and he was quickly followed into the box by Sgt. Healey, who verified his recovery on 19 March of the holster and cartridges from the nearby canal opposite St Mary's Wharf. Sgt. Healey drew the attention of the jury to what in the course of this narrative will be seen as significant, possibly crucial, evidence. He pointed out not one but two quite separate areas on the inner side of the holster flap where markings had been scratched out.

Henry Clarke then took the stand for what he must have expected to be quite an ordeal. Despite Marshall Hall having asked hardly a dozen questions of the witnesses so far, those in court who knew him or knew of his abiding interest and understanding of weapons must have been on the edge of their seats in anticipation of fireworks to come.

Clarke was taken through his evidence by Maddocks, and handed the bullet that the prosecution claimed had been the cause of the girl's death. He said he had examined it and it was 'a .455 calibre bullet which had been adapted for Army service cartridges, for use in a revolver; it was originally a black powder bullet'. Again, these were hardly the words that he had used in his original police statement. Continuing, Clarke told the court that since early in 1915 the authorities had used such bullets with cordite. Shown Exhibit 7, the cartridges and blanks recovered from the canal by Sgt. Healey, Clark said that he had extracted a bullet from one of the cartridges and compared it with the bullet shown to him earlier by the police. They were identical. The blank cartridges had been loaded with powder only. Happy that the necessary comparison between the bullet found in the lane and those recovered from the canal had been made Maddocks sat down, and left Clarke to the mercies of Marshall Hall.

Establishing an early and worthwhile point, Marshall Hall questioned Clarke on the quantities of such bullets since their introduction – as long ago as the Boer War. Clarke agreed that the bullet, Exhibit 6, was of that standard pattern; he could not say even approximately how many had been manufactured. Marshall Hall put it at thousands of millions, and Clarke could not disagree. Taking out a favourite magnifying glass Marshall Hall induced Clarke to agree with him that the bullet showed certain marks which would indicate it had been fired from a rifled barrel. Marshall Hall made sure that the point was not lost on the jury, and turned to the jury box as he addressed the witness: 'This bullet might then just as easily have been fired from a rifle as from a revolver.' Clarke agreed.

Clarke also agreed with Marshall Hall that the velocity of a bullet increased in proportion to the length of the barrel from which it was fired, but he was, surely surprisingly for such a common weapon, unable to say what the length of the barrel of a Webley-Scott service revolver might be. The barrel of a Webley-Scott Mk VI service revolver was, as Marshall Hall well knew, some 6 in in length, considerably shorter than any rifle barrel. Satisfied that the point was all but made, Marshall Hall moved on. Clarke was unable to say what length of barrel this particular bullet had passed through, but he agreed with Marshall Hall that the use of cordite greatly increased the velocity of a bullet. A bullet fired from a service revolver might easily travel some 1,000 yd and would even at 50 or 60 yd penetrate 1 in, perhaps 2 in, of deal. Clarke also agreed that the entrance hole made by such a bullet would be small and that the exit hole would be comparatively larger, yet when asked by Marshall Hall if he did not think this particular exit wound at 1½ in by ½ in to be unusually small. He replied that he did not.

There followed a lengthy discourse between gunsmith and defence counsel about the possibilities of such a bullet being deflected in flight, perhaps by a tree or fence, and still having sufficient velocity to leave an exit hole such as that found on the deceased girl. Clarke, and here one detects increased hesitancy and confusion beginning to temper his answers, agreed with Marshall Hall that such a bullet travelling at great velocity would be hardly deflected by coming into contact with something along its path of flight, but he thought that in this case the exit hole showed that the bullet had been deflected from its end-on position. Then, perhaps growing a little unwary, he agreed with Marshall Hall that the exit wound indicated the bullet's velocity had been very little diminished.

Marshall Hall, careful not to confuse the issue by speaking of calibres, then threw perhaps his most telling question at Clarke, the answer to which cannot have been misunderstood by the jury. 'Have you ever seen a human being who has been shot at a distance of within five yards with a service revolver?'

'No, Sir.'

'I suggest to you that the effect of such a bullet [presumably as that found by Hall] on the skull of a human being is almost to blow the side of the head off.'

'It depends on the velocity, Sir.'

'Of course it does,' snapped Marshall Hall.

The sharpness in Marshall Hall's voice at this point has always been considered to be a measure of how satisfactorily he believed the cross-examination of Clarke to be proceeding, but in the light of today's knowledge and a possibility which may very well have been fully appreciated at the time by Marshall Hall, that sharpness may in fact have been a measure of his annoyance at Clarke's reintroduction of the importance of velocity in such a case when perhaps he had hoped for a very non-committal reply from the gunsmith. Undeterred he continued his cross-examination. Would the part of the head struck not also have been of some importance in determining the size of the wound, Clarke agreed that it would. Then once again, emphasizing a point made earlier, Clarke agreed that such a bullet could have been fired from a rifle as well as a revolver. Clarke also agreed that the discharge of a cordite cartridge would make a sharp penetrating noise, and would have been audible over a very long distance in quiet surroundings. Once again the suggestion from Marshall Hall was that the bullet found by Hall and now produced as Exhibit 6 had been fired from a distance, possibly with a rifle, and certainly not, as the prosecution maintained, at short range with a service revolver. Marshall Hall's last suggestion, however, was perhaps a little more devious than was noticed at the time. Certainly its inference was not apparent to Clarke, and in all probability was not appreciated by the jury. Marshall Hall had referred to the noise that a cordite cartridge might make upon discharge, Clarke had not corrected the inference, but Marshall Hall knew perfectly well that in his original statement to the Leicestershire police, Clarke had said that the bullet found in the lane had been 'fired with black powder', not cordite, a statement that he had repeated at the inquest, some seven months before the discovery of the holster and its contents in the canal. Clarke had further said in that original police statement that 'it certainly was not a service bullet'. It had not been until the magisterial hearing of 24 March some five days after Sgt. Healey recovered the holster that Clarke had said the recovered cartridges were charged with cordite. The one that he had examined, he deposed, had carried the Government mark (so undoubtedly charged with cordite) and the bullet which he extracted from it was 'identical' to that found by Hall, the very same that he had earlier stated had been fired with black powder.

Hoping to repair a little of the damage done by Marshall Hall's questions, Maddocks rose to re-examine Clarke – who agreed that a revolver barrel was also rifled and that the bullet showed marks which were consistent with it having been fired from a revolver. He also agreed that a badly worn revolver barrel could diminish the velocity and penetrating force of the bullet. This seems a strange piece of re-examination, since all Marshall Hall's efforts had been designed to show that the wound showed all the hallmarks of being caused by a bullet of high velocity, one capable as he put it 'of passing through one perhaps even two inches of deal at considerable distance'; and rifling of a barrel served to increase velocity and accuracy. Would the wound, asked Maddocks, have appeared so clean if it had been caused by a bullet that had struck a hard surface and ricocheted? Clarke thought not, and yet only moments earlier he had told Marshall Hall that he thought that the bullet had been deflected from its end-on position. This re-examination seems even more strange when seen against the brief that Maddocks held. The prosecution's position was that the bullet, to have taken the path they believed it had taken, would have had to be fired from the field and could not have struck a hard surface first. The prosecution had therefore already discounted the ricochet theory.

Sir Thomas Horridge interjected. 'Do you', he asked Clarke, 'see anything inconsistent in the condition of the bullet with its having passed through the head of the dead woman, and then having had its course arrested by the turf where it joins the metalled edge of the road and being found at 17 ft away?' 'No.'

Clarke saw nothing inconsistent in that, despite the fact that the bullet, to its discoverer at least, appeared to have been kicked along and trodden on by an animal, and was found in the middle of the roadway, nowhere near the turf of the verge.

Would his Lordship put one more question to the witness, asked Marshall Hall. Would the witness expect to see any scorching of the skin of the face if the bullet had been fired from

A recent photograph of the murder scene, taken looking towards Gaulby. Today there is a tarmacadam surface

within 6 or 7 ft of the victim? Clarke's reply to the judge was that he would not. Again, there was the suggestion from Marshall Hall of the wound having been caused by a bullet fired from a considerable distance.

All in all this was an interesting and enlightening piece of cross-examination by defence counsel, that sustained the suggestion that, contrary to the prosecution's case, Bella Wright had not been killed at close range by the bullet found nearby, but that her death may have been the result of a bullet having been fired from a considerable distance, and that the bullet could have been discharged from a rifle and not from a revolver, especially not from the .45 calibre barrel of a Webley-Scott service revolver. Marshall Hall's colourful question to Clarke, of the likelihood of such a bullet fired from such a weapon being capable of blowing off the side of the victim's head, together with the admission extracted from Clarke that he had never seen someone who had been shot within a range of 5 yd with a service revolver, may have left the jury with just the impression that Marshall Hall sought, that he had himself seen many such victims.

The true effect of Marshall Hall's cross-examination of Henry Clarke cannot be firmly established. How much thought the jury gave to it during their deliberations has never been disclosed, but that Marshall Hall was on familiar ground is evident. The underlying fund of knowledge that defence counsel possessed is still obvious today. Much of that knowledge he could not utilize in the defence of Light; indeed, he would only have been able to fully demonstrate it had he appeared not for the defence but on the prosecution benches.

The last witness to give evidence before the court adjourned for lunch was Walter Francks, a motor agent and cycle repairer with premises at No. 43 St Stephen's Road, Leicester.

Mr Francks's deposition was virtually word for word as given at police court. He knew the prisoner, and had carried out work on a green B.S.A. deluxe cycle for him. He had last handled the machine in the spring of 1919 when he had repaired the tyres and fitted a pair of black mudguards, and generally put the cycle in good order. He was able to identify the main exhibit as part of the cycle on which he had worked. The back pedalling brake mechanism was then handed to Mr Francks, who proceeded to explain its function to the court. Cross-examined by Marshall Hall, the witness agreed that at the time when he had last seen the cycle it looked as though it had been stored away.

The case for the prosecution was drawing to a close, and the afternoon of Thursday 10 June saw the last few witnesses take the stand, only one of whom would face cross-examination.

Most of those in court had spent the luncheon adjournment in discussions of the case so far, and in speculation about what possible answer the defence had to such a damning catalogue of evidence, albeit circumstantial. Ronald Light himself must have been much occupied during the break, anticipating, perhaps dreading, what the afternoon would bring. He knew that now his own instructions had been passed to his counsel, he had little to fear in his examination-in-chief. He would have his say, his chance to impress the jury, but by going into the witness box he knew he must face perhaps many hours of cross-examination, and of that he must have felt some trepidation. Marshall Hall spent those last few minutes as the final prosecution witnesses trooped in and out of the witness box in preparing for his examination of his client, deciding how best to phrase those questions in accordance with the instructions he had so belatedly received.

The first man to take the stand that afternoon was Harry Cox, the cycle dealer and repairer. In much the same words he had used at police court, Cox said that the prisoner had brought his green B.S.A. bicycle to his shop for repair on 2 July. At that time he had said he had been an officer in the Army, and had taken a month's leave, but his firm had told him to have another week or two on full pay. He was in Leicester to visit some friends. In repairing the cycle, Harry

Cox told the court of his accidental breakage of the old cable, of the fact that it had been replaced, and that the prisoner collected the cycle, returning it to the shop once again on Friday 4 July in order for Cox to adjust the new cable. When collecting the cycle for the final time on Saturday 5 July, the prisoner had said that he was 'fed up with messing about the town' and was 'going for a ride in the country'. At that time the prisoner was wearing a raincoat and was badly in need of a shave. Having read a report of the murder in the paper, Cox said that he had contacted Supt. Bowley. When shown the bicycle, Cox was able to recognize patches that he had put on the tyre; he also testified to having identified the prisoner at Cheltenham on 4 March.

William Saunders, manager of the Champion cycle shop in Leicester deposed that on 1 March he had examined the bicycle frame (Exhibit 3) and at first had failed to find a number where he expected it to be, in the seat pillar lug. The number had been filed off. Upon further inspection he discovered a number, 103648, in the upper part of the front fork.

Supt. Levi Bowley then deposed that he had received information of the death of Bella Wright on 6 July 1919. The first police bill, which offered a reward and gave a description of both the green bicycle and its rider, was dated 7 July. The bill was circulated throughout England, Scotland and Wales on 8 July. On 4 March 1920 the witness had gone to the prisoner's home.

Marshall Hall's only question of the afternoon brought the answer from Bowley that it was the police who had asked the newspapers to give publicity to the description of the man who had last been seen in the company of Bella Wright.

The arresting officer, Det. Supt. Taylor of the County force, told the court that on 4 March he had, in company with Det. Sgt. Illes of the Gloucestershire Constabulary, gone to a college at Cheltenham and asked Light what had become of the green bicycle. His reply was: 'I never had a green bicycle.' The prisoner had also at first denied having one from Orton Bros. of Derby although he later admitted this, saying he had sold it years earlier. Taylor deposed that he had told the prisoner his answers were unsatisfactory, and the prisoner had been taken to Cheltenham police station. The prisoner had, said Taylor, later asked to see him and had said: 'What is this stunt?' Later he had said: 'I sold a bicycle to Mr Bourne, of Wilmot Street, Derby'. The prisoner had also spoken of selling another cycle. When charged, the prisoner had said: 'It's absurd.'

Det. Sgt. Illes corroborated the statement made by Taylor about the interview with Light at Dean Close School, and his subsequent removal to Cheltenham police station where Light had been identified by Harry Cox. Illes stated that after the identification had taken place, he personally escorted the prisoner back to the charge room. As they walked back Light had said to him: 'My word, that fellow had me spotted all right.'

Sir Thomas Horridge, finding that his laboriously pencilled longhand notes were on one point deficient, asked that the gunsmith Henry Clarke should be recalled. Quite why the judge should have sought the word of Clarke when the word of the doctor involved in the case would seem to have been more appropriate, it is impossible to know for sure; but it may be that once again Dr Williams had left the court and could not be easily recalled. The judge also knew from the court calendar that Illes had been the final prosecution witness. So it was that Clarke again took the stand and told the judge that the wounds to the head of the deceased girl could not have been self inflicted.

In the light of Sir Gordon Hewart's observation that Archie Ward was expecting to be demobilized by August of that year, it may come as a surprise to realize that Archie Ward had been served with a subpoena by the prosecution, though he was not in the event called to give evidence. He had been invalided out of the Navy on 4 June 1920, and had moved back to Leicester where he was living at Aylestone Grange Cottage. He was in court with other members of his family to hear those words spoken by the Attorney-General.

The closing of the prosecution's case is a point of some confusion, one might say another minor mystery. Sir Gordon Hewart's biographer, Robert Jackson, writing in the late '50s, said that the Attorney-General's professional participation in the trial extended to only his opening speech and examination by him of one or two of the earlier witnesses. He further states that having received a telegram from Lloyd George on the evening of the first day at Leicester requesting his immediate return to London, Hewart followed the proceedings in Leicester while assisting in the drafting of peace proposals. It is not possible to establish exactly why or even if Hewart received a telegram from Lloyd George. Telegrams were always considered to be the property of the recipient and the Post Office kept copies for only three months. As previously stated, Sir Gordon Hewart's papers were reported stolen by his wife after Hewart's own death. Lloyd George's papers were not helpful on this point, but the cabinet is known to have met on Friday 11 June to discuss Irish policy. However, at least one man present at the trial of Light was of the opinion that not only was the Attorney-General present at the close of the prosecution's case on the afternoon of the second day, but that he was also present for most, if not all, of Light's examination-in-chief, though not for his cross-examination.

Edgar Bowker, Marshall Hall's faithful clerk, writing in 1961, possibly with greater freedom than he had felt when in 1947 he published his first book of reminiscences, states that on the afternoon of the second day it was the Attorney-General who stood and declared that the case for the Crown was complete, and that after the Attorney-General's brief statement a silence hung over the courtroom for some moments before Marshall Hall rose to open the defence.

CHAPTER 14

Rex v. Light

THE CASE FOR THE DEFENCE

The long awaited handwritten instructions from Ronald Light to his counsel by which the defendant accepted, albeit unstated, the responsibility of going into the witness box, read as follows: 'Will you please ask me to tell the jury in my own words exactly why I did not come forward? I shall say I was dreadfully worried, and for some days was quite dazed at such an unexpected blow, and could not make up my mind to come forward, and hesitated for days. I could not give the police any information whatever as to how the girl met her death. If the police and papers had only stated the known facts, and asked the cyclist to come forward, I shall [*sic*] have done so, but they jumped to wrong conclusions, and I was frightened when I saw I was wanted for murder . . . Let me do this in my own words.'

Marshall Hall, ever one to appreciate the studied dramatic moment, and always at his most splendid when the odds were stacked against a success, rose slowly to his feet, and in that beautifully modulated voice spoke quietly but perfectly audibly: 'My Lord, I desire to call the prisoner.'

Ronald Light, his face of a deathly pallor and with his pencil in his hand, apparently without any hesitation stepped the short distance between dock and witness box, accompanied by the two warders who had sat in the dock with their charge throughout the proceedings. He took the oath in what was variously described as a boyish, a high pitched and a feminine voice.

Throughout the following pages which cover Light's own evidence I have sought as far as possible to use his own words, particularly concerning his time on the Western Front, any injuries he may have received at that time and any revolvers that he may have owned. Bearing in mind the non-existence of a trial transcript, these words are based on various London, Leicester and indeed other provincial contemporary newspaper reports, and on comments made at the time and since by several people present throughout Light's testimony. I feel this represents as fair and accurate an assessment of the defendant's own words as it is possible to obtain.

Marshall Hall began by taking the defendant back to his childhood. In a quiet voice Light proceeded to tell the court that he had been born in October 1885, and had joined the Army in 1915. Examined on the accuracy of Ethel Tunnicliffe's evidence, he said that he could not remember the letter he had sent to her. He did not have a revolver in April 1915, and had first owned one in July 1915. When asked how he had acquired that revolver, Light said he had bought it from his commanding officer, a Major Benton. It had been 'an ordinary Webley-Scott Service revolver'. He had, he said, taken that revolver with him when he first went to France in November 1915. Light admitted that at the time he left for France he left behind a B.S.A. green-enamelled bicycle at his mother's home, and that parts of that bicycle were exhibited in court.

'When did you come back from France first?'

'Either at the end of January or the beginning of February 1916.'

'How long were you in England at that time?'

'Well, the next time I went to France was in November 1917.'

'What was your capacity at that time?'

'I was a gunner in the Honourable Artillery Company.'

'When you went to France as a gunner had you a revolver?'

'I took my revolver to France with me.'

'Were you allowed to have a revolver as a private?'

'Well, you could not wear it of course.'

'How long were you in France after you went with the Honourable Artillery Company?'

'November 1917 to August 1918.'

'What happened to you in August 1918?'

'I left the battery and passed through a casualty clearing station at the base.'

'How did you come to be sent there?'

'Oh, I was sent there for shell shock and deafness; I have been deaf ever since.'

It might be apposite to mention here that at one point Ronald Light was requested by the judge to speak up, something that a great many of the deaf and hard of hearing apparently have little difficulty in doing, as it is so difficult for them to know how loud they are speaking.

Light proceeded to relate to the court that he left the clearing station after twenty-four hours, then spent a day or two at the base before being sent back to England as what he described as 'a stretcher case'. Marshall Hall wanted to know what he brought back to England.

'Well, I came across in my pyjamas and my sole possession was what they call a dolly bag.'

'What became of your revolver?'

'It was taken away from me with all my other kit and left behind at Corbie.'

'Have you ever seen that revolver since that time?'

'Never.'

There had been, said Light, a holster which he had taken with him the first time he had gone to France, but not on the second occasion. At that time the holster together with the rest of his kit had been sent from his last camp to his home. When shown the holster which Sgt. Healey had retrieved from the canal, Exhibit 8, Light admitted it was the holster he had owned. He had not, he said, any idea how the scratch marks on the holster had been caused. It was not he that had caused them.

Marshall Hall again referred to the time of Light's last return from France to England, when Light claimed to have been carried to this country 'on a stretcher'. Light told the court that after his return he was at Wharncliffe Hospital, Sheffield for about a month and a half, and afterwards spent a month at convalescent camp at Worksop, before rejoining his command depot at Ripon. He had been posted to a reserve unit and than at the end of January (1919) he had been demobilized and returned to his mother's home in Leicester, where but for a short time he had remained, unemployed. After his return home he had brought down his green bicycle from the boxroom. The tyres were in a perished condition, partly rotted away. Generally, said Light, he repaired his cycle tyres himself, but he had had a lot of trouble with them. On 2 July 1919 he had, he agreed with Marshall Hall, taken the bicycle to Cox's for repair but he said he could not remember telling Cox that he was on holiday and that he was receiving full pay from a London firm. Rather, said Light, he had told Cox that he was having a holiday, meaning that he was unemployed.

'On the Saturday, did you say to Cox that you were going for a run in the country?'

'I cannot say, I may or I may not have done.'

'Did you on that day go home for your tea.'

'Yes.'

'What time did you leave the house after your tea?'

'Somewhere around half past five.'

'How were you dressed?'

'I was wearing an old suit.'

Sir Edward Marshall Hall K.C., dubbed 'The Great Defender', photographed in his seat just in front of the dock at Leicester Castle court

'Something similar in shape to that which you are now wearing?'
'Yes, very similar.'
'I will ask you just once, was there in that suit any pocket in which you could have carried a service revolver?'
'Certainly not.'
'Had you in your possession at that time, any revolver?'
'No.'
'Have you at any time ever possessed any revolver, other than the one that you bought from your commanding officer?'
'No.'
'Had you at that time any ammunition?'
'Yes, between thirty and forty rounds.'
'And were those rounds .455 calibre for use in the service revolver?'
'Yes.'
'Did you also have blank cartridges?'
'Yes.'
'Are these cartridges produced here today yours?'
'As far as I know.'
'On that Saturday, after you left home at 5.30 where did you go?'
'I went to the home of some friends of my mother's in West Drive, for a strap. When I got there the house was closed up and so I went for a ride into the country.'

'Which way did you go?'

'I passed through Oadby. I do not know the district too well. I carried straight on along the main road until I came to Great Glen, then I turned off the main road and rode towards Little Stretton.'

'Did you pass through Evington on that outward journey?'

'No, I did not go anywhere near Evington.'

'On that night did you meet either of those two little girls who have given evidence here?'

'No.'

Further questioned, Light said that after reaching Little Stretton he had taken the first road to the left, back towards Leicester. He was part-way down this road when he consulted his watch and found the time to be about 6.45 p.m. He did not want to arrive home early and so decided to ride round by a longer route.

'Had you any fixed time in your mind as to when you intended to return home?'

'I intended, then, to get in between eight and half past.'

'Having decided, what did you do?'

'I turned into the road on the right.'

'And does that bring you into what is called the "upper road"?'

'Yes.'

'In the "upper road" did you see a young lady riding a bicycle?'

'Yes, after I had gone some distance.'

'Which way was she riding?'

'As a matter of fact when I first saw her, she was standing by her bicycle at the roadside.'

'What was she doing to it?'

'She was bending over it.'

'Did you know her; had you ever seen her before?'

'No. Never.'

'Did you know the village of Gaulby?'

'No, but I knew there was a village in that direction, I had ridden through it.'

'I want you to tell his Lordship and the jury in your own words what took place when the young lady spoke to you on the "upper road".'

'As I came up to the young lady she was stooping over her bicycle. She looked up as I approached and asked me if I could lend her a spanner. I had no spanners with me and I just looked at her bicycle. As far as I could see from what she pointed out to me there was a certain amount of play in the free wheel, but as I had no spanners I could do nothing.'

Light said that he had then ridden on with the girl down a steep hill. They had dismounted and walked up the next hill together, getting back on their machines at the top of the hill and riding on together once again until they came to a village. He had asked the name of the village and she had told him that it was Gaulby, and she was going to see some friends there. She had said 'I shall only be ten minutes or a quarter of an hour.' They had, he said, ridden into the village, and he had accompanied her as far as the house to which she was going.

'Had anything been said one way or the other about waiting?'

It can only be seen as perhaps a Freudian slip that one reporter in court that day filed Marshall Hall's last question as: 'Had anything been said one way or the other about courting?' It is clear, however, not only from other reports but from Light's own reply that the word was indeed 'waiting'.

'Well, nothing in so many words, but when she said she was going to see some friends and would be only ten minutes or a quarter of an hour, I took that as a sort of suggestion that I should wait and that we should ride together.'

Light said that he had waited in the lane between the houses and the church for about ten minutes or a quarter of an hour, during which time he walked with his machine up to the church and to his left back towards Leicester. He had got on his bicycle intending to ride straight back to Leicester, but had found the back tyre was flat. He had made his way to a nearby gate where he pumped up the tyre and sat on the gate to see if the tyre would keep up, but it had gone down again and so he had had to mend it.

'Shortly after you had seen that the tyre was flat, did you see someone?'

'Yes, a man in a field.'

'How long did you stay by that gate pumping up and then mending your tyre?'

'Just about an hour.'

'What time would it have been when you finished mending your tyre?'

'About a quarter past eight. I knew it was late, but before riding home to Leicester I thought I would ride round the triangle to see where the girl had got to in the interval.'

This refers to what might be loosely described as a triangle of land formed in the centre of Gaulby village, which had near its apex at the 'church end' of the village, a finger post giving directions to Leicester. The gate to which Light referred was close to the finger post and a short distance from the church.

Light went on to say that he rode back to the house where he 'just saw her coming out'. He was riding his bicycle, and it was downhill outside the house.'

'What did you do?'

'Before I got to the cottage I dismounted and walked to the gate.'

'Did you speak to the girl?'

'Yes. I said: "Hello, you've been a long time. I thought you had gone the other way."'

'Did you know her name or her home?'

'No.'

'Did you call her Bella?'

'No.'

'When did you first know her name?'

'When first I read it in the accounts in the newspapers.'

Light agreed with Marshall Hall that outside the cottage he remembered the girl doing something to her bicycle. He had also had some conversation with the witness Evans and apart from his not having said the name 'Bella', he agreed that Evans's evidence had been fairly accurate. He and the girl had left the cottage together, walking uphill with their cycles until they neared the church. From here they rode on together. He had had to stop to pump up his tyre, during which time he said the girl 'rode very slowly ahead'. Having caught the girl up, Light admitted to having had some conversation with her concerning bicycle tyres: 'I told her that while she had been in the house I had been repairing my bicycle tyre, and I said that it had got in a very porous and bad state having been laid by so long. She told me the first thing I knew about her. She said she never let her tyres get in such a state and that she was employed in a tyre factory and could get them cost price.'

Shown a map of the area, Light indicated a turning to the left a little way after passing the Kings Norton turning, also to the left. It was at that second crossroads that he said he turned to take the road to the right which would have brought him on to the 'top road', but the girl dismounted and then so did he. She had said, he deposed: 'I must say goodbye to you here; I am going that way,' meaning the road to the left. Indicating the road to the right, he had asked: 'Isn't this the shorter way to Leicester?' She had said: 'I don't live there.' Light said he had replied: 'Well, I must go this way, because I am late already and with this puncture I may have to walk part of the way home.'

'Did you shake hands with her or anything of that kind?'

'No, we were standing some distance apart.'

'What time would this have been?'

'Well, it was about ten minutes after we left Gaulby, I do not know the time.'

'What was she doing when you last saw her?'

'She was standing. She was just starting to move off on her bicycle.'

'Did you ever see her again after you parted?'

'No.'

It had taken him, said Light, until just before 10 to get home, he had had to stop several times to pump up his tyres, which had gone down about every five minutes. It had got so bad that he had had to walk. Here the judge intervened:

'You agree that the Saturday Mary Webb spoke of was the Saturday this girl was killed?'

'Yes, my Lord.'

Asked about the first news he had received of the death of the girl, Light said he had first heard about it on Tuesday (8 July) when he had seen the *Leicester Mercury*.

'I saw that someone had been killed. I saw the description of the bicycle and the man, and came to the conclusion that it must have been the girl that I had been with.'

He had, he said, moved the bicycle from the kitchen to the boxroom ten days or so after his mother had gone to Rhyl.

'You made the fatal mistake of not communicating with the police?'

'Yes.'

A question from Sir Thomas Horridge: 'Did you tell a living soul?'

'I told no one.'

Continuing, Ronald Light said that he had read in the paper that the bullet fired was a bullet of heavy calibre from a service revolver. He found out that Cox had given information and a description of the bicycle to the police.

'Except that you could have told the police what you have told us, could you have given them any assistance as to the person who committed the crime?'

'No, or I should have done so.'

'Did you do anything to the bicycle till Christmas-time?'

'Yes. In October I threw the bicycle away.'

Sir Thomas Horridge asked 'Had you ever ridden it since the Saturday night?'

'No, my Lord.'

In answer to Marshall Hall, Light said that he did not think he had gone out on the Sunday following that Saturday; neither did he think the puncture had ever been repaired. In reply to the judge, Light said that he would normally have repaired the puncture himself on the Monday, but he was busy because his mother was going away on the following day. In fact she had left about 11 a.m. on the following Tuesday (8 July). He had, he said, seen the evening paper at about 6 p.m.

Light's examination-in-chief ended when Marshall Hall asked if he had done anything to the bicycle before throwing it away: 'Well I took away a lot of the loose parts from it and I loosened the nuts and bolts.'

There can be little doubt of the sensational effect that Ronald Light's evidence had had upon the court. Guided by Marshall Hall he had admitted to everything with which the prosecution could possibly connect him. He was, he said, the man on the green bicycle; the machine was his, and it was he who had taken the cycle to be repaired. It was he who had later thrown it away after removing some loose parts from it, and filing the identifying marks from the seat pillar lug. He agreed that the holster and cartridges were his. He freely admitted to having met the girl whom he now knew to be Bella Wright on the upper road on the evening of her death.

He had accompanied her as far as the Gaulby cottage, had waited in the village, and had ridden away from Gaulby with her. He admitted to seeing the 'man in the field' and of having a conversation with the witness Evans. There, however, Light's admittance of the prosecution's case ended, and it was there that the indictment fell short; for there was nothing, absolutely not one jot of evidence, to place him on that stretch of the Gartree Road at the time when Bella was killed. Further, the prosecution had offered not one single piece of evidence to link Light to Bella before the evening of her death, and Light had denied quite categorically that he had so much as even known her name until he read it in the newspaper after her death. In its sheer simplicity the line taken by Marshall Hall, and indeed Light, was brilliant; but could this man, a 'stretcher case' after his last service on the Western Front, stand up to the rigours of cross-examination, and by whom would the ordeal be orchestrated – for as Marshall Hall sat down the now vacant seat on the prosecution benches must have been plain to see.

Those in court spellbound by Light's answers to his counsel must have been somewhat perplexed when, after a hurried consultation with Francis Sims and with Norman Birkett, Henry Maddocks rose in order to answer a question from Sir Thomas Horridge. Maddocks understood that the Attorney-General would not be back in Leicester for the remainder of the case. The deepest sigh of relief ought to have emanated from Light himself, but there is no report of even a flicker of interest from him. He knew he would still have to face cross-examination from Henry Maddocks, a shrewd and experienced lawyer, and from the less experienced Norman Birkett. But in reality the premature departure of the Attorney-General cannot be seen as anything but a bonus to the defence, as Marshall Hall, ever an admirer of Hewart's lucid and masterful grasp of a case and of its pertinent minutiae, would have been the first to admit.

As previously indicated, the full story behind Sir Gordon Hewart's departure for London is still something of a mystery. It has been stated that his professional participation in the trial ceased with the examination-in-chief of one or two of the earlier prosecution witnesses, but that he was in court to hear at least some, perhaps the most significant part, of Ronald Light's examination by Marshall Hall is apparent from the comments made in later years by Edgar Bowker. As soon as Light entered the witness box, Bowker noticed that the Attorney-General began to make notes, but as Light time and time again admitted to the prosecution's main points against him, Bowker noticed that the Attorney-General had laid down his pen and was in whispered conversation with his juniors. By the time that Marshall Hall sat down, his examination of Ronald Light complete, Gordon Hewart was no longer in court. Why, then, did he leave Leicester in the very middle of a major murder trial, a trial which did not over-run its expected course and one in which he need not have been engaged at all? In later years Bowker remembered that he, together with others involved in the case were given the news of the Attorney-General's departure for London later that same evening, the reason given at the time being that he was needed in the House of Commons to take part in an important debate. Perusal of Hansard reveals that the Attorney-General, if he were present in the House, most certainly did not take a vocal part in any debate in the House during any of the three days of the trial at Leicester. That he had left the Bell Hotel is certain; that he had returned to London would seem probable; but what could have made him abandon the prosecution of Light is still a mystery. Why had he come to Leicester in the first place, particularly if there was the slightest chance that he might be called away. If that possibility existed at the outset on Wednesday 9 June why begin the case? Why not hand it over at that point to another treasury counsel, who could have taken on the prosecution of Light with equal distinction? Perhaps the two most eminent and certainly the names which spring first to mind are Sir Richard Muir, who prosecuted Crippen, and of whom Crippen justifiably and prophetically had said: 'I would rather it were to be anyone but him.' There was also Sir Archibald Bodkin who, a little over a month after the trial at Leicester, would himself be appointed Director of Public Prosecutions. Both men at the time of the Light trial were formidable Treasury prosecutors and every bit as capable as the Attorney-General himself. Both would have struck fear into the heart of any man on trial for his life. It is interesting to note that the then Lord Chancellor, F.E. Smith, writing of Hewart in 1924, said that he always made it plain the only forensic career for him lay in London. Inevitably, as Bowker later recalled, some in Leicester drew their own conclusions about what precipitated the Attorney-General's premature departure; not all those conclusions were charitable in Bowker's view, but it is difficult not to draw conclusions now – in all probability the same conclusions that were arrived at in 1920.

If there was a precise time during the trial of Light when the Attorney-General was present in court and reached a decision to leave, it must have been just before the examination of prosecution witnesses passed into the hands of Henry Maddocks, which was certainly the case when young Valeria Cavan took the stand. This being so, it would appear that the Attorney-General made his decision some time before Miss Cavan was called, and after Marshall Hall's dramatic announcement that as to identity or ownership only the testimony of the two girls would be challenged. The Attorney-General was absent from the courtroom when the luncheon adjournment was taken, but came back to listen to part of Light's evidence. Can it be he was convinced by what he had heard that the case was lost? He must have always known the full extent of any weaknesses in the prosecution case, but perhaps having those weaknesses brought home to him so early in the case was enough for him to consider leaving Leicester. Did he really throw in the towel? Clearly that is what some staying at the Bell that night thought, and indeed would say in later years, and it is difficult at this late date not to agree with that conclusion. Gordon Hewart was ever a petulant man and it appears something of a poor loser.

Before we leave the mystery surrounding Gordon Hewart's departure, there is one other small and relevant mystery. Francis Sims had attended court that day despite feeling very unwell. At the conclusion of the proceedings there was, according to Bowker, a discussion between the D.P.P.'s representative and the remaining prosecution counsel; and yet when Francis Sims left the court he wrote the following letter to the Deputy Director, back in London:

Dear Stephenson,
    We have finished the case for the prosecution . . . the speeches and summing up are for tomorrow.
    I have kept to the case today although I had to consult a doctor who says I have a temperature and may be ripening for an attack of influenza. He has prescribed for me and is to see me tomorrow, but at this time of writing six o'clock, I am feeling very poorly indeed.
Yours sincerely,
Francis J. Sims.

Possibly Francis Sims had informed the Deputy Director of Hewart's premature departure earlier the same day; perhaps it had come as no surprise to either man. Certainly Stephenson's reply would seem to indicate that the line taken by the defence had come as a greater surprise than had Hewart's departure, abrupt as it now appears:

Dear Sims,
    . . . As to Light I cannot believe that the jury will give credence to his evidence, ingenious though it is.
Yours sincerely,
Guy Stephenson.

*Francis Sims, principal assistant to the D.P.P. and
the Chief Constable of Leicester, Edward Holmes,
arrive at court*

In the absence of the Attorney-General, the responsibility of cross-examination of Light fell chiefly on the shoulders of Henry Maddocks, assisted by Norman Birkett. Undoubtedly as Marshall Hall came to the end of his examination of Light, from Maddocks's own point of view the timing could have been better. In the event he had to begin his cross-examination immediately, not able to consult with Norman Birkett until the court adjourned for the day. Throughout the legal fraternity housed at the Bell Hotel that night, there would be a general feeling of sympathy for Maddocks and Birkett. Bowker thought that almost as much sympathy was felt for Maddocks as for the defendant. It would be a hard night for the depleted prosecution team, as the two men burned the midnight oil in an attempt to find a way of undermining the evidence of Light following what appears, surprisingly enough, to have been a totally unexpected move by the defence – a move which Guy Stephenson apparently was not alone in thinking to be 'ingenious'. The prosecution team would be joined in court at 10 the following morning by Hugo Young K.C. who, if consulted, does not appear to have taken any active part in the proceedings. It is possible that Norman Winning was also called in to advise.

Maddocks began his cross-examination of Light with questions about his time in the Army. In reply Light said that he had relinquished his Army commission on about 1 July 1916, and had later gone back out to France as a gunner, returning to his home in August 1918.

'As a gunner you would not be allowed to take a revolver with you?'

'Yes. We were not allowed to wear one but I actually had one.'

Sir Thomas Horridge asked. 'If you were known to have had the revolver with you, would you have been allowed to keep it?'

'I really cannot say, my lord.'

Light denied that he had ever received any training in the use of revolvers but admitted that he had practised with one at Buxton and that Ethel Tunnicliffe had often accompanied him. He did not think he had written one letter to her, but two. In those letters he told her that he could not get the revolver in the bag of the motor cycle that he intended to ride when he went to see her. He had sent the revolver on to await his arrival at Derby, but was prevented from getting to Derby and so wrote her the second letter asking that she should bring the parcel to Leicester.

'What did you want a large service revolver for while you were spending a weekend at Derby or Leicester?'

'I brought it here because I wanted my father to see it.'

'Was your father going to Derby when you sent the revolver there?'

'No, but I was going to Derby on the Saturday and then on by train to Leicester on Sunday.'

'Could you not have sent the revolver to your father?'

'Well, I could have done so.'

'And why did you not?'

'Because I happened to send it to Miss Tunnicliffe instead.'

'You might have addressed the parcel to yourself at your father's home?'

'Yes, I might have done that.'

Questioned about the revolver that he claimed to have bought from Major Benton, Light replied that he had probably bought it in the July. 'I suppose he has been killed?' remarked Maddocks, who knew perfectly well that he had not. Marshall Hall was quickly on his feet:

'I rather protest at my learned friend's assumption that Major Benton has been killed.' Light replied to Maddocks that he had bought the revolver for £3 from Major Benton of the 141st Fortress Company, Royal Engineers, at Buxton.

In actual fact the police had traced Major Norman Benton. It had taken some time, for the Major was away from his home at Leamington, but he was eventually interviewed. He could recall selling a Webley revolver for £3 to an officer whose name might have been Light, but he could not recall the incident clearly enough to know the man's name definitely. There is no indication that Benton was ever given the opportunity to identify Light, or indeed if he would have been able to do so. The enquiry seems to have ended on that one interview, possibly because at around that time the Chief Constable had finally received an answer to his persistent letters to the War Office, letters in which he repeatedly requested information regarding service revolvers which may or may not have been served out to Light before his first service in France.

'Did you take the revolver out to France with you when you were with the Honourable Artillery Company?'

'Yes.'

'That same revolver?'

'Yes.'

'When did you leave the holster at home?'

'When I went to France the second time.'

'In November 1917?'

'That was when I went out.'

Light had said in his evidence-in-chief that the holster had been sent to his home from the last camp he was at before being sent to France for the second time. Now he was agreeing with Maddocks that he had left it at home.

'Where did you carry the revolver, in your pocket?'

'I never had occasion to use it.' Then, perhaps remembering Marshall Hall's question about the type of suit he had worn on 5 July 1919, Light added: 'I could not carry it in my pocket, I never tried.'

'With regard to both the holster and the cycle parts, there never had been the slightest doubt that they all belonged to you?'

'Never the slightest doubt.'

Further questioned, Light said that from the middle of April until the middle of June (1919) he had been helping a man to build up an insurance business which had failed. During that time he had gone out each morning on his bicycle. No, he had not helped the man up until 5 July, but had had nothing to do since the middle of June – although he had gone out almost daily. He agreed that he had taken the bicycle on several occasions to be repaired by Mr Francks, and agreed with Maddocks that Mr Cox's shop was further from his home than the shop owned by Mr Francks. He denied having told Cox that he was visiting friends in Leicester or that he worked for a London firm, but said that he had told Cox he lived in London. Cox had not asked him for his Leicester address and, having had no occasion to do so, he had not given it.

'Where is the cable of the cycle?'

'In the canal.'

'With which part of the bicycle did you throw it in?'

'I am sure I cannot say; it was such a small thing.'

Light admitted to having taken the back-pedalling mechanism of the brake off the bicycle frame and having thrown it separately into the canal. It was, he said, somewhere in the canal between where the recovered parts had been recorded on the plan exhibited in court.

'Did you throw them all in on one occasion?'

'Yes, all on one night.'

Light agreed with Maddocks that he had filed off the number from the cycle frame. He had done that shortly before he had decided to throw it away. Asked when he had disposed of the bicycle he said: 'The only way I have of recollecting that is that it was shortly after summertime had finished. That would be in October.'

'What did you do all this for, Mr Light, in October?'

'In view of this case, I wanted to get rid of the machine.'

'Did Mary Webb ask you what had become of the bicycle.'

'I do not think that Mary Webb asked me anything about it.'

'Did you tell her you had sold it?'

'I told my mother that I had sold it.'

Light agreed with Maddocks that from 5 July until the time that he disposed of the cycle, no one had suggested that he was the person who had committed the murder, but he said all the newspaper accounts said that the man who had ridden the green bicycle had also killed the girl.

'At any rate, no one came to you and accused you of being the person?'

'No.'

Yet when pressed by Maddocks, Light could not say why he disposed of the bicycle at the time that he did. He admitted to the holster having been second-hand at the time he acquired it, but he denied knowing of any name upon it. He further denied that he had been on the lower road on 5 July, and he asserted that every word the two little girls had said was untrue.

'Do we understand that the statements made by these two girls are untrue, whether the incident to which they refer happened on that day or any other day?'

'I never saw or spoke to these girls on any occasion.'

That was the extent of Maddocks's cross-examination by the close of proceedings on that second day. A brief consultation between the judge and Marshall Hall indicated that he would be calling no more witnesses, hence the wording of Sims's letter to Guy Stephenson. While the jury prepared for their second and last night under the scrutiny of the police, a large crowd watched as the black maria carrying Ronald Light back to jail for what he must genuinely have hoped would be his last night in confinement, pulled out of the castle yard. It would return with its single occupant at 9 a.m. sharp the following morning.

* * *

FRIDAY 11 JUNE 1920

As might be imagined the Castle courtroom was crowded for what was hoped would be the final day of the trial of Ronald Light. The defendant, wearing the same blue serge suit that he had worn on the two previous days, was brought into court and the judge immediately indicated that he should be conducted not to the dock but direct to the witness box. There would be no other witnesses called for the defence, but there was still much to get through if the jury were to be spared another night away from their homes. In the event it was a close-run thing, and for some time a third night of enforced seclusion looked to be a distinct possibility.

The plan of the area to the east of Leicester was handed to Light and he pointed out to the court that he had marked the route he claimed to have taken on 5 July by a series of arrows.

In the very first few minutes of Light's evidence that morning it was necessary for the judge to remark once again on the quietness with which he answered Henry Maddocks. After having had to repeat one of Light's answers himself in order to be sure that the jury had not misheard, Sir Thomas Horridge addressed Light directly: 'I would advise you that it is in your own interests to speak a little more loudly.'

Asked by Maddocks if he had known that there was to have been a hot supper at 8, Light said that suppertime varied but that he was naturally told before he went out what time supper was to be. As far as he recollected, on that evening his mother had told him that supper was to be at 8 and he had intended to get home about that time.

'How long have you lived in Leicester?'

'My parents have lived here all my life, and I have been in the habit of coming here for many years.'

'When you went out daily on your cycle, did you go for many rides in the country?'

'No, I did not.'

Light said that he had first experienced trouble with his cycle on the road where he met the girl at about 6.45 a.m., after he had already ridden about 7 or 8 miles. The 'bad place' that Cox had repaired was on the outer cover and not on the inner tube. Light then, in compliance with a request from Henry Maddocks, marked on the plan the spot where he said he had met the girl. He agreed with counsel that he had turned away from Leicester, and rode on for about half a mile before seeing Bella Wright.

'Where did you intend going?'

'Through Gaulby, and getting on to the main road for Leicester at Houghton on the Hill.' He knew, he said, the way to Houghton.

Here the judge intervened, remarking presumably on the fact that Light had referred to Gaulby by name: 'He said in his evidence-in-chief that he did not know the name of the village, but knew where it was.'

Further questioned, Light said he attended to the girl's cycle for two or three minutes. He had no tools with him except three small tyre levers and a repair outfit. Afterwards they had ridden together into Gaulby. He agreed that they had spoken together as they rode along. The girl had asked him if he had come through Stoughton, and he told her that he had come through Great Glen. He did not think he had told her that he came from Leicester, had not told her his name, where he lived, where he was going, or what time he wanted to be home. The girl had told him nothing about herself before going to Gaulby; he had not asked where she was going or how long she had been riding. It was, he said, 'no business of mine'.

'By the time you got to Gaulby, it would have been about a quarter past seven?'

'It would be between a quarter and half past seven.'

'Was it not time for you to be turning back for supper; if you wished to get home at eight o'clock, wasn't it time to turn back?'

'At that time I was not thinking of turning back; I was thinking of going on to Houghton, I could have got home for eight if I had ridden straight on by Houghton.'

'How many miles was it from Houghton to home by the shortest route?'

'Between seven and eight miles.'

Pressed by Maddocks, Light said he had no idea where the girl lived or wanted to go. For all he knew she might have lived on the other side of Gaulby.

'In that case it would have been futile for you to wait for her?'

'But for the fact that she told me that she would only be a few minutes. I assumed that she would be going back the way she came.'

'Were you so interested in the girl that you would wait and see her when she came out of the house for the purpose of accompanying her home?'

'I was not.'

Light claimed that he had not ridden on to Houghton after mending his cycle because by then it was late and he had wanted to go back by the shortest route. In reply to a question from the judge, why he had not gone back by the shortest route immediately after his bicycle was mended and not gone on waiting for the girl, Light replied: 'When I had finished mending my machine I rode round the triangle to see if I could see anything of her, before going back the

George Measures' cottage, where members of Bella's family last saw her alive

shortest route.' He agreed that he had then seen the girl by the gate with some men. The judge wanted to know: 'Did you say "Bella" at all?'

'I never said Bella,' claimed Light.

Reading from his notes of the previous day's proceedings, Maddocks asked:

'You have been a long time. I thought you had gone the other way.' Which way did you think she was going?'

'I thought she might have gone the other way round the triangle, and I had missed her.'

'What did she say?'

'I don't believe she replied at all.'

'If no arrangement had been made for you to meet later on, don't you think this was a funny way of putting it?'

'Well, the last words she said to me were that she would be only a quarter of an hour.'

Moving on to the point where Light claimed to have parted from the girl, Maddocks wanted to know if all the girl had said was: 'I go this way.'

'No. She said: "I must say goodbye to you here, I am going that way."'

'Having waited some time for her, did you say anything to that?'

'I said: "Isn't this the shortest way to Leicester?"'

'And what did she say to that?'

'She said: "I don't live there."'

Referring to the road where the body of Bella was found, Maddocks asked: 'Did you know that was quite a lonely road?'

'I should not say it was any lonelier than the road we were on.'

'There are two gates at the entrance from the upper road, are there not?'

'I could not tell you.'

'You heard Mr Measures and Mr Evans say that it was about a quarter to nine when you left the house?'

'When I left her at the gate road it would be about twenty to nine.'

It seems odd here that Light should refer to the route that Bella took as the gate road, when only moments earlier he had told Maddocks that he could not tell him if there were two gates at the entrance to the road; yet he thought the road to be no lonelier than the top road, which would seem to indicate that he knew both roads equally well. He would later claim, though, not to have used the bottom road since his schooldays.

'I take it then that it took you an hour and twenty minutes to get home?'

'I reached home rather before than after ten; it took me about an hour and ten minutes to get home.'

Light admitted that on his journey home, especially after passing through Evington, he had seen a great many people on the road. He could not remember, however, if he had seen anyone as he rode through Stoughton village. He would later say that he had made no attempt to trace anyone who may have seen him pushing his bicycle that evening. Questioned by Maddocks about the condition of his cycle as he rode home, Light said that he 'had a slight puncture' yet he claimed to have 'walked for the greater part of the way'. He had not looked at the tyre at home to see what the puncture was like, and he did not know whether or not he had told Mary Webb where he had been. He had not told his mother where he had been.

Henry Maddocks then turned his attention to the early reports of the death of Bella Wright:

'I understand that it was on the Tuesday that you heard of the death of Bella Wright? . . . Did you see the notices asking for information concerning the man with the green bicycle?'

'I saw what was said in the newspapers. I did not see the handbills.'

'Why, Mr Light, did you not give information that it was you?'

'Because at first I was absolutely dazed about the whole thing, and I did not think clearly about it, and I could not make up my mind what to do.'

'Did you see the *Leicester Mercury* on 8 July?'

'Yes.'

Light was handed a copy of the paper, but said it was not the account that he had read. Marshall Hall then handed up a clipping from the *Leicester Mercury*, and Light agreed that it was that specific account he had first seen. It was the first he had known of the death of Bella Wright.

'Why', asked Maddocks, 'could you not have given the police an explanation that you were the man with the green bicycle who had been with the girl on that night?'

'Because everyone apparently jumped to the conclusion that the man with the green bicycle had murdered the girl.'

Here Sir Thomas Horridge again addressed Light: 'Do you not see, that if you had gone to the police and told the true story, if a true story it is, that you would at once have put them off a false trail and enabled them to look for the real murderer. You said yesterday that you could not have done any good by going to the police. Do you not see that you might have told them: "I was the man with the green bicycle; I left the girl at the corner", and it would have put them on to the real person, possibly, or at any rate they could have made other inquiries?'

'I see it now, of course. I did not deliberately make up my mind not to go forward. I was astounded and frightened at this unexpected thing. I kept on hesitating, and in the end I drifted into doing nothing at all.'

'But you could have said to the police: come and search my house, I have no revolver; and you could have shown them that you had no pocket in your clothes in which a revolver might have been put.'

Throughout this exchange between judge and prisoner it would have been possible to hear the proverbial pin drop. Everyone in court hung on the defendant's every word, but Light seems hardly to have been worried by the obvious implications in the judge's comments. He showed not the slightest discomfiture when he answered: 'I could not think clearly of those things then, my lord.'

Light agreed with Maddocks that had he gone to the police they might have been able to find people between Evington and Leicester who had seen a man wheeling a green bicycle. Might they also not have been able to see if it was true that the bicycle tyre was punctured, Maddocks wanted to know, and perhaps Light's reply shows just a hint of irritation: 'That bicycle has not been touched from that day to this.'

'You do not mean that?'

'I mean by that, I have never done anything to the inner tube.'

'Did you think yourself at the time that your story would not be believed?'

'I did not think so.'

Once again the judge directly questioned Light: 'Were you on affectionate terms with your mother?'

'Yes, my lord.'

'Finding yourself in this difficult situation, innocent and having had nothing to do with it, did you go to your mother for advice on what to say about it?'

'No, simply because my mother went away on the morning before I read about it.'

'When did she come back?'

'A fortnight later.'

'When she came back did you go to her?'

'No. One of the chief reasons why I did not come forward was that I did not want to worry my mother.'

That Catherine Light was indeed still ignorant of the murder when she left Leicester for Rhyl on 8 July would seem to be borne out by a passage from a letter that Maddocks would a little later ask Light to read out.

Light admitted that he recalled Mary Webb mentioning the murder to him, but he thought that she did so later than the Tuesday. He had not at that point said that he was the man on the green bicycle because he had not made up his mind to come forward and tell the whole story.'

One can almost detect a note of sarcasm in Maddocks's next question: 'You would surely think that Mary Webb your old servant, would at any rate believe you?'

Not in the least shaken by Maddocks's obvious reference to the fact that Mary Webb's evidence aided the prosecution in their case against him, Light replied: 'Certainly she would.'

Maddocks's next question, though full of implications pertinent to the green bicycle case, may, indeed should, have been taken by Light to refer to other events which will be detailed in a later chapter:

'Does it come to this, that in your own mind the facts that you alone knew, have made it difficult for you to explain your movements on that night and to be believed?'

'I really don't see what you mean.'

Maddocks, whose own frustration can only be appreciated in the full knowledge of all information regarding Light, was not at liberty to persist and indeed would have been grossly in breach of judges' rules had he done so, could only fall back on caution: 'In your own mind were you afraid to tell of that journey and of your conversation and accompaniment of Bella Wright; was it because you thought they would not believe you and that it pointed to you having had something to do with her death?'

'No, I did not think that at all.'

Once again the judge intervened, and in reply to him Light simply said: 'I did not think it would be difficult to get people to believe what I said.'

'Don't you see, it is even more extraordinary that you did not go and tell people?' Horridge pointed out.

'Well, it would have meant unpleasant publicity and that was what I shrank from. I did not realize what a difficult position I was putting myself in.'

Horridge, wishing to be perfectly clear on the position that Light claimed to have taken, asked: 'It comes to this, then, in order to prevent your own publicity you were not prepared to give information for the discovery of a very serious crime?'

'I could give no information whatever, my lord, as to the cause of the death.'

'You could have given information to the police. You could have said: "You are wrong about the green bicycle, it was not the man who rode the green bicycle". Do you not think that it would have been of great help to the police?'

'I see it now, my lord.'

Further questioned by Maddocks, Light agreed that he knew on the Tuesday (8 July) when he read the local newspaper that he had a revolver holster in the box room. He also agreed that Mary Webb may have seen that holster. Yes, on 5 July he had carried a raincoat over his shoulder; it had since been sold and he had made no attempt to get it back. The coat he had worn on that day, an odd one said Light, had also been sold. He could not remember whether or not the trousers that he had worn had been sold. Eager to elicit every fragment of information from the accused, Sir Thomas Horridge learned from Light that the items had been sold to a wardrobe dealer in Leicester by the name of Mrs Ridgeway.

In reply to Henry Maddocks, Light said his mother may have written to him from Rhyl asking for news of himself and of the murder. No doubt he was more than a little surprised when Henry Maddocks produced the letter which police had found in a drawer in Light's bedroom, and handed it up to him. The letter was on notepaper headed 'Morville Private Hotel, Rhyl', and began 'My Dearest Ronald'. Asked by Maddocks to read out a marked passage fom the letter, Light read: 'What is this Stretton cycle mystery, we are all interested in it here.' The letter was signed: 'Your Loving Mother, Catherine Light.'

Asked why, after receiving that letter he had not written or gone to Rhyl to tell his mother of the events of 5 July, Light simply reiterated that his mother was of all people the last he wanted to know about it, and that it was to save her worry that he did not come forward. She would, he claimed, of all persons have accepted his word. Moving from Light's relationship with his mother back to the green bicycle, in reply to Maddocks he agreed that he never rode it after 5 July, and that he had moved it up to the box room.

'You had by that time, then, made up your mind not to be identified with the green bicycle?'

'No, I cannot say that I had. I put it up in the box room because I had read about this case.'

'Did you put the bicycle in the box room in order to avoid being identified by it?'

'Yes.'

It was, said Light, dark when he went to the side of the canal with the bicycle. He had filed off the number and loosened parts before he left home. If it had been found, he had not wanted it traced to him. The holster had been dropped into the canal at the same time as the cycle parts. He had not known, he said, that when Supt. Taylor questioned him at Cheltenham that parts of the bicycle had already been found. When asked why he had said that he had never had a green bicycle, he replied: 'I said the first thing that came into my head.'

Maddocks put it to Light that when Supt. Taylor asked if he had had a green bicycle from Orton Bros at Derby, it may have occurred to him that his identify had been discovered. Why then had he said that he had sold the cycle years ago?

Light replied: 'Well, I had drifted into this policy of concealing the fact that I had been out riding on that night and I had to go on with it.' For the same reason, he said, he had also denied being in Mr Cox's shop. Once again Maddocks wanted to know if Light had been approached by anyone suspecting his identity: 'Up to that day you had been concealing the parts of a bicycle and your identity, but your identity up to that moment had never been challenged, had it?'

'No.'

A brief discussion followed in which the judge agreed with Marshall Hall that a man was quite entitled to reserve his defence. 'If a prisoner sits tight before the judge and jury, I think he is often a very wise man,' observed Sir Thomas Horridge.

There ended Maddocks's cross-examination of Light. It was a little before twelve noon, and in all Light had faced five hours of what can only be called restrained and, in consequence, unspectacular questioning, designed above all to test his assertions of his policy of concealment and – since it was all that the law allowed in the circumstances – a few questions specifically designed to rattle the prisoner. Rarely had there been any hesitation in Light's replies; only twice had the defendant seemed at all inconvenienced by Maddocks's questions. On each occasion when asked if his identify had been challenged before he consigned the green bicycle to the canal, he had answered with uncharacteristic brevity. This would only be apparent otherwise when Marshall Hall re-examined him about his father's death and his mother's ill health, and the burden that he himself had been to her. It would seem perhaps of the greatest significance that the only question to which Light could offer no answer whatever did not come from Maddocks, but was yet to be posed by the judge at the end of Light's re-examination by Marshall Hall, who began with questions about Light's parents: 'Tell my lord and the jury about your mother. I believe your father died as the result of an accident?'

'Yes.'

'Your mother has had a great deal of trouble, then?'

'Yes.'

'You have been the cause of very great expense to her in one way and another.'

'Yes.'

'What is your mother's physical condition?'

'She has been under the doctor for many years, she has a bad heart.'

Then, for the last time, Marshall Hall turned to Light's time in the Army, picking up Light's own words concerning his health when he returned to this country after active service in France with the Honourable Artillery Company: 'You were, I think, invalided home suffering from "shell shock" in August 1918.' Light agreed, adding that at that time his nervous system had been upset. He had, he said, not been the same since. 'To your knowledge, have you ever seen the spot where this young girl's body was found.'

'I do not remember that I have been along that road since I was a boy at school.'

In reply to Marshall Hall, Light said he had no idea where the girl had lived or where she was going when he left her. He agreed that the holster that he had dropped into the canal had been an officer's holster and that as a private he would not have been allowed to wear a holster with a revolver; but he did not think that should a revolver be found in a private's haversack, it would necessarily be confiscated. He very seldom went out on Sundays and he did not always take his cycle when he went into town. In July of the previous year he had been advertising for employment and had also answered a great many advertisements.

Light was again shown the holster and when questioned by the judge said that the revolver had left a certain amount of space in the holster; it had not been a dead fit. He had not taken the holster back to France with the revolver because he had not wanted to carry the extra weight.

Questioned by Sir Thomas Horridge about the time that he had waited in Gaulby, Light said that he had waited only a quarter of an hour in the village and had then spent another quarter of an hour on the outskirts of the village mending his puncture before riding back through the village. Then the judge moved to what had transpired between the defendant and Bella Wright. 'I am asking you for all that passed between you about your parting. Have you told us all that passed between you?'

Light was silent.

'Have you told us all the conversation that passed between you about your parting?'

'Oh, yes, that was all, my lord, yes.'

Light, having recovered his composure, said he had heard no shot as he rode along the upper road. He had disposed of his coat and raincoat 'probably about Christmas', and his mother had sold a lot of her things at the same time. It had been his oldest raincoat and one he had kept for cycling.

His ordeal over, Light was escorted back to the dock by two warders. He took with him the pencil that he had had with him in the witness box throughout his cross-examination, and with which he had intermittently toyed during questioning. If he had felt any nervousness then he had hidden it well; there had been but the occasional cough and easing of his shoulders. In all other respects he had appeared perfectly composed, nervous about only a handful of questions, the real significance of which was in all probability known only to himself besides counsel. If Maddocks had hoped to rattle Light into panic, and unplanned and uncalled-for admissions, he had been disappointed.

Light has always been accorded praise for his excellent showing in the witness box, for his cool head and his consistent and unchanging answers to counsel's questions. The true measure of quite how cool a witness Light was can only be understood in full knowledge of the difficulties which had faced him not only over those five hours in the witness box, but indeed throughout the whole of the previous eleven months since Bella Wright had met her death. It is no exaggeration to say that, innocent or guilty, Light would have been presented with the same difficulties – of which the jury could not be told and would not influence their judgement of the case. These difficulties burdened Light throughout his hours in the witness box and yet the jury's eventual decision, after listening to counsel's speeches and the judge's summing up, would perhaps be most influenced by what had already been said, and more importantly how it had been said, by a man who may be the most confident and composed prisoner ever to stand accused of wilful murder in the twentieth century. Undoubtedly intelligent, Ronald Light's memory and intellect had stood him in good stead throughout the long hours of his examination, much of it from the bench. If he truly 'had never been the same' since his Army service, it is entirely unlikely that he could have stood up so well to what will be seen as a particularly restrained but enlightened piece of cross-examination, one that more than justified the amount of midnight oil burned throughout the previous Thursday night at the Bell Hotel by Maddocks and Birkett. There was, however, still some way to go before the jury's verdict would be announced.

CHAPTER 15

Rex v. Light

CLOSING SPEECHES

Henry Maddocks, perhaps making the most important closing speech of his forensic career, began by reiterating what his chief, Sir Gordon Hewart, had said at the beginning of the trial; that this was without doubt a case of murder, not suicide. It was abundantly clear that sometime between 8.50 p.m. and 9.20 p.m. the girl had been shot by someone using a revolver of a large calibre. Sir Edward Marshall Hall had, said Maddocks, put forward the idea of accident. Sir Thomas Horridge intervened here to say that it was not his understanding that Sir Edward had raised the possibility of an accident as a defence, merely as a possibility. Picking up the thread, Maddocks said that it was for the jury to consider the possibility that by accident, either directly or by a ricochet, the bullet had killed the girl. Against the theory of accident he pointed out that the bullet had been travelling in an upward, not a downward, direction and that if anyone had been practising with a revolver at that hour of the night then it would have been heard by someone. The prisoner, said Maddocks, was seen with the girl within thirty-five minutes of the body being found; to the prisoner there had never been any mystery about the green bicycle. Three days afterwards, with suspicion pointing to the owner of the bicycle, the prisoner had said 'that he knew what inference would be drawn by the police in the absence of an explanation'. The prisoner had admitted ownership of the bicycle but he had dismembered it and some parts had never been found. To what Maddocks called his 'wonderful silence' the prisoner had added deception; at the first opportunity the prisoner had had to explain the matter he had told a lie. That, claimed Maddocks, was the mind of the man the jury had to judge.

Maddocks stated that Light had reserved his evidence until the last moment, so that the prosecution had not known what his defence would be: 'Until the prosecution knew, and that was only yesterday, how could they produce any evidence?'

Since it was widely broadcast at the time that Light would offer an alibi, and indeed the prosecution probably thought that to be the most likely course, any evidence which would have placed Light anywhere near the lane where Bella met her death or on the road back to Leicester after the time of her death, would surely have been of tremendous help to the prosecution. In the event any such information would have proved to be of equal importance in the light of the defence which was eventually promulgated. In either case, Light's movements on that Saturday evening after Bella's death should have been considered to be just as important as his movements before her death. For three whole months before the commencement of the trial, the prosecution had known that Light was the man with the green bicycle, and had known the address to which he went on that Saturday evening. The first person Francis Sims interviewed when he arrived in Leicester had been Mary Webb, who had already told the police what time Light arrived home and what his appearance was at that time; more importantly she told the police that he had claimed his bicycle had broken down on his way to Highfield Street. Upon receipt of that information it became imperative that the police should trace anyone who had seen a man either riding or pushing a green bicycle anywhere between the spot on the Gartree Road where Bella met her death and the house in Highfield Street to which Ronald Light returned. Furthermore, had Harry Cox not at the very outset of the enquiry told the police that the man with the green bicycle had said he was staying with friends in Leicester, and from that might the police have not suspected that the man, together with his distinctive bicycle, might make tracks back to Leicester – just as Light eventually admitted to having done. It seems, therefore, a lame excuse to offer at the eleventh hour that the prosecution had only had since the previous day to adduce evidence in rebuttal of Light's eventual defence. Maddocks's final question to Light had been: 'Have you made any attempt to find out if there were people on the road between Evington and Leicester on 5 July who saw you wheeling your bicycle?' He might more pertinently have asked Supt. Taylor if the police had managed to locate, during the three months before the trial, anyone who had seen a man answering to Light's description either riding or pushing a bicycle through Evington or near Highfield Street late on the evening of 5 July; for the route that Light took and the opportunities afforded him along that route were of primary importance.

The prisoner had, said Maddocks, failed to cover his traces. Now he took the only course open to him, claiming to know nothing of the shooting and to have been so bewildered and dazed that he had not known what to do. It was, said Maddocks, for the jury to say whether they believed his story.

Once again Sir Thomas Horridge intervened. He reminded Maddocks that whether the prisoner's story was true or false it still fell to the prosecution to make out beyond all reasonable doubt that it was the prisoner's hand that had committed the crime.

Moving to Light's conversation with Harry Cox on the morning of Saturday 5 July, and obviously touching on the possibility of premeditation, Maddocks said it was not for him to comment on whether or not the prisoner had anticipated anything. The evidence given by the two little girls corresponded completely with the description of the prisoner, and it had been established that he was upon the road that they mentioned, at about the time they met him. After some discussion between the judge and counsel as to whether the Stretton Road and the Gartree Road were one and the same road, Maddocks decided not to proceed on this point, which is surprising because the police at Leicester (in communication with Francis Sims) had stated quite clearly that from the point where the girls said they saw the prisoner, he could quite easily have reached the road he claimed to have used before the meeting that took place between himself and Bella Wright. That much, as Maddocks might have pointed out to the jury, was all there on the plan before the court.

The prisoner, said Maddocks, had said he had never seen the girl before, and who could give evidence to the contrary? The girl was dead! If he did not know the girl, but had an appointment to meet her when she came back (from visiting her uncle), then it was easy to imagine a motive. The prisoner had admitted waiting about for nearly an hour; he had had to admit that much because he had been seen. The jury as men of the world would find many matters to consider in this. Maddocks reminded the jury that both Measures and Evans had deposed that the prisoner addressed the girl as 'Bella', which showed the prisoner and the girl were on such terms that he could do that. Maddocks, quaintly perhaps even for those days, pointed out that to wait so long for a girl whom he claimed not to know, might indicate that the prisoner was 'saying something which was not accurate'.

The girl had been shot, but could they rely on the prisoner's statement. No one heard the shot, and the prisoner said he did not hear it, yet it amounted to saying that a quarter of an hour after the prisoner said he left the girl, she was 'found shot with a heavy calibre revolver cartridge'. What a terrible coincidence for the prisoner that the bullet was of 'a special kind', made for use with black powder and adapted for use with cordite – and that cartridges containing bullets of the same kind were now known to have been in the prisoner's possession. The prisoner had claimed to have no revolver; if the prisoner had not remained silent a search of his house would at once have shown that to be the case. Now they only had the prisoner's word for it. Evidence had been given that the prisoner had asked a lady to take a parcel, containing a revolver, secretly to his home for him in 1915. Why had there been that secrecy? As to the holster, the prisoner had given his explanation of why he kept it at home and why he took the revolver away. Why take to France a revolver he would not be allowed to wear? And if he had taken it why did he not take it 'in the only receptacle in which he could wear it'? That was something, said Maddocks, for the jury to consider with the greatest care.

Turning to the moment of the girl's death, Maddocks spoke of it as 'this terrible deed', and commented that speculation on how the deed was done could not help the prisoner or the prosecution. He went on to make the only comment throughout the whole trial and investigation that indicates the location on the *Via Devana* where Bella was found could be reached from where Light claimed to have parted from her just as quickly, or perhaps even more quickly, by taking the alternative road through Little Stretton and turning back on to the Gartree road. Maddocks put it like this: 'Whether the prisoner did or did not accompany, or perhaps ride round and meet her, whether he made overtures to her and was repulsed, and whether in a moment of madness, he produced a revolver to terrorize her and shot her so that it would not come out must be a matter for pure speculation.'

When the prisoner arrived home, said Maddocks, 'he prepared those at home for the silence he was to maintain'. The prisoner had neglected to repair the punctured bicycle tyre either on Sunday, Monday or the Tuesday morning. It might be said that before the news was made public that a green bicycle was connected with the case, the prisoner was preparing for the defence he set up. The significance was, maintained Maddocks, overwhelming.

The prisoner had claimed not to know the spot where the girl had been found: it might have been miles away. 'Would not an innocent man go and inform the police that he left the girl just outside the village?' The prisoner can only have been dazed because if he had given the explanation that he now gave he would not be believed. Commenting further on Light's comment that he had been dazed, Maddocks spoke of the thoroughness with which the bicycle was broken up; 'This was not the work of an ordinary man, incapable of concocting a story, but of a very clever, deliberate man.' Coming to his peroration, Maddocks said it would be a calamity if an innocent man were convicted, but it was equally a calamity if a guilty man were allowed to go free. Could the jury accept this man's word? 'Having regard to all the circumstances, and looking at the facts, if you, the members of the jury think that you cannot accept his story then you will be obliged to do your duty to society.'

One can almost sense a feeling of relief in Maddocks as he resumed his seat. Left in Leicester to salvage as best he could a prosecution case that had, even before Marshall Hall's final speech, been considerably weakened by a brilliantly simple and, one would have thought, foreseeable line of defence. After all, the police had been able to bring no one to identify Light other than those who saw him on his journey earlier in the evening or with Bella as they rode into Gaulby, and those members of Bella's family who saw the couple as they left the village. It did not take a man of Light's intellect or Marshall Hall's incomparable experience to draw the conclusion that the police were entirely unable to produce even one person to testify that the couple were together after they left Gaulby. In all probability Light had recognized and could place everyone who was brought forward on identity parades, with the possible exception of Elizabeth Palmer's husband who had been driving his van and would have been somewhat hidden from Light's view; but Palmer had in any case failed to identify Light.

Maddocks knew full well that any strength in the prosecution's case lay entirely in circumstantial evidence, and the sheer magnitude of those points of circumstance must have given Maddocks his and his team hope that they would prove their case to the satisfaction of the jury. Sir Gordon Hewart had a phrase, 'the coincidences of truth are innumerable', but Hewart was not in court to exploit those coincidences; and however lucid and well marshalled Maddocks's arguments might have been, it is probably true to say that he would not have been able to put them to the jury with quite the same weight as the Attorney-General could have done. That those coincidences of circumstance could not be ignored would be borne out by the length of time the jury spent in consideration, but before the judge gave his summing up and the jury retired to their deliberations, there was Sir Edward Marshall Hall to be heard. Had the Attorney-General stayed the course, he would by right and tradition have had the last word, regardless of the fact that the defence had called no witnesses save the defendant. In the event it was Marshall Hall who rose to have the last word.

Immediately Sir Edward put the case to the jury in all its stark reality. However they might disguise the fact, there was no question that shortly into their hands would be placed the life of a human being; but he would not ask for sympathy, or ask for pity. He would merely deal with the case on the evidence and, after listening to counsel and to his Lordship if they the jury were satisfied beyond reasonable doubt that Ronald Light had killed Bella Wright on the night of 5 July, then it was their duty to the community to find him guilty.

It was, said Marshall Hall, a somewhat curious fact that in this case even the 'super-ability' of the Attorney-General could not present the court with a definite theory as to the commission of the crime. It had been suggested that the prisoner had made false statements to Cox. This presupposed premeditation, and the prosecution must accept the theory that the prisoner did not wish to go to a repairer that knew him, and put Cox off the scent as regards identification. If that were relevant to the charge it must mean that on that Saturday morning Light had made up his mind to murder Bella Wright. 'What was a man doing with a revolver on the Stretton Road, unless he went out for the purpose of committing some crime?' asked Marshall Hall. If the prosecutions supposition was correct then the prisoner had deliberately covered up his tracks to create a false identity. 'Did that suggest that he knew the girl before?' His evidence was positive: 'I did not know her', and what of the dead girl's statement? They had been told that she had said: 'I don't know the man, I have never seen him before. He is a perfect stranger to me.' Was that evidence not just as acceptable as the other evidence? Light's statement had not been contradicted, yet the prosecution asked the jury to believe that the girl did know the man, and had known him and had lied about it. 'What foundation was there for such a belief? The only tittle of evidence to support the belief that the man knew her was a casual conversation overheard . . . One witness said that Light had exclaimed "Bella, you have been a long time", and another "You have been a long time Bella", and upon this flimsy statement the jury is asked to believe that the two people were known one to the other . . . I ask you not to say that Light murdered an unknown girl without any motive whatsoever.'

Having first planted the idea in the minds of the jury that they and they alone would hold sway over the life of the defendant, Marshall Hall had taken his earliest opportunity to pose what must have been the foremost question in the minds of the jurors as Henry Maddocks had resumed his seat. Were the defendant and Bella Wright known in any way to one another before Light claimed to have met her on that top road when he said she asked him if he had a spanner. It was a point which must, if the defence were to succeed, be tackled with courage and resolution, for it embodied all that an advocate in Marshall Hall's position would have preferred to leave unsaid. That though, was a risk he could not run. The jury had to be convinced that the words of the girl herself spoken in conversation with her uncle were the truth. In his incomparable way, Marshall Hall was determined that the shadow of Bella Wright and the words she had used would be felt in that courtroom, and especially in the jury box, as though she had herself taken the stand.

Marshall Hall pressed on. The Attorney-General might say all he liked about the innumerable coincidences of truth, but the overwhelming difficulty in the case was 'the entire absence of motive, as between the prisoner and the woman'. The jury must, insisted Marshall Hall, consider very seriously before they said that this man murdered an innocent girl under the circumstances detailed by the prosecution. None of the witnesses had said one single word about the revolver. Surely such people 'who observed with such nicety' would have noticed the weight if it were concealed in the raincoat.

Of the evidence given on the previous day by Henry Clarke, the gunsmith, Marshall Hall was scathing. 'I have never heard such ridiculous evidence as that witness gave.' Referring to Clarke's supposition that such a lead bullet fired into the ground would bounce into the air at right angles and then fall to the ground, he said: 'I suggest, quite seriously, in spite of the doctor's evidence, that the wound in the piece of flesh produced could not have been caused by the bullet which has been produced, even had it been travelling nose on.'

At this point Marshall Hall paid a rather oblique compliment to the police on their handling of the case and of the absolutely fair way in which the identification had been carried out, but he was doubtful whether when the doctor produced the rather gruesome specimen now before the court from his little black bag, that the police knew anything about it. He went further: 'If I or my advisers had known of it, we would have had it submitted, by consent, to some great expert.' It seems certain, therefore, that the defence knew nothing of the specimen until the time when Dr Williams produced it in open court, but one cannot but share Marshall Hall's scepticism as to whether or not those police officers in charge of the case and representatives of the Treasury who were engaged in its prosecution knew of the existence of the specimen. What is certain is that Dr Williams was called back to Little Stretton by P.C. Hall, who pointed out to the physician what he took to be a bullet hole. Is it really likely that Hall then left before Dr Williams had completed his examination, and before he had removed the section of flesh from the face of the dead girl? Is it not far more likely that an officer as enthusiastic as Hall undoubtedly was, would not have stayed with the doctor until his work was finished? There is also the question of who held a candle to light the doctor's dissection if it was not the indefatigable P.C. Hall? It is therefore apparent that at least one member of the Leicestershire Constabulary knew from the outset of the existence of the specimen of skin taken by Williams from the face of the deceased girl.

That Marshall Hall was genuinely rattled by having been denied access to the specimen is made evident by his leaving the subject of the wound without further comment, when he might have been expected to reinforce his earlier statement that such a bullet could have been expected to blow off half of the girl's head.

Again he came back to the question of motive. The Attorney-General had, he said, made some suggestion of an improper motive. That was, maintained Marshall Hall, 'absolutely, definitely and finally negatived by the evidence; there was no sign of any struggle or of any molestation of the girl.' If it was suggested that the man had been rebuffed by word of mouth, 'a man of that class would have done what he wanted first, and shot afterwards,' but he was glad that there was not a tittle of evidence on that point, because the name of the girl remained unsullied. All the resources of the police had been unable to 'disclose a single person' who saw Bella and Light together near the place where she was found, close to Little Stretton church and within 200 yd of the nearby houses . . . 'or could give the court one particle of evidence to say whether or not they knew each other in any sense'.

Of the meeting that Ronald Light had claimed took place on the top road, Marshall Hall spoke in the restrained and stilted parlance of the day: 'They will never get rid of the power of sex; here is the story of a young man of thirty, and a young woman who had met.' Was that, he asked, not natural? 'Women may become more manly, and men more effeminate; you may take

Ronald Light, shown seated between two warders in the dock, listens intently. Seated in the row behind Light are: second from left, Ethel Tunnicliffe, Mary Webb, Muriel Nunney and, second from right, Valeria Cavan. Marshall Hall is at the extreme bottom right of the photograph

votes from men, but you cannot take away their sex; you may give woman the vote, but cannot alter her sex. In these episodes there is always a possibility of adventure without any suggestion of immorality. It is strange that the unknown attraction, sex, should dominate the world. Here was a charming girl, with a bicycle, not reluctant to have company and Light accepted her invitation to wait. He has been foolish and has possibly shown moral cowardice of the worst possible order, but it must be remembered that shell-shock destroys nerve vitality.' Was it not, asked Marshall Hall, 'quite understandable that the man, not wanting to alarm his mother, should drift into a policy of concealment?' The jury could read between the lines. The prisoner's mother suffered from heart disease, and very possibly the prisoner did not tell her what he knew for fear of disturbing her peace of mind. If lies had been told by the prisoner, where, he asked, was the evidence in rebuttal?

Stress, claimed Marshall Hall, had been laid upon the alleged concealment of the revolver in 1915. Was it suggested that as far back as that the prisoner had the murder of this girl in mind? It was of no moment in this case, only showing that the prisoner had once had a revolver – but that had not been denied.

Marshall Hall had been on his feet for about an hour when, not for the first or last time in his forensic career, he called the attention of the jury to the differences in the English and Continental systems of justice. In this country the presumption of innocence was accorded any defendant until the weight of evidence proved him guilty. Unless, he reiterated, they were satisfied beyond reasonable doubt that Light was guilty, then he was, by right, entitled to an acquittal, 'even if they were not disposed to accept his story with absolute confidence'.

This was vintage Marshall Hall. Clearly he was all but ready to launch into his frequently utilized demonstration, descriptively dubbed his 'scales of justice act'. This was a parody, some who saw it thought it a very moving parody, of that famous figure of Justice by Cedric Pomeroy that adorns the Central Criminal Court in the Old Bailey. Certainly it seems to have been a parody that many a jury thought worthy of consideration and even now, some sixty-odd years after his death, one can almost see the arms of the advocate beginning to rise, reaching out, his hands cupped in representation of those two scales of justice, his voice breaking as he appealed to one more jury on behalf of one more prisoner. There was one man in court that day who thought to capture the moment for posterity, but the movements of the press photographer at the back of the gallery were suddenly noticed by Sir Thomas Horridge. The trial was stopped, and Marshall Hall slumped back in mid-sentence on to his knifeboard seat, his train of thought broken, the nervous energy which had been building throughout his speech dissipated. For him, and doubtless for Ronald Light also, such an interruption could not have come at a more crucial time. The judge ordered the photographer, who to this day remains unidentified, to be brought down into the well of the court. There he stood somewhat sheepishly before the bench, as Sir Thomas Horridge ascertained that the man was indeed attempting to take a photograph. Horridge told him that he was lucky not to be sent to prison for contempt of court. The man's reply was that he had no idea it was not allowed, and to be fair, anyone seated in that courtroom throughout the trial might easily have gained that impression, so numerous were the photographs taken, many while the court was in session. Somewhat angered by the man's reply, which he clearly thought to be flippant, the judge replied: 'Of course you knew it was not allowed in a court of justice. If you talk like that I shall be tempted to deal with you more severely. Go away, Sir.' The man's camera and film were confiscated and the world lost what would have been a fascinating photograph.

The first written prohibition of photography in court came under Section 41 of the Criminal Justice Act of 1925. Before this it appears that on similar occasions individual judges took what action they saw fit within their own courts. Before the Act, however, a person taking or attempting to take a photograph in a court where a case was being tried, could most certainly be charged with contempt of court. At the trial of Light the photographer was indeed lucky, for the judge was a man of little patience who was once known to fine a juryman £10 for being just a few minutes late.

Turning to Marshall Hall, Sir Thomas Horridge – doubtless fully aware of the effect that the interruption had had on defence counsel – said: 'Do go on, Sir Edward.' For a second time the advocate rose to his feet and attempted to recreate the atmosphere that had prevailed before the interruption. For some time he spoke without his usual flair, the words falling lifelessly from his lips, but gradually he recovered, and spoke for the best part of another hour, following in all probability, his usual practice of speaking directly to each juror in turn until he believed he had won over that particular man, and only then moving on to the next. His peroration in defence of Light, accompanied by that favourite parody, was delivered with sufficient emotion to register in the quivering of the voice. Again Marshall Hall laid emphasis on that all-important presumption of innocence: 'I have to remind you gentlemen that this is a matter of life or death. Unless the evidence leaves you with no doubt, you will remember that in the one scale held by the finger of Justice is what is called the presumption of innocence, which is the British judicial system's most valued feature. You will not hesitate to make use of that if there is any reasonable doubt in your minds.'

An adjournment was called directly Marshall Hall finished speaking and he straightaway made his way to counsel's robing room. His clerk remembered him damning the photographer over and over again for the interruption he had caused, and being in need of the complete change of clothes that was habitually carried for just such a contingency – so drenched in perspiration was he after the efforts of not once but twice bringing his speech to its climax. For a man of Marshall Hall's advancing years, not enjoying the best of health and in all probability swathed as ever in bandages from ankle to groin, the extra energy needed to pick up the pieces of a ruined speech must have been a great strain on both mental and physical resources. Edgar Bowker in later years said that few who watched that day would have realized what an ordeal it had been and how much his chief had taken out of himself in his defence of Light. Not until Marshall Hall had drunk a cup of tea and smoked a cigarette with the aid of his habitual holder did he begin to calm down in readiness for the judge's summing up.

Marshall Hall himself once said: 'It is not the speeches one has to fear in a case, it's the witnesses that count.' Including the interruption it seems that Marshall Hall's speech lasted for something in the order of two-and-a-half hours, and was therefore considerably shorter than several speeches made by him in similar circumstances. In 1915 he had spoken for four hours on behalf of George Joseph Smith, a man who Marshall Hall believed to be guilty, and that speech is comparable with that in defence of Light, in that they both embodied far fewer emotional appeals to the jury than in many of his most notable and well publicized capital defences on which his reputation as 'the greatest defender' was founded.

It is rather doubtful that Marshall Hall ever rated his closing speech in defence of Ronald Light as one of the best of his lengthy forensic career, but so much groundwork had already been done and so many damaging points won that any satisfaction he took from the case probably stemmed from the first two days, and from the decision to keep the main line of defence a matter of guesswork until the eleventh hour. In addition to that invaluable groundwork there had been Light's own evidence, and more importantly, the confident manner in which it was given that made such a favourable impression on the court. Even old hands rated Light as a superb witness, one commentator thinking that he was the coolest man in court. It must be assumed that Light's firm and generally straightforward way of answering counsel's questions must have left an indelible picture in the minds of the jury, but would all his sanguinity and all that his counsel had asked the jury to believe be enough to save him? It would still be several hours before Light knew the answer to that burning question.

CHAPTER 16

Rex v. Light

SUMMING UP AND VERDICT

Sir Thomas Horridge began his summing up at precisely 4 p.m., and his half-hour speech is largely considered to have been extremely fair. That Light had to a great extent and for many months by his own admittance failed, for whatever reason, to come forward and offer the police the assistance that they sought obviously could not be ignored. His deceit and lies told to the police when they eventually discovered his whereabouts might be construed in one of two ways. Horridge put it like this: 'Is it a deception which in your opinion could have been practised by an innocent man, or do you think that deception points a certain finger to the actions of a guilty man. I don't want to influence you one bit, but I think that that question and the answer to it will largely help you to come to a conclusion in this case.'

Referring to Marshall Hall revealing to the court only at the eleventh hour a hint of what Light's defence would be, and knowing that but for Norman Birkett's error it would have remained a secret until the moment that Light himself stepped into the witness box, Horridge had this to say: 'The prisoner has had the advantage not only of skill but, might I say, the discretion which had been exercised by his counsel.' Sir Thomas Horridge would in fact later say to George Pleydell-Bancroft that he considered Marshall Hall 'did not make a single mistake'.

It was, said the judge, the duty of the prosecution to show beyond reasonable doubt that the hand of the prisoner shot the girl. That duty was such that it did not follow that because the jury disbelieved the prisoner's story they were to find the prisoner guilty: The prosecution had still to show to the jury's satisfaction that the prisoner was guilty. In deciding the question, though, if they thought the prisoner's story to be untrue that would be a large element for them to take into consideration.

George Measures' deposition was read through by the judge in its entirety. It included Bella's own words to her uncle that the man was a stranger to her. One must look, said the judge, at the probabilities of the story. The couple had been in each other's company for some time; the man had been in the village for 'well over an hour'. He had said that he had had no intention of waiting, so did the jury think it likely he would have been sent away by a conversation such as he had detailed?

If the prisoner was an innocent man and had gone to the police and told them of the girl to whom he had been seen talking, that at least would have shown they were on the wrong scent. It was, said Horridge, entirely for the jury to say whether it was credible that an innocent man should have behaved in that way. If, on the other hand, assuming the man to be guilty, did the jury think his behaviour compatible with innocence. If so, they were bound to give him the benefit of that possibility.

The jury should, said Sir Thomas, put all minor incidents out of their minds. They were not to trouble their heads about the two little girls on the road or about the allegation that the prisoner had made a false statement to Cox. The prisoner had certainly made false statements, about that there was no dispute, but it had also been stated quite truthfully that no motive had been proved. 'You must', said the judge, 'always look carefully at a case where there is no motive. In the absence of a motive the defence are entitled to say, "Why should the prisoner go and kill that human being".... In this case no real motive has been suggested.'

It may have been those few words spoken by Horridge that led in time to a belief that the evidence of the two young girls Muriel Nunney and her friend Valeria Cavan was in fact totally discredited at the time of the trial, but doubtless the judge wished only to point out that there were witnesses who could place Light and Bella Wright together far closer to the time of her death, and in that respect only the evidence of the two girls was perhaps of less importance than that of other witnesses. It is, given information now to hand, a sad thing that the evidence of those two girls has been given little credence, for it may point to the state of mind of Ronald Light as he rode into Gaulby village with Bella Wright, and later as he waited, pondering her last words to him before going into her uncle's cottage.

Did the jury, asked the judge, think the bullet found in the road was the one that caused the girl's death? Did they think that the prisoner had had a revolver out of which he fired that bullet? If the jury thought there was grave doubt about that then they were entitled to consider the fact that there was no motive.

In conclusion Mr Justice Horridge charged the jury that it was of supreme importance that an innocent man should not be convicted, but it was also of supreme importance that a terrible crime of this kind, if brought home to the prisoner, should not be allowed to go unpunished.

The jury retired to consider their verdict at a little after 4.30 on that Friday afternoon, and defendant and counsel alike prepared for what was to be a long vigil.

Afternoon became evening, and at a little before 7.45 p.m., when it had begun to look as though the jury would indeed have to spend a third night in seclusion, the judge recalled them and asked their foreman if there was any real prospect of them reaching an agreement. In those days it would not have been open to the judge to suggest that a majority verdict might be reached: that innovation was not introduced until 1967. In 1920 an agreed verdict by all twelve men had to be forthcoming, and if that were not possible then the jury could state they were unable to agree upon a verdict – then the case would have to be retried at a later date. In calling the jury back at that time in the evening the judge was, contrary to one contemporary comment, not being impatient but merely trying to establish whether or not he should adjourn until Saturday morning, not a prospect to please anyone engaged upon the case. In the event the jury foreman said that there was a likelihood that the jury could agree and requested another ten or fifteen minutes. Once again the jury retired, but only seven minutes later a flurry of excitement passed through the precincts of the court indicating that after what can only have been a very few more minutes of discussion, the jury were for a final time filing into court. The twelve men took their places and there are reports of them all staring straight ahead, which must have appeared to bode ill for the prisoner. It was always said that a jury about to acquit a defendant would readily, and perhaps with some relief, look directly into the face of that defendant, while a jury about to convict would if at all possible avoid the prisoner's eye.

The Clerk of the Court, George Pleydell-Bancroft, rose to address the foreman: 'Gentlemen, are you agreed on your verdict?'

'Yes.'

'Do you find the prisoner guilty or not guilty?'

'Not Guilty.'

'Is that the verdict of you all?'

'Yes.'

For the first time throughout the proceedings Ronald Light exhibited signs that perhaps, despite his confident demeanour over the three days of the trial, and indeed since the time of his arrest, he had after all feared for his life. From the time that the jury were led into court for the final time he had stood with the whites of his knuckles visible as his hands clutched the dock rail. As the verdict was announced he fell back heavily into his chair; some thought him near to collapse. As the judge ordered the prisoner's discharge and the door of the dock was opened, for a few moments Light hesitated. Wightman Powers spoke briefly to him, then after an initial shout of 'Congratulations, Mr Light' amid some cheering and one call from the public gallery of 'Money has won this case', Light stepped out of the dock a free man. The case of Rex v. Light which had cost the Treasury a total of £497 19s 6d in counsel's fees was at an end. Supt. Taylor walked up to Light and reportedly shook him heartily by the hand. Light was heard to say quietly to him: 'I'll see you some time.'

For some time Light stood in the courtroom between the dock and the public gallery. The crowds that were milling around outside on the Castle Green had heard the news of the acquittal and had taken up the cheering.

Light, however, was advised by the police to wait a while before attempting to leave the courtroom, and this delay gave the waiting corps of pressmen their first of several opportunities to interview Light. With a broad grin on his face and with that old confident manner fast returning, he told his eager listeners: 'I have expected this verdict all along.' Perhaps that was the truth. Certainly he would later admit to having had a bet on the outcome of his trial, a bet which needless to say he won.

When asked if he had any more to say, he replied: 'Not now, but everyone had been very kind to me.' When asked what he intended to do next he said, with a smile on his face: 'I've a jolly good mind to take a holiday.' Det. Supt. Taylor had had the same idea, and was to leave Leicester immediately for a short vacation.

One shrewd reporter, perhaps already better informed than most, asked Light: 'Do you intend to return to Dean Close School?' to which Light, with perhaps a touch of foreboding replied:

'I'm not sure they will have me back after this. Some of the things I did were damaging to me but, well, I wouldn't mind.'

As he left the courtroom several people shook Light's hand, and heard him remark: 'I'm thankful it's over.'

Sir Thomas Horridge was cheered as his carriage pulled away, and a few minutes later Light left the castle by a side door and, quite unnoticed by the milling crowd, with 3d borrowed from a friend, went to catch a bus for the short ride home to the London Road, from where he walked the few hundred yards to the house in Highfield Street where his mother had waited patiently for news of the verdict.

Mother and son would quickly be approached by reporters hoping for exclusive interviews. One reporter from the *Daily Sketch*, who persistently referred to Light as Lieutenant Light, found that his flattery paid off when he managed to secure an interview with both Ronald and his mother at their Highfield home later that evening Light told the reporter that he had 'felt confident from the start', and that the verdict 'was no surprise to him'. Catherine Light added: 'And I was confident too.'

Catherine Light, as a letter later written by Marshall Hall would show, had supported her son financially whenever the need arose. She would herself face another considerable account in respect of Light's defence, and would receive help from a friend. Therefore it stands in some contrast that no provision had been made for Light's journey home in the event of his acquittal. Such an oversight, if oversight it was, rather begs the question whether Catherine Light really was as confident of that acquittal as she had that *Daily Sketch* reporter believe?

In such a case it is inevitable that in the course of their enquiries the police will sometimes follow a lead that is misleading, and indeed sometimes amusing, if only in hindsight. The case of the green bicycle would provide one such interlude. During their search of Light's study at Dean Close School, the police came across a letter which held references to the 'Stretton'

A photograph of Ronald Light taken soon after his acquittal

A coup for the Daily Sketch *reporter, who secured this earlier studio portrait of Catherine Light that appeared alongside that of her son, on the day following his acquittal. The family likeness is quite striking*

bicycle. Much intrigued, Supt. Taylor and his men made exhaustive enquiries until they traced the writer of the letter, one Annie M. Harper, who by 1920 was married and residing in Kidderminster. It transpired that Annie Harper's maiden name had been Stretton and her family were manufacturers and hirers of cycles in Cheltenham. The company, Strettons Ltd, had their main premises (the Million Cycle Factory) in Bath Road, with three other branches around the town. They manufactured the 'Million' and the 'Cobra' cycle, and should any budding cyclist require assistance, Strettons taught them to ride free of charge on their cycling ground in Wellington Street, Cheltenham. It seems likely that Light's particular interest may have been the purchase of a new cycle to replace the B.S.A. deluxe machine which had been consigned to the murky waters of the canal back home in Leicester.

Following his release, Ronald Light's time was seemingly well taken up with the attentions of the press, for it was not until Wednesday of the week following his acquittal that he finally sat down to write a letter of thanks to Sir Edward Marshall Hall. In the way that symmetry and coincidence seem to follow these things, the day that Light chose to write his letter, 16 June 1920, was the very day that Harold Greenwood would be arrested at Kidwelly for the murder of his wife by arsenical poisoning. The defence of Harold Greenwood at Carmarthen in the coming November would mark Marshall Hall's next, and again successful, appearance in a capital case.

As previously stated, Marshall Hall's papers were at his request destroyed after his death, and so for the words of Ronald Light's letter and indeed for the content and sentiment of Marshall Hall's reply we are dependent upon Edward Marjoribanks's biography of Marshall Hall. The great defender, according to his habitual rule, would have requested Light to return his own letter to him. Majoribanks doubtless, therefore, read both letters in full, so it is a pity that probably because they contained information which will be revealed in a later chapter, Majoribanks felt it necessary to edit them for publication.

Leicester

16 June 1920

Dear Sir,

The very first letter I am writing since my release is, of course, to you.

I cannot find words to express how deeply grateful I am to you for your great and successful efforts on my behalf. It seems rather feeble to say 'Thank you' for saving my life, but I feel sure you will understand what I think. Your speech to the jury was simply great, and practically obliterated any previous impressions they had obtained from hearing Mr Maddocks . . . I shall always remember you with the deepest gratitude.

Yours sincerely,

R. Light.

Marshall Hall had a flat in Wimpole Street when in London, but his reply to Light's letter from his country house Overbrook, in Brook, near Godalming, Surrey, would seem to indicate that the advocate's reply was written at the earliest during the weekend of 19–20 June but more probably during the following weekend, for the letter leaves the reader with an impression that the writer gave a great deal of thought to its contents. Those who know of Marshall Hall's own personal tragedy may be tempted to see the letter as no more than the writing of a man who always had the greatest sympathy for any woman who, through no fault of her own or perhaps through her weakness, found herself to be the bearer of a heavy cross. Undoubtedly Marshall Hall did feel great sympathy for the widowed and invalid Catherine Light: Marjoribanks talks of him being haunted throughout the days of the trial by the thought of her sitting at home awaiting news of her son's trial for murder. There is an unmistakable sense of that concern in Marshall Hall's letter, but perhaps it is secondary to his own opinion of his correspondent. Even though, on first reading, the letter as edited states so little, in effect it says much more; and it gave the earliest indication (apart from Francis Sims' comment at police court on Light's gazetting from the Royal Engineers) that the impression of Light as an upright, honest and virtuous officer and gentleman was far from the truth. This distance between illusion and reality must have been known, if only in part, by Catherine Light and her maid of some eight years, Mary Webb. How much those women knew would have been a measure of how successfully Light stage-managed the dichotomy of his life. Some knowledge of his lifestyle, and even possibly an unwelcome personal involvement in it may finally have driven Mary Webb to risk the wrath of her employer at a time when she knew her days with the Lights were numbered. There is no evidence extant that Mary Webb was ever served with a subpoena, but it is certain and well documented that Francis Sims was concerned for her well-being.

It was with the woman who remained at Highfield Street that Marshall Hall's sympathy lay, and this is shown in his reply to Ronald Light:

Dear Sir,

Thank you for your letter, which I much appreciate. Quite apart from *the* matter which caused so much anxiety . . . may I in kindness and great sincerity express the hope that you will realize that life is a serious thing, and that work and self-denial are the only means to happiness. Please convey to your mother my sympathetic regards, and you will, I am sure,

157

forgive me if I say that you can best show your gratitude to me by making her life happier in the future than I fear it has been in the past. I am indeed glad to have been of service to you, and through you to her.

Yours very faithfully.

Edward Marshall Hall.

Reading between the lines of this letter it is clear that Marshall Hall was conversant with much of Ronald Light's past life, but it is obvious that when it came to his defence of Light he would not, indeed could not, allow that privileged information to bear in any way upon his eventual handling of the case. However, his acceptance of the brief must have been to an extent coloured by that knowledge, which in itself would ensure that his conduct of the case was more difficult than it might otherwise have been. The impossibility of Bigg not apprising Marshall Hall of that privileged information, which was obviously fully known to the prosecution, goes without saying, and that Marshall Hall was, despite being fully aware of Light's reputation, still able to give him the quality of defence that any man is entitled to receive under our law is obvious. If, however, by that knowledge the case was made more difficult for Marshall Hall then it must have been doubly so for Ronald Light himself. It must have meant that his five hours in the witness box were a far greater strain upon him than they would have been to a man of unblemished reputation, for had he unwittingly disclosed anything of his previous character on oath, the prosecution would have been at liberty to question him on that disclosure, and that would have resulted in the derogation of Light in the eyes of the jury.

Part of a letter which Marshall Hall wrote after Light's acquittal to one of his oldest friends, Sir Arthur Wing Pinero, the playwright and dramatist, indicates the difficulty he had in taking on the case. Again the letter, not in its entirety, is quoted by Marjoribanks. It would have been fascinating to read it in full, for the precise abridgement speaks volumes for Edward Majoribanks's propriety.

To a typically worded telegram from Sir Arthur Pinero, written in his usual witty and cryptic way, and which read simply: 'Congratulations on the Light which did not fail', Marshall Hall replied:

My Dear Pin,

I was so glad to get your telegram – for it spoke of rememberance [sic]. It was a desperate fight, and Horridge paid me a most unusual compliment, and I must say that his summing-up was most fair . . . The coincidence of the bullet was literally astounding, as I am convinced the bullet that was found within 17½ ft of the body never killed the girl; but the deadly thing was that the accused man had in his possession at the time identical bullets. True, as I elicited in cross-examination, they are made in thousands of millions, but, for all that, it was a coincidence. Absence of motive too, was a great asset. But for all that, I can assure you that it wanted handling. Personally, I think it is the greatest success as an advocate I ever had.

Yours as ever,

Marshall.

Despite Marshall Hall's words to Pinero, his own theories concerning the circumstances in which Bella Wright met her death must largely be a matter for speculation. He was amused in the weeks following the trial to read Trueman Humphries' assessment of the case published in the *Strand* magazine, the first account of the case in which the black raven was resurrected. There is no indication that Marshall Hall ever voiced his own feelings as to the innocence or guilt of Ronald Light, even when sequestered within a meeting of Our Society, of which he was a founder member and where he loved to talk of his successful defences. Not even, it seems, within that exclusive circle did he propound any theory of how Bella Wright met her death. His reticence may have been uncharacteristic, but in this case it was shared with the judge, whose comment concerning Light's right to reserve his defence even until the eleventh hour was widely reported, and who was never to make known his own views on the case. While that may not have been an unusual position for Horridge to take, for Marshall Hall to be so completely uncommunicative was indeed unusual.

The reasons why any advocate accepts such a defence as that in the case of Rex v. Light are multitudinous. There is no record that in this specific case anyone dared Marshall Hall to accept, or indeed even suggested that he had any obligation to do so, but he may have been to some extent deceived into believing that he and Ronald Light had both attended the same public school and thus felt himself to be under some obligation. As previously stated, after attending preparatory school in Leicester, Light went on in 1899 to Oakham School, but it has since been regularly and quite erroneously stated that he was a pupil at Rugby. The first published account of that misconception seems to have been made by Edward Marjoribanks in his biography of Marshall Hall, a book which it must be remembered was based on Marshall Hall's own papers and conversations which the advocate had shared with his biographer. There is, therefore, every indication that Marshall Hall had been told, and in fact believed, that in Light he would certainly be defending a fellow Rugbeian. How great an influence in his final decision to do so that false information had on him must be a matter for speculation.

Rugbeian or not, the defence of Light represented particular problems, because of his own personal background and Marshall Hall was always a man to relish a challenge.

Acceptance of the case resulted in Marshall Hall's believing the acquittal of Ronald Light to be the pinnacle of his forensic career, which before he had always maintained was his defence of Edward Lawrence at Stafford in 1909. That the less conspicuous difficulties in defending Ronald Light outweighed in the mind of the advocate the very real difficulties of defending a man such as Lawrence, who not only looked to be a man more than capable of murder but had immediately rushed from the scene of his lover's death to a nearby doctor's house to gain assistance for the dying woman, and who readily admitted to ownership of the revolver that killed her, may be seen as an indication of the depth of the black mood which clearly consumed Marshall Hall for some days after his first meeting with Bigg. It must also be a measure of the intractability of the case, of the dilemma which Marshall Hall faced in his acceptance of it and his prognosis of the eventual outcome.

Despite having secured an acquittal and acknowledging it to be his 'greatest success as an advocate', Marshall Hall's unusual silence concerning the guilt or innocence of Ronald Light was maintained consistently throughout the remaining years of his life and may be seen as almost certainly indicative that he held strong views on the actual commission of the crime and on the guilt or innocence of the man he had successfully defended. That singular and uncharacteristic silence must be allowed to speak for itself.

Yet might we not permit ourselves to wonder if Pinero's telegram of congratulations to Marshall Hall, which contained a simple play on Light's surname, also indicated an earlier discussion of the case? Marshall Hall was ever an avid reader of fashionable novels, and it is a fact that in 1890, a year in which due to the tragic death of his first wife Marshall Hall was at his most vulnerable and impressionable, Kipling was writing his first and not wholly successful novel *The Light that Failed*. The novel, which was to some extent written during visits by Kipling to his parents, who were staying in Wynnstay Gardens, only doors from Marshall Hall's own home, tells of the desperate love of Dick, a young soldier, for a young girl, Maisie. The novel opens with the two experimenting with a revolver, and results in Maisie almost wounding Dick as she fires the weapon.

Perhaps despite the obvious reversal of roles, Marshall Hall or Pinero or perhaps both had seen in the novel a possible parallel to the Light case. Perhaps they considered that just such an experiment had taken place on the *Via Devana* in 1919, and had resulted in the accidental death of Bella Wright.

But whatever Marshall Hall's thoughts, and we can but speculate, he may have taken note of the words of the dedication which Kipling put to his book (as distinct from other versions which appeared). The first stanza of that dedication is surely as apposite to Ronald Light as to the character Dick in *The Light that Failed*:

> If I were hanged on the highest hill,
> Mother o' mine, O mother o' mine!
> I know whose love would follow me still,
> Mother o' mine, O mother o' mine.

But Light was not hanged and, unlike that of Bella Wright, as Pinero noted, his light continued to shine.

CHAPTER 17

Ronald Light

OFFICER AND GENTLEMAN?

As Ronald Light stepped from the dock in Leicester's Castle courtroom a free man he had been asked by one wily reporter if he would return to his post at Dean Close School. Light had replied that some of the things he had done were damaging to him, and the school might not want him back. Light did not specify what those damaging things were, and he most certainly did not point out that in order to obtain his post as assistant mathematics master he had given the headmaster, Dr Flecker, a very false picture of his suitability. Following his arrest at the school in March 1920, investigations were set in motion to discover what manner of man the new assistant mathematics master might be, and a brief note, still extant, in the school record bears witness to the result of that investigation. The record states that Ronald Light was appointed to the staff on the strength of testimonials which turned out to be forged. It goes without saying that Ronald Light would never again cross the threshold of Dean Close School.

It is no longer possible to ascertain the exact extent of the deception within those forged testimonials, but it is fairly safe to assume that Ronald Light claimed to be a past pupil of Rugby School, which probably accounts for others later believing this to be a fact. Light had in fact very good reason to lie about his schooling, his employment and his Army career. The forgeries were without doubt in Light's own hand.

There is little known of Ronald Light's early childhood, but a friend of his, Barbara Allen, writing to relatives in Leicester in the 1960s, said that she was his only playmate – but really didn't care for him much'.

Perhaps the very first sign that George and Catherine Light had that their only son was to become a constant source of disappointment and worry came in 1902, when they were living in London Road, Leicester.

In later years the Oakham School record book would for some unexplained reason list its past pupil as Capt. Ronald Light, a rank he was never to attain. In 1902, however, the young Ronald was in his third year at the school and apparently progressing well enough academically; but that his interest was not confined to his books is obvious, for that year brought his expulsion from the school 'for lifting a little girl's clothes over her head'. Perhaps this would be seen today as nothing more than a boyish prank, but Light's behaviour has to be understood in the context of the day and in the knowledge that the girl was obviously very young, while Light himself was by that time well over seventeen years of age. There is no way of knowing if Light had previously received warnings about similar conduct, but his expulsion would only have come after careful deliberation by the school authorities; for expulsion was in those days a real castigation, one which could have a lasting effect on future educational and professional prospects. There may be many men who have achieved fame, fortune and respectability in varying degrees after just such an early act of censure. Of all examples perhaps that of the infamous Titus Oates, another Oakham man, is not out of place here. The son of a Baptist minister, he was expelled not only from his school but also from university, though still became a vicar in the Church of England and later a convert to the Roman Catholic faith. Expelled from his post as a naval chaplain for misbehaviour and from various seminaries, Oates was an inveterate liar and schemer, and probably a murderer too. Tried for perjury he was sentenced to life imprisonment and, as would Ronald Light, whose ego probably matched that of Titus Oates, eventually died in virtual obscurity.

After his expulsion from Oakham School it must have been plain to Ronald that in George Light he was fortunate to have a father who even if he never forgave, and it is certain he never forgot, nevertheless continued to give financial support to his wayward son to the extent that he was able, within the year, to take up a place at the City and Guilds College, London, and to afford lodgings there throughout his university years, and well into his years as an engineering apprentice with the Midland Railway in Derby.

Quite what effect his expulsion from Oakham had on Light can only be imagined, but it may well have served to blow up out of all proportion an incident which might in other circumstances have been cast from the boy's mind. The sexual connotation of the incident may in so young a mind have become inextricably associated with things unobtainable, forbidden and, consequently, perhaps particularly desirable. The incident may have become linked in Light's mind with conversations that he overheard at home, where it is apparent that he, and indeed his mother, lived under some pressure in order to maintain the respectability that Catherine Light understandably valued so highly.

In her own childhood Catherine Light had known the difficulties and sadness that a marriage between partners from totally differing backgrounds can engender. John Clifton, Ronald's grandfather, was well on his way to building his very successful legal career when he met and married Catherine Mullins, a servant girl in the employ of a victualler in Woolwich, where she had been born in 1834. She was just two years younger than John. The couple settled in the West Country and, as was common for those times, Catherine gave birth to her six children almost at yearly intervals. Ronald's mother, the second daughter and fourth child was aged fourteen when her mother died suddenly of what was described as 'sanguinous apoplexy' resulting in a fatal stroke.

At the time of her death Catherine was just thirty-nine years old, and had for several years been separated from her husband. Despite the fact that she was interred in the family vault at Bristol, her husband at the time of her death seems not to have known where she had been living. For some time after the couple split up, Catherine and probably her two eldest children had lived at the Bank Tavern in Bridge Street, Bristol; indeed her husband believed her to be residing there at the time of her death early in December 1874. Accordingly that address was entered on the cemetery burial board. The error was not corrected until 4 January 1875, when the deceased's last abode was altered to No. 57 Abbey Road, Torquay, Devon, upon information supplied by one Henry A. Cross.

Divorce in those days would have been out of the question for a man wishing to preserve a reputation, and it would seem that for whatever initial reason (perhaps their differing backgrounds, though there may have been another) the couple merely lived apart. Once the separation had taken place, the couple apparently had no contact and it seems that John Clifton saw nothing of his two eldest children, who may both have taken their mother's part. The effects of broken marriage on the children, including Ronald's mother, in those days of double standards and fragile respectability may well be imagined. Not only were they deprived of one parent, but they were also separated from two of their siblings. The need to present a respectable and acceptable face to the world was of great importance in the 1870s, and the sins of parents were often unjustly visited upon their children. It seems, though, that eventually the two eldest children were reunited with their father.

John was not alone and seems to have been well cared for during his final years for, by his will, he bequeathed not only his share in several horses and an amount of money, but also the proceeds of a substantial insurance policy on his life to Sarah Ann Crook, a widow of his own age whom he described as his 'housekeeper' but who had first stayed in his house as a visitor. The proceeds of a second equally substantial policy were by the terms of John's will paid to Sarah's son, Arthur Henry Crook, who bore the same names as the first-born son of John and Catherine. It is perhaps apposite here to mention that in later years it was written that *both* John Henry's sons were trained in the law; yet only Robert Clifton, his second son by his wife actually survived to an age at which he could read law. Both Arthur and Frederick Clifton perished at the tender age of seven. We might therefore reasonably deduce that John Henry's bequest to Sarah's son, the other Arthur, was well spent.

It would seem from the emergence of the Bank Tavern address that Catherine may for her last years, have returned to a way of life that she remembered from her days in Woolwich. It is not certain but seems possible that it was through her mother's connections with the victualling trade that the young Catherine Louisa met her own future husband, George Light, or Harry Light as he preferred to be known.

Early in 1881 George Light was staying as a guest of John Clifton at Upland House, Keynsham, and was there on the night that the 1881 census was taken, giving his age as twenty-six, and his birthplace as Denbigh, Flintshire. At the time of his marriage to Catherine, George was living in the parish of St Mary's, Leicester, which was conveniently near to his place of employment as manager of Ellistown Colliery and Sanitary Pipeworks at Ibstock, but well outside the diocese of Bath and Wells. Despite the fact that George apparently visited the West Country well within the statutory application period of three months before the marriage took place, it was not he but Catherine, who personally obtained the necessary marriage licence. At the time of his marriage George Light stated his father to be one Edward Brooke Jones, gentleman.

Extensive research has failed to trace any child by the name of George Henry (or indeed Harry) Light born either in 1856 (the birth date given on his memorial headstone), or indeed in previous or successive years in the area around Denbigh. Neither can any son born to Edward Brooke Jones be traced to that area in the relevant years. Records do reveal, however, that a child named George Henry Light was born in September 1856 in Millbrooke, Southampton. That child, the eldest of five children, was the son of Elizabeth (née Blake) and George Light, a brewer's labourer. Little is known of George Light and his wife Elizabeth, and the name of Edward Brooke Jones appears nowhere. There is, however, one puzzling reference to the child George Henry born to Elizabeth and George Light in 1856. The 1861 census for the parish of Millbrooke lists the couple as still residing in the same Redbridge cottage, and gives the age for their eldest child as twelve years, when in fact he could have been no more than six years of age at the time.

The details of the early life of Ronald's father must remain a matter for speculation. Quite how much Catherine knew of George's family or of his own early years, or indeed he of hers, we cannot know, but if either chose to have their secrets that may have added a burden to the marriage and their only son might have sensed from a very early age that neither of his parents came from the straightforward and respectable middle-class backgrounds that they had their friends in Leicester believe. Ronald Light seems to have been incapable of the diligence and industry so obvious in his father and here it may be possible to detect something of his maternal grandfather, the debonair John Henry Clifton, who is reported to have been a man who liked to enjoy life while leaving the real work to others. As will become clear, Light was capable of great deception, of inventing a false scenario to suit his own purposes and of sustaining deception for however long was necessary. From whom he inherited that talent, if it may so be termed, cannot be stated for certain, but that such trends in behaviour are frequently inherited or at least nurtured in our formative years is only too plain. It is possible that Ronald Light's mould was cast long before he set out for Oakham, where another facet of his character first surfaced.

Ronald Light seems to have progressed well enough during his years at university but if either parent was hopeful that the upset of 1902, which may have precipitated the family move to another house in the London Road, Leicester, was to be an isolated occasion, they would be disappointed. By that time Ronald Light may already have begun to develop an outlook on life which as we shall see, coupled with an abnormal preoccupation with sex, would have serious consequences.

By 1914 Ronald Light had spent four years in full employment with the Midland Railway at their Divisional Engineering Offices at Derby, as an engineering assistant. In April 1912 he had been elected as an associate member of the Institution of Civil Engineers, and from around 1910 he had regularly dated Ethel Tunnicliffe, who was employed as a tracer in the same office. Taking advantage of the eagerness of others to get into uniform to fight in a war which was expected to be over before Christmas, Light left his lodgings with the Morris family in Hartington Street, Derby, in 1914, claiming that he had given up his job and was going to enlist immediately. What Light did not say was that he had been dismissed by the Midland Railway when he had lied to his superiors concerning an incident involving a fire in a cupboard. Reading between the lines of the report it would seem that it was Light himself who was suspected of setting fire to the cupboard. A further reason given for his dismissal was that he was guilty of 'making rude figures on the lavatory walls', which would seem to be an infantile pastime for a man aged almost thirty.

Light once more returned to his home in Leicester in disgrace, and about this time, George Light suffered a breakdown in health. The family again moved house, this time to a larger and grander residence, Park View in Granville Road.

Although he presumably lacked a good character reference from his last employers but probably because his engineering qualifications were admirably suited to the work, Light managed to secure a temporary commission with the Royal Engineers' in February 1915. He took this up almost immediately. On 14 March he was posted to the Royal Engineers' School of Mechanical Engineering at Buxton. Light was not at the school primarily to receive any training in the use of firearms, but there is evidence that while there he had a revolver and did receive some training in its use. He apparently thought himself proficient enough to include Ethel Tunnicliffe, who seems to have visited the camp frequently, in practice sessions. The number and types of revolvers acquired by Light at Buxton and his next camp will be discussed in the following chapter.

On 27 September 1915 Light was transferred to the Royal Engineers' camp at Newark, where he would remain until he sailed for his first bout of overseas service on 13 November 1915. Second Lieutenant Ronald Light was given command of a section of the 152nd Field Company, Royal Engineers and supplied with a batman/driver named Ambrose. In 1920 the police at Leicester very much wanted to talk to Driver Ambrose, but they failed to find him. All that could be ascertained was that he hailed from Birmingham. The police had to make do with a statement from one Horace Aldridge who was residing at No. 21 Spar Road, Bermondsey and working as a news vendor. Aldridge told the police that he had served three and a half years in France attached to 152 Field Company, R.E. and remembered Lieutenant Light very well. He was, said Aldridge, 'my section commander all the time he was in that company . . . I used to see him daily . . . it was only a very short time, about three months.' As might be expected the police from Leicester were chiefly interested in any revolvers which Light might have had with him in France. Aldridge was able to tell them: 'I never saw him actually use or draw his revolver from the case but I am certain he carried a revolver as I could see the butt of it . . . all the officers carried revolvers.'

Ronald Light wearing the uniform of a Second Lieutenant in the Royal Engineers. This photograph was given to a London journalist on the evening of Light's acquittal, thus perpetuating the myth of Light as an officer and gentleman

A bald statement of fact entered by 152 Field Company's Commanding Officer Major Rundall in the company war diary leaves no doubt that Ronald Light was abruptly sent back to England; it reads simply: '24 January 1916. T/Lieut. R. Light R.E. transferred to England.' That the company commander was hardly expecting to lose one of his three section commanders is apparent from the fact that Light's replacement, Lieutenant G.W. Rudyerd, did not arrive from the company's base camp until two days later.

Exactly what Light did to deserve the Army's disapproval at this time is unclear. There is, however, a persistent and abiding rumour, of which this author has frequently been reminded, that while in France he assaulted a French post-mistress. Certainly as an officer and especially an officer in the Royal Engineers he would have had more opportunity than most to make the acquaintance of the local inhabitants; in all probability he was, as most officers were at that time, billeted in adapted village buildings. If there is any truth in this rumour then it would seem likely that the incident occurred in the vicinity of Pommier, in or around the village of Bienvillers, where Light's section seems to have been engaged in construction work along a salient, throughout the brief time that Light was their commander. It may be of significance that despite the urgency to complete the British trench system in the shortest possible time, that 3 Section, 152 Field Company, apparently found themselves on the day before Light's return to England with a day off. They were not allowed to leave camp, and spent the day in cleaning their billet. There exists the possibility, therefore, that, the section found itself temporarily without a commander, because Light had been removed so abruptly from his post.

The fact that it was not until 14 July 1916, four months later, that Light was ordered to give up his commission, would seem to indicate that any incident occurring while he was in France may not have brought about his final cashiering on 2 August. The theft of a gun at Buxton camp during Light's time may have had some bearing on the case.

There are two further incidents, both of which came to light at the time of the green bicycle investigation, which tell us something of Light's movements and conduct during the summer of 1916. The first incident relates to a local Leicester woman, whose name does not appear in Holmes's correspondence with Sims. She and Light first met in the summer of 1916 in the grounds of Victoria Park, Leicester. At that time she was thirty-four years of age and in business in Leicester. She was attracted to the 'Army officer' who told her that his name was Davis. Eventually the officer, who in later years would tell her his real name, booked a room at Thurnby and the woman stayed with him for four nights, cycling the short distance from Leicester each night. Light rode over from Leicester each evening on a motor cycle. All went well until the fourth night when, as Edward Holmes put it in the discreet parlance of the day, 'the lady had her courses'. When told of this her partner's mood changed, and he became 'very cross when the lady refused to let him have connection with her, she had to get up, dress and remain seated on a chair until morning'.

On the following morning the woman sent a telegram to 'Davis' telling him that her mother was ill, and that consequently she would not be able to go over to Thurnby again. Although he had given a false name, Light may have supplied the woman with a correct address, for that telegram was found four years later among his papers at Highfield Street. Obviously disturbed and intimidated by Light's behaviour the woman resolved to end the relationship, which apparently she was temporarily successful in doing. The two would, however, meet again and it would seem that, against her better judgement, the woman once again formed a relationship with the officer who, she would admit in a statement to the police in 1920, 'had fascinated her'.

The significance of this incident, pre-dating as it does Light's second service overseas when he claimed to have suffered shell shock, may give some insight into Light's attitude towards women – an attitude and a capability which were a part of the man himself, a part which by 1920 would result in both the representative of the D.P.P. involved in the green bicycle case and the police at Leicester being of the opinion that Light was 'of a depraved moral character'.

If the story concerning the assault on a post-mistress in France should prove to be true, then it would tend to confirm the apprehension which may have been felt by that Leicester woman in 1916. It is evident that it was during these months that Ethel Tunnicliffe's affections towards Light seem to have cooled, as their correspondence ceased. Why that should have happened is not precisely known, but bearing in mind that his fall from grace in 1914 had not ended their relationship it is possible that something she had learned of Light's conduct of a more serious nature, possibly coupled with his attitude towards herself, marked the end of their relationship. Perhaps it is significant that, for several years at least, Tunnicliffe maintained her friendship with Catherine Light, with whom she may have felt a certain empathy and some sympathy.

It is clear, therefore, that Light stayed for at least some part of the summer of 1916 in Leicester, but he spent, apparently unknown to his parents, August and part of September working as a farm labourer in the West Country. He had told his parents that he was in the process of leaving the Royal Engineers and joining another regiment. Although he was officially gazetted on 2 August, his name appeared on the Army list for that month; and it would not be until the issue of the September list that Light's name would no longer feature. Light's work on that West Country farm came to an abrupt end when he was strongly suspected by his employer of firing hayricks, a matter brought to the attention of Sims by the police in Leicester.

On 18 September Ronald Light again enlisted, this time as a gunner in the 309th Siege

Battery, Honourable Artillery Company. It would seem that he had returned to London from the west of England and had still not spoken to his parents, for on Tuesday 19 September, George Light, extremely worried by this time, travelled down to London in the hope of seeing his son, but was unable to locate him. By Wednesday evening he was back at home, where he was attended by his physician at 6 p.m.

At 6.45 a.m. the following morning George Light left the bed he shared with his wife in a first-floor front room. Having heard a noise which she later described as being similar to that made by a piece of furniture being knocked over, Catherine went in search of her husband. He was no longer on the first floor of the house, and her maids assured her that he had not gone downstairs. She then went to a spare bedroom on the second floor of the house, where she saw that the window was open. By this time Mary Webb had reached the front door, to find George Light in a stooping position, leaning against the door. Mary asked her master what had happened, to which he replied: 'I don't know, Mary.' When Catherine arrived on the scene her husband was lying in the vestibule, and she asked him: 'What were you doing; can you remember?' to which he replied: 'I went to look out of the window.' The doctor was called, but there was little he could do. George died of shock and internal injuries at about 9 a.m., having sustained a broken pelvis and three broken ribs, all on the right side of the body, seeming to indicate that during the fall of over 20 ft his body struck the portico over the open vestibule.

Naturally an inquest into the death was held. The coroner was one Edward G.B. Fowler who, four years later, would act as magistrate's clerk at the police court hearings into the charge facing George's son. George was, in the words of Edward Fowler, 'a respected friend'.

The doctor, Kirkland Chapel, gave evidence that he had treated George Light for some time for dyspepsia, gastritis and occasional insomnia, and that of late he had been 'worried and despondent'; but at their last consultation on the evening before his death he had seemed 'quite bright and cheerful'. He did not think the deceased had any suicidal tendencies.

Mary Webb told the coroner that George Light had been very worried, but otherwise she had noticed nothing unusual about him. She had come to the conclusion that her master had felt faint, had gone to the window for fresh air and had then fallen out. The coroner was at pains to point out that in her signed statement Mary Webb had said she had known George Light to faint before.

Catherine Light was not well enough to attend the inquest, held at the Town Hall, Leicester. Her statement taken at home, makes mention of the spare bedroom window from which George fell to his death. It was situated on the second floor, overlooking the New Walk. One of the side panes had a sash which enabled the window to be opened by raising the lower half. The window sill was about 2 ft above the floor of the room. She knew of no insanity in her husband's family but for 'the past few weeks he has been worried a good deal about our son'. Catherine went on to tell of her husband's fruitless trip to London and said that upon his return he 'seemed very worried', but she said: 'I do not think he would attempt to take his own life.'

It was, said the coroner, particularly painful for him to have to hold the inquest upon a respected friend. The jury recorded a verdict that death resulted from shock and internal injuries caused by falling from a window, adding a rider that they had found insufficient evidence to show how the fall occurred.

George Light was obviously depressed and extremely worried by his son's conduct. Perhaps the news of Ronald's cashiering may have been sufficiently distressing in itself, but it may be that it was the actual cause of that gazetting coupled with other reports of their son that had reached the Lights which may finally have been more than George could bear, coming as it did after Ronald's expulsion from school and dismissal from his appointment with the Midland Railway only two years before. Leaving aside his state of mind there is one more point which

Parkview, Granville Road, the last home of George Light, who fell to his death from a second-floor window in 1916.

must be considered, one which was important enough to result in the coroner referring to it in a note on the inquest papers. Had George simply wanted fresh air then he might have obtained it at one of the windows either in the couple's own bedroom or in any one of several adjoining rooms on the first floor; or he might have gone downstairs and into the back yard. It seems of relevance that he chose instead to climb up to the top floor of the house. In the absence of evidence to the contrary, the assumption has to be that George, faced by the shame or disappointment at his son's conduct, could face life no longer and chose to end it.

Ronald Light attended his father's funeral, held on 25 September at St Peter's church, Leicester. The grave, at Welford Road Cemetery, remained unmarked until after Catherine's death, when on her instructions a white cross was erected there. However, the cross was not fashioned from white marble as she had requested, but from an inferior white stone.

One might have thought that the death of his father in such tragic circumstances, being in all likelihood a result to some degree of his own behaviour, might have had a sobering effect on Ronald Light – might even have convinced him that he must turn over a new leaf, and behave less selfishly. One might even expect that Light could have given some thought to his invalid mother, now a widow and dependent for her peace of mind on her son's good conduct. Within eight months of George's death, any glimmer of hope left in Catherine's heart was to be destroyed completely; her only consolation must have been that her husband had not lived to know that day.

Following training, the main force of the newly formed 309 Siege Battery, Honourable Artillery Company joined the 88th Heavy Artillery group and sailed for France, arriving in Le Havre on 26 April 1917. Meanwhile the battery's reserve draft to which Ronald Light was attached remained in London.

It is understandable that by 1917 no man would have relished the prospect of service on the Western Front, but having donned a uniform there must be few who, without inflicting self-injury or absenting themselves, actively attempted to prevent that service taking place. On 3 May 1917 orders were received to the effect that the draft, which included Light, was to be moved up in readiness to sail for France. On the following day a telegram reached the reserve draft's commanding officer, appearing to have been sent from the War Office: 'Cancel departure of siege battery reserve till further orders.' As a consequence the reserve force H.A.C., including Light, did not move up and was held in London. At a later date Light's draft again came under orders to prepare for transit to France and again a telegram was received, this time purporting to have been sent by Lord Denbigh, officer commanding the Honourable Artillery Company. The telegram gave the order: 'Arrangements again cancelled. Keep siege battery in London.'

The telegrams were bogus, and the mandarins at the War Office decided to investigate. It was arranged for forty-three men, including Light, to take an examination paper in which certain words would have to be written, to allow the Army to examine the handwriting of all the men who could possibly have benefited from the draft remaining in London on reserve. A handwriting expert was called in and came to the conclusion that the telegrams were both in the hand of Gunner 625440, Ronald Light.

On Friday 27 July 1917, at Westminster Guildhall, Ronald Light faced a district court martial presided over by Lt. Gen. Sir Alfred Codrington who at that time commanded the Coldstream Guards. Gunner Light was charged with forging telegraphic orders and with improperly wearing military decorations, to which he pleaded not guilty. He was further charged with the improper possession of passes to which he pleaded guilty. He was said by the prosecuting officer, Capt. Watson, to have worn the Queen's and King's South African medals and the Tibet Campaign medal, to which he was not entitled. It is of interest to note here that at the time of his arrest in 1920, Light was in possession of several medals including the Military Medal, the Croix de Guerre, the Mons Medal, the Meritorious Service Medal and, perhaps most inappropriately, the Distinguished Conduct Medal, none of which was he entitled to wear.

Light, financially supported by his mother, was defended by one of the most notable and distinguished advocates of the day, Ernest Wild K.C., who received a knighthood in the birthday honours of the following year. Wild's answer to the charge against Light was that it was no offence to send a bogus telegram. It was not sufficient that there should be an attempt to deceive in order to constitute a forgery, which was defined as the making of a false document with intent to defraud. Therefore, suggested Wild, there could be no forgery without intent to defraud. Intent to deceive was not enough. Wild further proposed that as the telegrams were not public documents they were not covered by the Forgery Acts. To this defence, Capt. Watson replied that he proceeded under the Post Office Protection Act which had never been repealed. On the charge of improper possession of passes, which Light had admitted, he was formally found guilty. The decision on the two more serious charges was promulgated in due course.

Ernest Wild, no doubt sensing the mood of the court, spoke in mitigation of punishment. The accused was, he said, an only child of most respectable parents. He had been educated at the Imperial Engineering College in South Kensington and had gone on to London University, taking a BSc degree before the age of twenty-one, Wild stressed the responsibilities of Light's former position with the Midland Railway Company; he made no mention of the fact that Light had been dismissed from that position. Light had volunteered 'when war broke out' and had obtained a temporary commission with the Royal Engineers, serving in England and France.

With understandable brevity Wild referred to Light's gazetting of the previous year by saying that Light's commanding officer had 'requested his resignation on the grounds of lack of initiative'. From that moment, claimed Wild, Light had thought himself and his family disgraced and had become an entirely different man. The affair had, he said 'so told on Light's father's health that he was found dead outside his door'. Light's mother's health had also 'been badly affected'.

Wild's pleas may or may not have impressed the court. In the event Light was sentenced to one year's detention, and ought to have thought himself fortunate; for the district court-martial was empowered to impose up to two years' imprisonment.

While detained in military prison, Light learned that on 16 October the Council of the Institution of Civil Engineers had met in London to discuss his conduct. The council was undoubtedly already aware of Light's dismissal from the Midland Railway Company. They had apparently been tolerant of that and prepared to give Light a chance to redeem himself. The decision of the court martial was another matter. The minutes of the council bear witness to that and are quoted here in full.

> The Council were summoned specially to consider a statement by the Officer-in-Charge of the Military Records, dated 1 September 1917, relative to the conviction by General (*sic*) Court-Martial of Gunner R. Light, Honourable Artillery Company on certain charges; and had before them a statutory declaration made by Mr Frederick John Greasley, Assoc.M[ember] Inst. C.E. identifying 'Gunner R. Light' with Ronald Vivian Light B.Sc (Engineering) (London), Assoc. M. Inst. C.E.
>
> The Council being of the opinion that the offences referred to rendered Ronald Vivian Light unfit to be a member of the Institution, unanimously resolved that he be expelled and that his name be erased from the Register. [Fifteen members present.] The Secretary was instructed to give him notice of this action, in accordance with form G. of the By-Laws and to record the erasure for report by the Council at the next Annual general meeting.

Light's response to that notification is not recorded, but it is perhaps of significance that when police searched his rooms in 1920 they found no reference to the Council's decision, just as they apparently found nothing relating to his cashiering from the Royal Engineers, though documents concerning his original commission had been preserved.

Although sentenced to a full year in detention it would seem, however, that Light was held in detention for something under four months from the time of his court martial, for by mid-November he was on his way to France to join 309 Siege Battery, Honourable Artillery Company.

Whatever his purpose in attempting to avoid overseas service, Light must have been somewhat disappointed to find himself so soon on French soil. Doubtless he would have preferred to serve the full term of his sentence. It would seem likely that the sentence was only reduced because the relatively hard option of service at the front existed. It could be that Light's attempt to avoid the fighting in France was simply a measure of his fright, indeed of his cowardice. Alternatively there may have been a different reason behind the sending of those telegrams. If Light had found himself in serious trouble with either the French civilian authorities or the French military authorities before his abrupt transfer back to this country in January 1916, he may have had qualms about returning to France.

Light's service with the Battery has been detailed in a previous chapter as has his claim to have been invalided out of France in August 1918 'wearing pyjamas'. Nothing to substantiate those claims has been discovered, but from 24 August to 22 October 1918, with a short break at a convalescent camp, Light was certainly a patient at Wharncliffe War Hospital, Sheffield. For a picture of his health at that time we are dependent upon a letter from Dr Robert Gordon, Medical Officer at Wharncliffe, in reply to enquiries by Chief Constable Holmes in 1920:

> Gunner R. Light 625440 was admitted to Wharncliffe War Hospital on 24 August 1918 with deafness. He had been in a heavy howitzer battery for 10 months.
>
> Progressive deafness for three months, associated with ringing noises in both ears.
>
> He was not deaf before joining the Army. He was in the Royal Engineers and was then transferred to the Siege Battery and the deafness appears to have come on in the last three months.
>
> [Apparently here Dr Gordon means the last three months of Light's service in France with the H.A.C.]
>
> The deafness was probably due to heavy shell fire. There is no definite disease of the ears. Treatment prescribed, rest.

Shell-shock, always a rather vague expression, has over the years become an emotive term. It conjures up a picture of a man whose nervous system has been partially or totally destroyed by his experience of warfare, and who, in the severest stages of the disorder, is unable to carry out the simplest tasks, and suffers from bouts of severe giddiness, depression and sleeplessness, gradually becoming more withdrawn and isolated. Contrary to popular belief neurasthenia in several forms, as a result of trench warfare, was recognized as early as 1916. Army authorities have recognized for many years that men with a poor sense of motivation are far more likely to be affected by psychological damage than their more highly motivated comrades; thus it is that conscripts are more susceptible than regular soldiers. Since Light took positive action to avoid being sent to the Western Front it may be assumed that his sense of motivation was extremely low.

Difficult as it is to draw conclusions in such a matter, there were, by 1918, specialist hospitals established which dealt with the more severe cases of shell-shock. Wharncliffe was not one of them. It would appear from his report that Dr Gordon was more than satisfied he had correctly diagnosed Light's illness. Had he been in any doubt he could have entered the quite usual comment 'NYD(N)' which meant 'Not yet diagnosed (Nervous)'. That he neither entered a diagnosis of neurasthenia in any form or registered his own uncertainty would seem to point to the fact that in Light's case the only symptom which he displayed was deafness as a result of the noise of the guns fired by his own battery and the explosions from incoming German shells, rather than distress resulting from the scenes which he witnessed. The deafness was treated, and its severity or otherwise must be set against the brevity of Light's time with the battery and the relatively quiet time his battery experienced during Light's posting in France. Also significant is Light's ability to speak quietly by the time of his trial, which would seem to indicate that his recovery was quite successful.

An incident which occurred in 1918 while Light was at Wharncliffe Hospital perhaps indicates that his expulsion from public school may not have been the result of a childish prank, but an ominous warning of things to come. In the summer of 1918 an ambulance driver (who remains nameless in the police report given to Sims, based at Wharncliffe and living in the vicinity, invited Light back to his home for tea, but Light was to abuse this act of hospitality. While he was there Light made sexual advances to the man's fifteen-year-old daughter. No charges were brought but the hospital authorities were informed, and the man forbade Light to have anything to do with the girl in the future. We may consider that girls of fifteen these days are often well able to take care of themselves. Perhaps some girls in 1918 were no less worldly, but the fact that the ambulance driver felt constrained to report the incident indicates that the incident was seen as serious, and was against the girl's wishes. That it was brought to the notice of the hospital authorities must be a measure of the ambulance driver's conviction that Light had indeed seriously molested his young daughter.

After leaving Wharncliffe, and spending his final weeks in uniform at the Army's depot at Ripon, Light was finally demobilized in February 1919 and, despite her son's repeated falls from grace, Catherine seems once again to have taken him back into her home, this time in Highfield Street, the smaller house to which she had moved in May of the previous year – when she learned of her son's impending court martial and the expense which it would entail. Here Light resided until he took up his appointment at Dean Close School in Cheltenham, ten days after the date of the official end to the First World War. Light appears to have picked up the threads of civilian life with little difficulty. He found no full-time employment, but that was not unusual at a time when thousands were returning to the cities from the Western Front. He had the added difficulty in that he possessed no genuine character reference from his last civilian employer and his record in the Army had been abysmal. Light seems to have spent most days out of the house. As she would state in court in 1920, Mary Webb believed him to be helping a friend build up an insurance business, which occupied him throughout the spring and summer months of 1919. It would seem that it was this same friend who allowed Light to borrow a motor cycle from time to time. Since Light never owned one of his own it is possible that the same friend was in the habit of lending him a motor cycle before 1919. As early as the summer of 1916, when Light is known to have met the woman at Thurnby, he had the use of a motor cycle on each of the four nights.

Towards the end of June 1919 the same woman met the man she had known as Davis, recognizing him immediately despite his unkempt appearance, when he approached her in Hinckley Road, Leicester. The man, who was riding a bicycle, told the woman that he had been demobilized, and said that his real name was Ronald Light.

Considering the woman's previous experience of Light, it has to be assumed that he could be most persuasive in his dealings with women, for that same night they again met in Western Park, where they stayed for about an hour. The woman was at some pains to point out in her statement to the police that nothing improper took place. She then received a letter from Light making an appointment to see her, but it was an appointment she did not keep, having no desire to rekindle the relationship. But that the relationship did begin again was borne out in March 1920. When the Leicester police searched Light's room following his arrest they found the telegram which the woman had sent to him four years earlier, and traced the woman to the home of her married sister in Salford. By the time the police found her she was heavily pregnant and extremely concerned to keep the fact of her pregnancy from the rest of her family in Salford and Leicester. The woman, by then thirty-eight years old, told the police she expected to be confined within the week, and that Ronald Light was father to the child she carried. Whether or not these claims were true must be a matter for speculation, as must the possibility that Light himself knew of those claims. It must, however, be asked what possible gain there could have been for the woman in falsely claiming to carry the child of a man already in police custody on a charge of murder, especially since according to Chief Constable Holmes she was at some pains to prevent her family learning of her condition. If in fact the woman did carry Ronald Light's child when the police spoke to her in Salford in early March 1920, then in all probability she was already pregnant at the time that Ronald Light admitted to riding into Gaulby with Bella Wright.

There seems to exist little evidence that Light had friendships with other men. The friendship with the ex-officer whom he claimed to be helping with his insurance business seems to have come to an end; yet Light spent most of his days and apparently many evenings away from the Highfield house. When the police searched the room he used at his mother's home and his room at Dean Close School they found scant evidence of any conventional hobbies or interests other than a stamp album and collection of bird's eggs which had in all likelihood been preserved since Light's schooldays. What the police at Leicester did find, and what was considered to be evidence that Light was of a depraved moral character, was a quantity of 'indecent literature' which included several advertisements for 'protectives', ten indecent prints and a parcel of ladies' underwear addressed to an unmarried woman at an address in Bonsall Street, Leicester. The literature, the photographs and the parcel might be overlooked but for the apparently growing catalogue of Light's activities with the opposite sex. By the time of Light's arrest in March 1920 he was already well known to the police at Leicester, and when he was committed for trial at the Summer Assize it was known to the police in Leicester that their colleagues of the Essex force held a file on Ronald Light, which indicated he was connected with a case of illegal abortion in Southend.

It is clear that from the evening of Bella Wright's death, Light never again rode the green bicycle. He always claimed that it was the wording of the newspaper articles, and one particular article of 8 July, which convinced him that as the man who had walked out of Gaulby village in full sight of Bella's family he was also the man whom the police sought in connection with her death. He admitted disposing of the green bicycle because it connected him with the girl; and he thought that his story would be believed. Yet it becomes apparent that less than three months after Ronald Light read that article, he felt safe enough to venture out of the house and commit at least one serious sexual offence close to his own home.

Ronald Light with Catherine Light's terrier, a photograph which appeared shortly after Light's acquittal

Before his eventual arrest for Bella's murder, Light spent some time in the custody of Leicester police, concerning a separate enquiry. On the evening of 28 October 1919, just over three months after Bella's murder and at a time when the description of the man with the green bicycle was still fresh in the minds of everyone, Ronald Light was taken by one Constable Beaver to Clarendon Road police station in Leicester, where he faced allegations of improper conduct with a young girl. She was only eight-and-a-half years old, and the daughter of a traveller who resided in nearby Howard Road, Leicester. This respectable residence was adjacent to Victoria Park and only a very short walk from Light's own home in the Highfields district.

At first Light denied the allegations, but after further questioning he admitted to an offence against the child and apologized. Doubtless to protect their child from any further unpleasantness her parents decided that they would not press charges, and consequently Light was allowed to leave. For the second time in a little over a year Light would not face the consequences of his sexual penchant for young girls.

The offence against this girl was seen by the police at Leicester to have a possible connection with a series of complaints they had received which centred on the Spinney Hill district of Leicester, all pertaining to indecent exposure. From the night of 28 October, 1919 and over the following fortnight, the police kept Light under surveillance, but he was not observed to repeat his earlier offence, either in Spinney Hill or elsewhere.

In the knowledge of this event it is evident that the depositions of fourteen-year-old Muriel Nunney and twelve-year-old Valeria Cavan must be taken seriously as a true representation of a pattern of behaviour which by the time of Light's trial, although entirely inadmissible as evidence, was well known to the police in Leicester.

The hidden significance behind a question put by Henry Maddocks in court may be appreciated: 'May we understand that the statements made by these two little girls are untrue, whether the incident to which they refer happened on that or any other day?' Light would have seen the implications of this, but replied with his usual sang-froid:

'I never saw these girls or spoke to them on any occasion.'

As he stood in the dock charged with the wilful murder of Bella Wright Ronald Light was already known by several in that courtroom to be a liar, a forger, a poseur and a child molester; he was suspected of much more. It may be that his unkempt appearance of late summer and autumn in 1919 was a calculated pose, a disguise. How could anyone have associated such a dishevelled character with the upright, law-abiding ex-officer of almost exemplary character, the war hero who had suffered shell-shock in the defence of his country, the man who stood in that dock and convinced the jury of his innocence?

CHAPTER 18

Corpus Delicti

Even given that it took place in 1919, there can be little doubt that the death of Bella Wright, having first been considered to be a case of nothing more than accidental death, was investigated rather less thoroughly than it should have been. Dr Williams, by his own admission a man who knew little of gunshot wounds, probably did his best, but the full consequences of that misunderstanding may now never be realized.

When discovered, the body was moved from the roadway, as was the dead girl's bicycle. No attempt to note the position in which Cowell found either body or bicycle was made until after 10 a.m. the following morning, when Hall called Cowell back to the scene. It is possible also that Cowell inadvertently tidied the clothing as he laid the body on the grass verge. He supposed that the girl had fallen from her bicycle, so may have accepted that a certain amount of disarrangement in her clothing was to be expected. It is also possible that, left to guard the body while Cowell went to fetch help, the two men Naylor and Deacon may also have moved the body. There is no record that they were questioned about their actions on that night, but it is reasonable to suppose that either or both may have helped to place the body on the milk-float. It may be, therefore, that up to four men had handled the body even before the arrival of Dr Williams, who made only a cursory examination of it at the scene and later at the 'chapel'. The four men all had one advantage over Dr Williams, as they saw the body before the light faded.

In reassessing a case like this, where the prosecution offered no evidence of a relationship between the girl and the man who was charged with her murder, and where the defence would ask why a man should kill a woman who was virtually a stranger to him, any evidence to show that the girl was involved in sexual activity shortly before her death becomes of paramount importance. However, Williams's investigations seem to have been limited to whether the girl had been sexually assaulted, or was suffering from a sexually transmitted disease.

Constable Hall himself noted in his report that no check for signs of sexual interference was made at the first two examinations, and although Dr Williams was called back by Hall on the evening of 6 July it appears probable that his interest was confined to the newly discovered gunshot wound. Therefore it would have been about forty hours after the discovery of the body before any examination of whether sexual intercourse, by force or consent, took place shortly before death.

Dr Williams was able to state that he believed no struggle had taken place between the girl and her assailant, because her skin was of such a fair complexion that she would have bruised easily, and no such bruising was found. The fact that Bella also wore a bow fastened with a flimsy pin which was still in place gave further support to his findings.

In his autopsy report Dr Williams stated that there was a 'vaginal discharge' that was 'not sufficient to indicate syphilis'. He could not say whether gonorrhoea was present, and indeed was unable to decide what the nature of the discharge was. He therefore stated it 'could have been of natural causes'. What he meant by this he failed to stipulate, presumably because his investigations did not extend beyond the possibility of sexual assault.

It is worth noting that by the 1920s there was a test, albeit not always reliable, which, by the use of a filtered ultra-violet lamp, showed the presence of seminal fluid on clothing. Obviously this apparatus would not have been available to Dr Williams, even if he had the specialist knowledge that the test required, which is unlikely. There was, however, an alternative method

175

that could have been utilized. It was reported as follows in 1843: 'Some of the stains on the linen . . . were considered to be stains caused by spermatic secretion. Digested in water, they yielded a turbid solution of a powerful odour, and when submitted to a powerful microscope, spermatozoa were detected.'

We cannot know what results would have been obtained if clothing worn by Bella at the time of her death had been promptly and more extensively examined. But it is clear that even in 1919 a forensic pathologist would have been able to present a far more accurate report to the coroner. If a report had included the finding that sexual intercourse had taken place only a short time before Bella's death, it is not impossible that more emphasis would have been placed on investigations concerning male friends and acquaintances of the dead girl. Indeed, had that been the case, no other course would have been open to the police. In the event, the police seem largely to have directed their efforts towards establishing the ownership of the green bicycle, the investigation only coming to life after Enoch Whitehouse made his vital discovery in February 1920. Before that discovery the case had seemed to have become hopeless, as is made evident in a letter received at Scotland Yard by F. Trevor Binham from an address in Leicester: 'I have read the papers in this case with considerable interest and am returning them to you as I have very little hope that the murderer will ever be caught.'

With the advantage of modern research and the knowledge that only limited police investigations were conducted concerning Bella Wright's friends and acquaintances, it may be profitable, even though some seventy-three years have elapsed, to return to basics and examine all aspects of the *corpus delicti*. Light's own statements and admissions should also be re-examined, and also those made by others concerning weapons he may have had in his possession on 5 July 1919, to evaluate the part they may have played.

It may also be useful in the light of today's superior understanding of ballistics and, in particular, the damage which can be expected from bullets of various calibres, to consider the gunshot wound sustained by Bella in relation to the bullet found at the scene. Before we move on to the details of the case, however, it is necessary to dispose once and for all of the black raven found by Hall and the stories that surround it. Hall stated at the inquest that the bird 'died by gorging itself with blood'. It was Det. Supt. Taylor, however, who took steps to discover how the bird had come to fall dead in a field adjacent to the lane where Bella's body was found. The bird was found some time after 10 a.m. on Sunday 6 July, and before the inquest on the afternoon of Tuesday 8 July. Taylor himself opened up the bird, and was quite satisfied that it had died by gorging itself with blood, as its crop was full of new blood. Finding no gunshot wound, it seemed clear that the bird had choked to death.

That surfeit of blood together with the bird tracks found by Hall at the scene of the murder are undoubtedly the basis for the rather macabre ideas detailed in a previous chapter, but it is impossible to establish satisfactorily where the fresh blood in the crop of the bird originated. Since it rained during the night of Saturday 5 July, it seems hardly likely that any blood left on the *Via Devana* after the removal of Bella's body would have been of a quantity or consistency to cause the death of a large bird in this manner – though it was still possible to detect traces of blood as late as 11 July, when many people who attended Bella's funeral took the opportunity to walk from Stoughton to Stretton to view the scene of the murder. It is clear from the dissection carried out by Taylor that the bird was not the victim of a sportsman's bullet, although this must be seen, at best, as an amateur assessment, and his conclusion was borne out by the police, who were satisfied that there were no sporting guns in use at around the time Bella met her death. Is it even remotely possible that she was shot by someone out rooking whom the police failed to trace? The answer is clear. The bullet that killed Bella Wright was fired from a distance of probably no more than 6 ft. The 'minute specks of an unspecified

metal' referred to by Dr Williams at the inquest and the trial, which he found embedded in the
skin around the entry wound, were certainly part of a particulate pattern – minute scrapings
from the cartridge case, cap and possibly the bullet, produced as the gun was fired. Such
particles do not precede the line of the bullet, but follow it, so are only noticeable on the surface
area, be it skin or clothing. They do not exist around a wound caused by the discharge of a
revolver at very close range, or where a shot was fired from more than about 6 ft away. At
anything over that distance the metal fragments have fallen away harmlessly. It is very unlikely,
therefore, that Bella died as a result (as was cleverly suggested by Light's counsel) of an
unfortunate ricochet, or a bullet which had already travelled a considerable distance and was
almost spent. Where the body was discovered the grass verge was 9 ft wide and the hedge was
over 4 ft thick, the distance from the edge of the road to the far side of the hedge being more
than 13 ft, greater than could be travelled by any metal fragments if a gun had been fired in the
field. It seems likely that Bella died exactly where she was found, as there was a pool of blood
beneath her head and no trail of blood leading to the spot. There can be no doubt that her
assailant knew of the result of that fatal shot, for the victim was only a few feet away as the
weapon was discharged.

There is one point that indicates the shot was not fired with the muzzle almost touching
Bella's skin, as scorching of the skin occurs in such circumstances, while the particulate pattern
is not present. Williams deposed that he found no such powder burns.

At the trial Marshall Hall succeeded in persuading Henry Clarke, the gunsmith, that the bullet
produced in court was equally suitable for firing from a rifle as from a revolver. Considering the
conflicting evidence given by Clarke, we would be justified in taking his testimony with a pinch
of salt. Far more eminent in the field of ballistics than Clarke was Robert Churchill, who was of
the opposite opinion. Marshall Hall apparently considered calling Churchill for the defence,
since it was clear from an early stage that he would not be called for the prosecution.
Accordingly Marshall Hall consulted Churchill before travelling to Leicester, and after
examining the bullet Churchill told him that the bullet was not suitable for firing from any rifle.
From the number of grooves and the direction in which they ran, the bullet could only have
been fired from a Webley revolver. It is hardly surprising that Marshall Hall decided not to call
him for the defence, as he would have made an excellent prosecution witness, and it is rather
puzzling that the prosecution decided to rely on the much less experienced Clarke.

Clarke's evidence was nothing if not confusing. He told the coroner that the bullet produced
by Hall was a 'No. 44 . . . a foreign bullet', but by the time of the trial he described it as a '.455
calibre bullet . . . originally a black powder bullet . . . adapted for Army service cartridges'.

There exists one other important description of that bullet, written by P.C. Hall himself soon
after he produced it, which consists of a simple note of its measurements and appearance.
Bearing in mind that Hall himself suggested the bullet had been trodden on and kicked by an
animal, his measurements may not be entirely accurate but are worthy of mention. He states that
it had three grooves at the base and to have measured $7/8$ in in length and $7/16$ in in diameter. In
comparing these dimensions with those of a .455 calibre round as issued by the Army for many
years before and during the First World War, it is clear that the length lies within the tolerances
for the .455 but that the diameter is somewhat smaller than the normal tolerances given for a
.455 round. The dimensions given by Hall would seem to more nearly reflect the calibre of a
number of revolvers of foreign manufacture which were common at the time. For instance, the
1883 model German 11 mm service revolver, though obsolete by 1914, is known to have still
been in use in large numbers in the First World War and was described as being .43 in to .44 in.
(Hall's measurement equates to a diameter of .437 in.) Perhaps Clarke's first description of the
bullet was after all his most accurate assessment.

While rifle bullets have pointed tips and are required to travel long range with streamlined flight, a revolver bullet (and especially any bullet supplied to the Army for use in the Webley service revolver issue of the First World War) would have had a round soft nose for greater stopping power. A .455 service bullet as described by Clarke at the trial of Light would have been of an actual diameter of .454 in. It would have weighed 265 grains, would have had a conoidal base cavity and three canalures (circumferential grooves), and a striking velocity of 580 ($\pm$ 30) ft per second at 10 yd. It was designed to stop a man in his tracks, not simply to wound but to ensure he was unfit to fire back. Such a bullet was, as suggested by Marshall Hall, well capable of penetrating an inch or two of deal. His words to Clarke that such a bullet 'might almost have blown the side of the head off' were rather theatrical, but were not unreasonable. Such a bullet fired at full velocity, say 600 ft per second at something like arm's length, would cause greater damage to a human skull than that sustained by Bella Wright. Effective as the .455 Webley service revolver was, though, it had a mighty kick which took a lot of getting used to, which jerked the muzzle somewhat violently in an upward direction. Therefore an attempt at a head shot at anything over point blank range would require either considerable luck or immense confidence on the part of the marksman.

Ronald Light claimed that he had not received any weapons training while with the Royal Engineers, but a police report to Francis Sims indicated that he had actually been given some training. It also appears that Light himself felt proficient enough to pass his skills on to Ethel Tunnicliffe, whom he took with him on practice trips to the firing range, which would seem to indicate that if nothing else he had an interest in weaponry. However, his own opinion of his skills in any field may have been exaggerated.

At his trial, Light admitted to having bought one revolver for £3 from his commanding officer while he was at Buxton. Maj. Norman Benton confirmed this. A letter sent from Chief Constable Edward Holmes to Francis Sims later in the enquiry elicited that while at Newark, Light 'swore to the purchase of a service revolver and cartridges for same' at the depot stores. This was apparently verified by Adjt. Lt. Burton, the officer commanding Clothing and Equipment.

Light said he thought he bought the revolver from Maj. Benton in July 1915. His time at Newark commenced on 27 September of that year, and so it would seem that by 13 November 1915 when Light sailed for France, he already owned at least two revolvers.

By 1920 Lt. Burton was in Gibraltar and for some inexplicable reason was not called to give evidence at the trial, where his deposition, when seen in context with Light's own admission that he bought a revolver from Maj. Benton, could have been of immense importance to the prosecution. Light was able to say that he left one revolver in France when he was invalided out. One wonders how he would have explained away a second revolver. It remains a mystery why the prosecution failed to seriously address the question of precisely how many revolvers Light had owned before July 1919, and how many he still owned at that date.

Turning to the revolver that Ethel Tunnicliffe admitted to taking down to Light's home in Leicester, again there is nothing to indicate exactly what type or calibre of weapon this may have been. The only description we have of it comes from Ethel herself, who described it as large. Light said that he was unable to get it into the bag of the motor cycle which he intended to ride down to Leicester, but, as Maddocks insinuated and as the police were fairly certain, there were other reasons why Light could not risk leaving the Buxton camp with the revolver in his possession. In 1920 the Leicestershire Constabulary's investigation revealed that during Light's time at Buxton, a fellow officer had found his own revolver to have been stolen. There was a strong suspicion in Buxton at that time that 2nd Lt. Ronald Light was responsible for the theft of that revolver, either acting alone or in concert with Ethel Tunnicliffe. It may well be that the parcel which Ethel Tunnicliffe admitted receiving by post from Light and later took to Leicester to be opened by Light in her presence contained that stolen revolver. It is fair to say, though, that the police seem not to have been certain the parcel ever travelled by post at all. Certainly, as Maddocks's questions showed, there was no real reason, if the revolver was legitimately owned by Light, why it should not have been sent direct to his father in Leicester. It is impossible to say at this late juncture whether or not Ethel Tunnicliffe was anything more than a courier in 1915. The police at Leicester clearly thought it possible she may have been more directly involved in the suspected theft. Certainly she had remained loyal to Light after his dismissal from the Midland Railway, and working as she did in the same office it is likely she would have known every detail of that dismissal. In the event Ethel Tunnicliffe's affection for Light does not appear to have been seriously shaken until 1916, when possibly Light's conduct proved to be more of a personal affront.

We have only Light's word that he chose to leave a service holster behind in England when he went to France for the second time and he never satisfactorily explained why there were areas on the holster which showed signs of having had a name erased. He could not of course be questioned about how, when he was released from military prison and sent over to France, he was able to take a revolver that he claimed to have in his possession at that time. He admitted the holster had been sent to his Leicester address from his last camp. That must have been at the time of his imprisonment, and so it is inconceivable that the contents of the holster were not sent to Leicester at the same time. If, however, we accept Light's word that on leaving for France for service with the Honourable Artillery Company in November 1917 he took a service revolver with him, and if we further accept that that particular weapon was confiscated and left in France we still have the possibility that one, if not two, revolvers remained in England and in his possession at the end of the First World War.

We have the further consideration that those revolvers may not all have been of the same heavy .455 calibre, for why would a man want to own two, possibly three, identical revolvers? Light may have been a thief, but there is no evidence to support a theory that he was a compulsive thief intent in amassing an arsenal of weapons of identical type. It is more likely that Light possessed revolvers of differing types, any one of which might need to be considered in investigations into the death of Bella Wright. It may be that the obsessional interest by the police and the prosecution in a bullet which they came to believe was of .455 calibre, a theory which was all the more acceptable after spent and live ammunition belonging to Light was fished out of the canal, served only to blind them to the realities of the case and specifically to the dimensions of the victim's fatal wound.

Let us look once again at that wound – which five men saw and failed to recognize for what it really was. At least one of those five men, P.C. Hall, having just returned to the force from service on the Western Front, must have seen many a gunshot wound. It is unlikely that in his years in the trenches he had never witnessed an injury resulting from the discharge of a British service revolver. He would surely have had some idea of the weight and size of .455 lead bullet and the damage that could be inflicted by one. Yet Hall said he was first alerted to the fact that Bella's death was not a cycling accident by Dr Williams's statement that death was caused by a sudden haemorrhage, an assessment with which even as a layman he could not concur, rather than by the nature of the wound. When that exit wound was eventually discovered, the sheer neatness of it ought to have alerted the police and their expert witnesses to the impossibility of the wound being the result of a .455 calibre bullet. Dr Williams stated that he thought the wound had been caused by the bullet produced by Hall, but later admitted to Marshall Hall that he was no expert in gunshot wounds. That he had some misgivings about the assessment of the wound is borne out by his written suggestion to Chief Constable Holmes that an expert forensic pathologist should be called in. Quite why Holmes and his team were so reluctant to have the opinion of an expert must remain a matter for speculation, but clearly the lack of such an opinion must have coloured the whole enquiry, perhaps even ensuring that those engaged on the enquiry, obsessed with the theory that the girl's death was caused by a heavy calibre bullet fired from a service revolver, were blind to other possibilities, and failed to see the significance of various items which would come into their hands later in the enquiry.

The skin puncture wound was so small that an ordinary pencil could just penetrate it, according to Dr Williams's deposition. However, he also said that 'there was a small round hole in the base of the skull through which a lead pencil would pass', stating on oath that the hole was 'clean cut'. Where skin may shrink, bone obviously cannot. For the exact size of the exit wound we are again dependent upon Dr Williams's reports and depositions, which thankfully are remarkably consistent. By the doctor's reckoning the exit wound measured a mere $1\frac{1}{2}$ in by $\frac{1}{2}$ in. Was an exit hole of these diminutive proportions, however, likely to be the result of a .455 bullet passing through the head of the victim?

The results of a test to compare the relative damage caused by a .455 bullet fired from a Webley Mk.VI revolver with a bullet of smaller calibre is to be found in an Army Small Arms Committee report. The test, using sheep skulls, gives a clear indication that the .455 made a far larger entry hole, caused a far larger passage, and on exit the hole caused was considerably larger than that on entry. The entry hole made by the .455 was not clear cut, and there was also a good deal of vertical splintering of the bone with the .455 which was absent with the smaller calibre bullet. Internally the .455 caused far greater destruction of surrounding tissue than did the smaller calibre round. In his autopsy report Dr Williams notes simply that 'the brain was much lacerated', but he does not speak of tissue being destroyed in any quantity.

Bullets can behave oddly on coming into contact with a skull. There is an instance of a bullet entering a man's head, making a complete circumvolution of the skull, exiting and leaving the man, if not exactly well, certainly still very much alive. It is impossible to know for certain at this late date whether the bullet that killed Bella Wright passed cleanly through the head in a straight line or travelled around the head before making exit through the upper third of the right parietal bone. What is certain from Dr Williams's autopsy report is that the entry hole made by the bullet was clean cut, which suggests it was made by a bullet travelling at supersonic speed, around twice the speed at which a .455 bullet might be expected to travel. Such a bullet, apart from the hole made by passage through tissue, might also be expected to produce a considerable shock wave which in muscular tissue may produce a temporary cavity, but in relatively unstable tissue such as the brain can produce damage which could be described as lacerations. The internal damage to Bella's head would not appear to resemble that which might be expected from a .455 bullet travelling at about 600 ft per second, but seems far more in keeping with a bullet capable of supersonic speed, perhaps something in the order of the more slender .22 long rifle round. At a weight of only 40 grains (.083 oz), a muzzle velocity of around 1,200 ft per second and, being an unjacketed lead bullet, demonstrating some mushrooming on first impact with bone, it would result in a larger, though not considerable, exit wound, more of the order described by Dr Williams. Fired from a rifle, the .22 long rifle round is dangerous at up to a mile. Fired from a target pistol it is remarkably accurate at 25 yd. A versatile and readily available ammunition it was, by the years of the First World War, used together with other higher and lower powered .22 rounds in vast quantities by the Army for training purposes, not only as might be expected in .22 target pistols but also, and of possible significance here, by the addition of a simple device in the familiar Webley Scott Mk.VI service revolver.

Ronald Light admitted to having bought a service revolver for £3 from Norman Benton, and he certainly swore to the purchase of one service revolver and suitable ammunition. As we have seen it is not inconceivable that Light may have owned other types of revolver or pistol, possibly of foreign manufacture, which would not readily fall into any category labelled service revolver. We know of the revolver stolen during Light's time at Buxton, but we do not know its calibre. So it transpires that by the end of the First World War Light probably possessed, by one means or another, at least two revolvers which might or might not be classed as service revolvers. Since it is unlikely that he would own up to three identical revolvers, it becomes necessary to look at what was available within the broad description of service revolver. It seems sensible to confine ourselves to what might reasonably be described by Light, his counsel and indeed the prosecution at his trial as a service revolver and by Ethel Tunnicliffe as a 'large revolver', which may have fitted inside the brown leather service holster fished from the canal by Sgt. Healey.

Light took up his temporary commission with the Royal Engineers in 1915, the same year that the .455 Webley & Scott Mk.VI revolver was officially introduced. It varied little from its predecessor, the .455 calibre Webley & Scott Mk.V which, at 38 oz weighed one ounce more. Both guns were 11 in in length overall, and had a 6-in barrel. Either gun might have been referred to in 1920 as a service revolver or a 'large revolver'. The Mk.VI was made in huge quantities: Webley had a contract to deliver 2,500 weekly. There was also a bayonet attachment available which, though not officially adopted, was bought privately by many officers.

As might be imagined, the training of thousands of men in the use of an arm of .455 calibre was expensive. It was also incompatible with training on indoor ranges. Therefore, in order to give recruits some preliminary practice, a small calibre version of the Mk.VI was introduced. It was designed to take the far more economical .22 calibre cartridge. In appearance it bore great resemblance to its parent arm. It weighed 38 oz, was again 11 in long overall and had a round, 6-in barrel. It has been described as an accurate and well-balanced weapon, but as far as training a man to use a .455 Webley Mk.VI it was nigh on useless, for in firing there was a total lack of recoil. Again, the .22 practice version of the Webley Mk.VI might readily have been described in 1920 as a service revolver and might, considering its size and weight, just as easily be adjudged by Ethel Tunnicliffe to be a large revolver which, relatively speaking, it was.

Ronald Light might therefore within the various descriptions of service revolver and large revolver have owned any one or more of three models, and those models could have been of .455 or .22 calibre. All three models were made by Webley, all were bought in quantity by the Army and all were readily available for private purchase by officers.

Let us look once again at the head wound sustained by Bella. Though it seems more likely that the wound sustained was caused by a small calibre bullet, it is not possible to state unequivocally that Bella was shot by a .22 round, but the possibility exists that Light had the means to fire bullets of .22 calibre in addition to bullets of the heavier and more destructive capability, the .455 round. By his own admission he disposed of many of these .455 rounds after the death of Bella Wright.

Light admitted at his trial to having owned a service revolver. In the knowledge that he spent time in military prison following his court martial immediately before embarking for France with the Honourable Artillery Company, his story of having taken the revolver with him, but not the holster, seems less than convincing. If, however, we choose to believe that Light only ever owned one revolver, a service revolver of .455 calibre, then we must ask ourselves a simple question. Is it possible that Ronald Light, using a .455 service revolver, could have fired a bullet which produced the fatal but comparatively unobtrusive head wound as described by Dr Williams? Regardless of the obvious evidence of a particulate pattern and the absence of powder burns, the likelihood of the wound being the result of a ricochet, the possibility of the bullet being all but spent when it hit the girl all become irrelevant when we consider that by the use of a very simple device, the successful and effective firing of a .22 bullet from a service revolver of .455 calibre was entirely feasible.

In 1881 a device was invented that effectively reduced the calibre of a given arm and rendered it suitable for use with less expensive, smaller calibre ammunition. Morris Tubing, nowadays referred to as a sub-calibre training device, was simple to use and in the early years of the century quite popular. Availability of the tubing during the First World War was probably unlimited and virtually unrestricted. The smaller ammunition that was freely available at a far lower cost than heavier calibre ammunition added to the growth and popularity of what became a much imitated device. Originally intended for service rifles, by the First World War the idea had been taken up for use in revolvers. The idea was a simple one. Lengths of tubing sleeved into one or more chambers of the cylinder together with a similarly bored tube inserted into the barrel of the revolver effectively reduced the calibre of the weapon. Questioning Light about the revolver that Ethel Tunnicliffe had admitted taking to Light's home at Leicester, Maddocks asked: 'What did you want a large service revolver for while you were spending a weekend at Derby or Leicester?'

Light's answer bears the ring of truth: 'I brought it here because I wanted my father to see it.' It may be significant that by the time of the trial Light's father was dead and could not be questioned about the revolver. It is certainly significant that Maddocks did not take Light up on the admittance. Light had heard Ethel Tunnicliffe's evidence, and knew that she had already told the court it was she who took the revolver to his home. Had she not said that if she had known what the parcel contained she would not have taken it from Derby to Leicester? Having just dealt with questions concerning his skill with a revolver and his claim that as a lowly gunner in the Honourable Artillery Company he had taken a revolver but not a holster to France, Light was clearly discomforted. His disclosure that it was he who had taken the revolver to Leicester was, in the light of Ethel Tunnicliffe's evidence, superfluous, and may have slipped out while Light's thoughts were concentrated on the revolver itself. The prosecution made nothing of it; indeed Maddocks then pursued a line of questioning which concentrated on the other possible ways in which Light might have conveyed the revolver to his father. He had claimed earlier not to have had room in his bag for the revolver, and had thus been prevented from personally taking the weapon to his father. It is noticeable that he was not asked how he managed to get the revolver back to camp in order to take it with him when he went to France with the Royal Engineers. Difficulty in explaining that might have shown that the revolver Light wanted his father to see was in fact not the one which Horace Aldridge remembered seeing in France.

It may be that Light was more than thankful he was never questioned about what aspect of that revolver might have been of interest to his father. It may be that it was a perfectly ordinary Webley Mk.V or Mk.VI, but it could have been a .22 Webley Mk.VI practice model, or a .455 service revolver fitted with a sub-calibre training device which rendered it suitable for firing .22 calibre rounds. Might George Light's interest, as a fellow inventor of no mean achievement, have lain not in the original weapon itself but in the ingeniousness of the adaption?

It was certainly no part of Light's defence or obligation to bring to the attention of the police any .22 or small bore weapon, adapted weapon or ammunition that may have been in his possession at the time of the death of Bella Wright, but such was the strength of the belief within the police force that the bullet produced by Hall was indeed the one that had killed the girl, it may have proved difficult for anyone to convince the police otherwise. That belief was further reinforced when Sgt. Healey presented his haul of .455 calibre cartridges from the canal, and Light admitted ownership. Without that admittance ownership could never have been traced back to him, so why he did say they were his is something of a mystery. Of course the green bicycle had been traced to him, but there were no tell-tale marks of ownership on the holster and the cartridges were, as Marshall Hall pointed out, produced in their millions. Both the cycle and the holster and its contents were found in the same stretch of canal, but then so was a whole mountain of scrap metal. Could it be that Light only disposed of incriminating items which were pinpointed specifically by the police in their enquiry and consequently in the press following Bella Wright's death – namely the bicycle and ammunition of a 'heavy calibre'.

It is now possible to disclose that when Light was arrested in Cheltenham, he was actually in possession of a revolver. There in Light's room, among more mundane possessions which included letters from his mother and a cheque book, Det. Supt. Taylor found a small revolver and small bore ammunition. A communication between Chief Constable Holmes and Francis Sims around the time of Light's arrest indicates that an explanation was given to the police that the revolver had been found in the possession of one of the schoolboys and confiscated by the headmaster, who had handed the items to Light as he was in charge of the school armoury. It was further explained that the small bore ammunition belonged to the school. Quite who gave the police that explanation is not known, but perhaps it was given by Light himself: it was not substantiated by any signed deposition taken from the headmaster, or any member of staff, and there is no evidence that a verbal deposition giving this explanation was obtained from anyone other than Light. In a murder enquiry such as this, where a revolver was actually found in the possession of the accused man, it was at least remiss of the police not to investigate the circumstances of the explanation they were given. Perhaps this is a measure of the certainty of the police that they were searching for not a small revolver but a revolver of heavy calibre. The inference that the words 'small revolver' probably means that the revolver was of small bore rather than small in size is absolutely inescapable, particularly since the ammunition was stated to be small bore; but so sure were the police that they had already found the bullet that killed Bella, they failed entirely to see any significance in Light being in possession of a revolver of any other type. As master in charge of the school armoury at Dean Close, Light would have had more opportunity than most to conceal or exchange a revolver. An inventory of the school's armoury may have made interesting reading, but there is no evidence that any such inventory was made.

That in time the police at Leicester came to believe in the existence of a weapon which may have been the one that killed Bella Wright is apparent from correspondence which passed between Holmes and Sims after Light's acquittal. That a prosecution for perjury was also considered is equally apparent. Only Light himself and Ethel Tunnicliffe gave evidence regarding any revolver that Light may or may not have owned. Tunnicliffe, though obviously suspected by the police of involvement in the theft of a revolver at Buxton, would seem not to fall into the frame since by July 1919 her relationship with Light had cooled considerably. She was still living in Derby and probably knew little of his movements or of his possessions. It seems unlikely that by 1919, three full years after her patience with him seems to have run out, that she would have been prepared to perjure herself in order to aid Light. This gives rise to the possibility that both Ethel and Light himself transported a revolver to Leicester from Buxton. It seems, therefore, that it was Light himself who came close to prosecution for perjury following the receipt of a document by Edward Holmes and in consequence an investigation by his deputy, John Allen. Needless to say neither the document nor Allen's report is extant in available files, but should they ever come to hand they will make fascinating reading. In the absence of both documents the relevant letters that passed between Leicester and Richmond Terrace are quoted here in full. It must be of some significance that the letter of 23 June 1920, almost a fortnight after his acquittal, carries just the one word, heading – Light.

On 22 June 1920 Edward Holmes visited the office of the Director of Public Prosecutions in

Richmond Terrace, London. He took with him a document, which he left with Francis Sims. The importance of the document to Holmes is borne out by the fact that he made the visit personally, when he might easily have entrusted the task to one of his younger lieutenants. That the subject of the document was also of importance to Sims is borne out in his letter sent to Holmes on the following day. It was marked 'Confidential' and headed 'Re – Light':

> With reference to your call of yesterday and to the document you left with me I beg to say that we have been in consultation with the Attorney-General as to what use if any should be made of the information contained in that document and that he has decided that a prosecution for perjury should be instituted if the necessary evidence is forthcoming.
> In these circumstances and for reasons which you will appreciate, I think it is desirable that such suggestions as I have to make in the matter should be verbally either to yourself or to Supt. Bowley and I shall be glad if one or the other of you can make it convenient to attend here for this purpose say on Friday next the 25th inst. at about noon. I shall be glad to know by wire if I may expect you.

In response a telegram (P.O. No. 2104) was duly handed in at Hinckley at 11.16 on the morning of Thursday 24 June: 'Hope to attend about noon tomorrow, Friday, Holmes.'

For the second time in four days the Chief Constable personally made the journey to London rather than trust discussions to his subordinate. Predictably the meeting of 25 June between Sims and Holmes is not documented and probably never was, but on 17 July 1920, Holmes received a report from his deputy and duly acted upon it. His words to Sims were these: 'I enclose report which tells its own story.' Sims replied to Holmes on 19 July 1920, as follows:
'I acknowledge receipt of your letter and enclosure. I regret in the circumstances mentioned by Mr Allen the course of procedure which has been discussed between us appears to be impossible. The matter must rest where it is unless any further or precise information should come to light as to the whereabouts of the weapon. Mr Allen's comments have been laid before the Attorney-General who quite agrees with the view stated above.'
The belief by both Holmes and Sims in the existence of a weapon is clear, as is the lack of firm evidence which might have led the police to that weapon. The originator of the information could have been any one of a number of people. The police then, as now, were used to receiving letters from cranks, but that this particular document was considered to be of value is obvious from the way in which both Holmes and Sims together with Gordon Hewart treated the information that it contained. Whether or not the existence of the document ever came to the knowledge of Light is not certain, but it is reasonable to think that he may have been interviewed by the police in the course of their enquiries. Light was no fool, though, and however cautious the questioning he would have realized that the police had insufficient evidence for a charge to be brought. It is not inconceivable that the police actually told him they believed in the existence of the weapon, and warned him that if its whereabouts should ever become known he would face a prosecution for perjury. It is said that after the trial Light boasted of having 'got away with it'. Although there is no real evidence of this, it would seem to be in character that Light should boast. There is also a persistent rumour, again totally unsupported by evidence, that a signed confession was made by Light and salted away carefully in a police safe in Leicester, where more than one serving police officer in later years claimed to have seen it. None of them, sadly, could produce it.
There is one other indication that Light came to know of the suspicions of the police concerning the existence of a weapon, and as a consequence of this that he had been guilty as

charged. In the mid-1940s a cleric writing of his younger days as a prison chaplain in Leicester referred to there being a strange sequel to the case, one that he tantalizingly failed to reveal. He claimed that those who knew of the sequel felt it to show that vengeance does in fact pursue the evil-doer. That vengeance may have visited Ronald Light in the form of Edward Holmes, deputy Allen and a document concerning the weapon which killed Bella Wright, but this must remain a matter for speculation until firm evidence of the circumstances surrounding the findings of the police in the days following Light's acquittal comes to hand.

Fortunately, not everyone is as reticent as this Leicester cleric and, as will be seen in the next chapter, at least one Leicester citizen was, even in her eighties and with her memory as sharp as ever, regularly discussing her own involvement in the case and, more importantly, her knowledge of Ronald Light and Bella Wright.

CHAPTER 19

Fateful, but First, Meeting?

A man may be, as Light undoubtedly was, an inveterate liar, a poseur who needed to impress his own imagined importance on others, guilty of assault, and in possession of a weapon and competent in its use, but it is rare for even such a man as this to murder a woman who is unknown to him. We must therefore question Light's claim that Bella was, before the day of her death, totally unknown to him.

Bella Wright's 'fiancé' Archie Ward, had two sisters, Gertrude and Sally, both of whom were close friends of Bella and probably looked forward to the time when she would become their sister-in-law. Of the two sisters it was Sally who was best acquainted with Bella. They were closer in age and worked side by side in the same department at St Mary's Mill and, as girls will, they frequently discussed how they spent their free time and with whom.

Gertrude Ward, aged fifteen when Bella died, lived in and around Leicester all her life. She never forgot Bella and until her death in the late 1980s she repeatedly told a remarkable and unchanging story.

It was a story that Gertrude would relate to her family and to anyone who had an interest in the case. At one point Gertrude contacted a local newspaper and an account of her story appeared, yet today her memories of a case in which she and her sister probably played a crucial part is almost forgotten. It is possible that without evidence of corroboration Gertrude Ward's story could have been dismissed. But it is possible to reveal now that there is vital evidence in support of the information that Gertrude and Sally Ward could have given the police, evidence which would have greatly strengthened the case against Light. It might not be an exaggeration to say that the testimony the two sisters could have given, together with a deposition which was placed in the hands of the police in the early days of the enquiry but disregarded could have resulted in the conviction of Light for the murder of Bella Wright. Far from being the fanciful ramblings of someone who remained on the fringes of the case, the story that Gertrude Ward repeated was told with some chagrin by a woman who understood it was too late to avenge the death of a good friend. It was a story told of an age when a father's word was final and two young girls bowed to advice not to get the family involved, and to leave it to the police who knew best. Such advice must have seemed all the more sound after the arrest of Ronald Light, when surely the police and the courts could be trusted to see that justice was served.

In the months following the death of Bella Wright, the police claimed to have questioned all her workmates and friends concerning any and all acquaintances that she may have had. It is clear, though, that more could have been done by the police to obtain information that would have indicated that Bella and the man on the green bicycle were, in fact, known to one another. This information was there for the taking.

Sally Ward seems to have been a young woman of some courage and determination, capable of taking steps that she felt warranted even at some risk to herself. From the police point of view both Sally and Gertrude ought to have been questioned carefully and at some length, as they were doubly connected with Bella Wright. They were better placed than most to know how Bella spent her time while she waited for Archie to be demobilized.

In later years Gertrude Ward would recall that for many weeks before Bella's death there had been a series of conversations between her elder sister and Bella during the hours they spent together on shift in the same department at St Mary's Mill. Bella had told Sally that a man had

186

An old photograph of Shady Lane, Evington, a haunt for lovers and sweethearts. Few of these trees survive today

waited for her on occasions as she returned home to Stoughton from Leicester. The man had spoken to her several times and she had told him that she was about to be married. More importantly, Bella claimed that she had asked him to stop attempting to see her, in effect to stop waiting for her; but apparently he was most persistent. Bella told Sally that the man usually waited for her at a spot known locally as Shady Lane, which was an avenue lined with sycamores leading from the Gartree Road to Evington. Originally a route to divert traffic away from Stoughton Grange, the avenue became increasingly popular as a meeting place for lovers. As surviving postcards from the period reveal, Shady Lane was a secluded and romantic spot.

Gertrude's story then moves to a day she and Sally spent with Bella in Leicester. They were on their way to have photographs taken at Gales Ltd of Granby Street. As the trio walked down Granby Street towards the studio, Gertrude recalled Bella turning excitedly to Sally and saying: 'There is that soldier, you know, the one that waits for me.' Looking across the road, Gertrude saw that the man to whom Bella referred was with three other soldiers; she further remembered that her sister Sally whom she described as 'having a hot temper' wanted to cross the road and remonstrate with the soldier on her friend's behalf. Sally was of course mindful of Bella's agreement with her brother Archie, and was probably keen to see that nothing came between the couple. She intended, she said, to tell the soldier to keep away from Bella. Gertrude recalled that it was Bella herself who prevented Sally from crossing the road, by pulling her back and saying that perhaps the soldier would not bother her again. Sally advised Bella to confide in her father and let him deal with the man, but Bella replied she could never induce her mother or her father to talk about boyfriends, and in any case she was certain in her own mind that the man would not persist in trying to see her.

After Bella's death, and when it became apparent that the police would not be making an early arrest, Sally's thoughts turned to the soldier whom Bella had pointed out that day in Granby Road and of whom she had so often spoken. It becomes evident at this point in the story that not only could Sally have identified the soldier whom Bella claimed had repeatedly pestered her in Shady Lane, but that in addition she knew where the man lived, information that in all probability was also given to her by Bella. It seems reasonable, therefore, that she may also have been aware of the man's identity. Whether or not Sally had already discussed the situation with her father we cannot know, but it seems unlikely that the family had not discussed who might be responsible for such an untimely death. In the event it must have seemed to Sally that the police were making heavy weather of the investigation and she decided, according to Gertrude, to conduct her own enquiries. The police handbills and the newspapers pointed to the man the police sought owning a green bicycle. Sally recalled that the soldier she had seen in Granby Road owned a bicycle but she was not certain whether or not that machine was green. She was determined to find out, and persuaded her young sister to accompany her. Sally's plan was to call at the man's home and say to him that she had heard he had a bicycle for sale and that she might be interested in purchasing it. It may be imagined that any young girl about to face the man whom she suspected of killing one of her best friends might have experienced at least some trepidation – certainly the younger Gertrude was more than a little frightened by her elder sister's intentions and decided to err on the side of caution by remaining on the nearby street corner while her more intrepid sister carried out her plan of campaign. Gertrude watched as Sally walked boldly up to No. 54 Highfield Street and knocked on the door. The door was opened to her by, in Gertrude's words, 'the housekeeper', presumably Mary Webb. Sally asked if the master of the house had a bicycle for sale, to which she received the reply: 'I don't think so. I think the one he had must have been sold because I heard him getting it down from the boxroom, but if you leave your name and address I will ask him.' Sally, loath to comply with this suggestion and eager to make her exit, replied: 'Oh, leave it for now. I'll get in touch.'

In assessing Gertrude's account of her sister's actions it is worth looking at what was said both by Light and Mary Webb concerning the disposal of the bicycle. Light himself claimed to have thrown the bicycle, the holster and its contents into the canal 'all on one night'. He said that he did so 'shortly after summer-time had finished . . . that would be in October'. Summertime ended on 29 September in 1919, which may or may not support Light's statement. Mary Webb, on the other hand, told the police in 1920 that she 'happened to miss the cycle about December last year'. There was a good reason why Light should have remembered October 1919 vividly, as he had spent some part of the end of the month in police custody. That alone may have convinced him it was necessary to dispose of, rather than simply conceal, the bicycle, but did he do so at that time or (as now seems more probable) several weeks later in December? Mary Webb first missed the cycle 'about December', and since she had the run of the house and we may presume could have entered the boxroom whenever she pleased, it is likely she would have known about it if the bicycle had been disposed of in October. During her examination-in-chief, Mary replied to Maddocks: 'As well as I remember, it [the bicycle] was brought down [from the boxroom] just before Christmas.'

It was not only Mary Webb who believed the green bicycle was still at the Highfield house as late as December. Marshall Hall, who had after all taken his instructions from Bigg and belatedly, and briefly, from Light himself, posed the question: 'Did you do anything to the bicycle till Christmas time?' Perhaps that was a slip of the advocate's concentration but Light's reply was predictable: 'Yes, in October, I threw it away.' Since Light was taken into custody by the police on 28 October it is certain that if this was the incident that decided him to dispose of the cycle, then his earliest opportunity of doing so would have been in mid-November: he first had to gather together the holster and the cartridges which he claimed to have kept in the boxroom, and also he spent some time in removing 'a lot of the loose parts' from the cycle, and erasing the frame number. All that may not have taken Light long to complete, but we know that throughout the first two weeks of November Light was under close police surveillance every time he left his home. He could not have thrown anything into the canal during that time without the police knowing about it.

Samuel Holland told the police of a suspicious man he had seen bending down attending to a cycle near where the green bicycle was dragged from the canal, in either November or December 1919. Holland described the man's cycle as having two lamps; Mary Webb told the police that she remembered the green bicycle had two lamps. The weight of evidence would therefore seem to indicate that it was as late as December before Ronald Light finally disposed of his tell-tale bicycle, but if he had waited so long, what event or circumstances can have precipitated such action at that late date?

At the time of Sally Ward's visit, Mary Webb believed the cycle to have been taken down from the boxroom and sold, but did she as a result of the visit check whether or not the bicycle was still there? Did she discover it was the All Weather Raleigh cycle that Light later stated he had sold to a friend in Leicester that she had heard Light bringing down from the boxroom before Sally's visit? Mary Webb later said that she had asked Light just before Christmas what had happened to the bicycle and that only at a later date did he tell her it had been sold. Mary Webb had told Sally that she would ask Light about the cycle, yet Light denied he ever told Mary Webb he had sold it. He said he had told his mother of the sale, and claimed that Mary Webb asked him nothing in connection with the bicycle. Again, why should Mary lie to the police and to the court on that point? If indeed she told the truth, why should Light deny having had that conversation with her? It seems likely that the green bicycle was a topic of conversation between Light and Mary Webb on at least two occasions in later 1919. It may be that both of those conversations, one directly and one indirectly, were prompted by the visit of young Sally Ward. Bearing in mind that Mary was only able to tell Sally she had heard the bicycle being brought down, she had not actually seen it being carried down the stairs; and yet she later told Maddocks that the green bicycle was brought down by 'Mr Ronald' who took it out and returned without it.

It is worth remembering that, by his own admittance, Light disposed of a quantity of clothing, including the raincoat and jacket which he had worn on the day of Bella's death. That clothing was disposed of in that same month of December. If Light is to be believed in his statements that he disposed of the cycle and the holster and ammunition in October, then why not dispose of the clothing at the same time?

Light was quite unable to give Maddocks any reason for disposing of the bicycle. Maddocks had two questions for Light, both of particular interest when we consider the effect that Sally Ward's visit may have had on him:

'Up to that day [when Light disposed of his bicycle] you had been concealing the parts of a bicycle and your identity, but your identity up to that moment had never been challenged, had it?'

'No.'

'At any rate, no-one came to you and accused you of being that person?'

'No.'

Nevertheless, with that visit from Sally Ward it may be that Light had felt that things were beginning to close in around him, and it is notable that it was in December, just before Christmas, that he took the first steps to move away from Leicester. Around that time he contacted Dr Flecker in Cheltenham in the hope of obtaining a teaching post at Dean Close School.

There is a further suggestion that Bella may have been approached by Light at an earlier date, and this came from a deposition given by Mary Wright to Albert Hawkins of Scotland Yard on 18 July 1919. Hawkins and his sergeant returned to London long before the arrest of Light, and in consequence of that it may be that the police in Leicester failed to see the significance of Mary Wright's statement, given, as it was, some months earlier, to an officer from the Metropolitan police rather than to the local force. Following Light's arrest, however, Mary's statement should have been reassessed.

In her statement Mary Wright recalled a conversation that she remembered having with her daughter when the family had yet to move to Stoughton and were living in Braunstone:

'I remember about twelve months ago, or maybe longer, Bella came home after having a ride on her bicycle and said: 'What do you think? When I went down Braunstone Lane I had an officer fall in love with me and get off his machine, a motor cycle. He asked me who I was and I told him I was a labouring man's daughter. He said what a nice girl I was and said by my nice ways and looks I ought to be in a nicer position than a labourer's daughter.' I advised her to have nothing to do with him and I never heard her mention any more of that incident and I certainly never did [mention it] again.'

In that deposition Mary Wright stated that the meeting between her daughter and an officer took place about a year before July 1919. We have seen that Light occasionally borrowed a motor cycle from his ex-officer friend. Light had been gazetted out of the Royal Engineers in July 1916, and his entitlement to wear an officer's uniform obviously ceased at the same time; yet Mary Webb told the police that for part of 1918 Light was at home in Leicester, and that during that time he sometimes wore an officer's uniform and went about riding a motor cycle.

The obvious inference is that the man whom Bella described to her mother was indeed Light. Mary's advice to her daughter to have nothing more to do with the officer may well have been ignored; the excitement Bella felt at the time is evident in her words to her mother and she may have had difficulty in resisting his approach. Light would have needed little encouragement. Perhaps only when he became persistent and possibly more demanding did she try to dissuade him from trying to see her. If Bella had gone against her mother's advice it could account for her remark that her parents could not be persuaded to talk about boyfriends. Her reluctance to allow Sally Ward to remonstrate with him could be indicative that the relationship had gone further than she cared to admit, and she may have been at pains to conceal this from the Ward sisters. It may be that in the first place Bella was rather flattered, perhaps even a little overawed by the attentions of 'an officer' and a man many years her senior. Perhaps in the absence of Archie Ward a mild flirtation was a welcome distraction, and it is not likely she would have been put off by the difference in age between herself and Light. That difference was almost exactly mirrored in the ages of Bella's own parents.

The extent of the relationship between Bella and Light would have been far more easily explored then than is possible now. Light's whole character and attitude to the opposite sex, known to the police by 1920 ought to have been spur enough to encourage the force to make exhaustive enquiries about the possible existence of a relationship between the couple.

If both Mary Wright and Gertrude Ward told the truth, then it may be supposed that Bella Wright's relationship with 'the officer', slight as it may have been, had at least survived the Wright family move to Stoughton from the opposite side of Leicester, for Shady Lane is in close proximity to Bella's Stoughton cottage home.

A further indication that the officer Bella described could have been Light is shown by one more fact and one more deposition. When the police searched Light's room after his arrest they found almost everything that in any way represented the respectable side of his life – everything from which he drew pleasure and perhaps pride. But the uniform of a Second Lieutenant in the Royal Engineers was not found, even though Light had taken pride in wearing it. Perhaps he had disposed of the uniform in December 1919, because although there was no mention of an Army uniform in the police handbill, in time it may have been seen to link him with the death of Bella Wright. What Light could not have known was that to the police his ownership of the green bicycle would take priority over enquiries concerning a relationship he may have had with Bella, which was suspected (and pointed out to the police) by James and Margaret Evans. Margaret told the police that she had pointed out to Bella that a man was waiting in the lane outside the cottage. Bella had replied: 'I wonder if it is the man who overtook me coming along the way; he said he came up from Great Glen.' At the time it struck Margaret Evans as odd that 'she [Bella] did not at any time get up from her chair to see who the man was'. Clearly Margaret gained the impression that her cousin did not look out of the window as she already knew who the man was, that he was waiting for her and that he would still be there when she emerged. After watching Light and her cousin walk away from the Gaulby cottage, Margaret was more convinced than ever of the couple's relationship, saying to her husband: 'She must have known him.' James had replied: 'Of course she did.' Neither husband nor wife can have left the police in any doubt about their suspicions. In fact, Margaret told the police she was sure they were acquainted 'by the sort of familiarity between them', and, also because when the man spoke to Bella she did not answer, but 'went very red and confused'. During the visit George Measures was equally sure of his niece's friendship with the man. He had said to Bella: 'You must know something about him, I know.' She had replied that the man was a perfect stranger, and in some ways he may have been, for Bella clearly felt no qualms about being alone in Light's company. Perhaps, as she had indicated to her uncle, she intended to outrun Light: 'I can easily get ahead of him,' she had said. 'I can easily give him the slip.' As we have seen one witness testified that when he first saw the couple on the top road the woman was riding some way ahead of the man, and he was shouting to her. Perhaps Bella had indeed outrun Light before their arrival at Gaulby.

What actually happened in the time it took Bella to reach the spot where her body was found can only be a matter for conjecture.

If there is the slightest chance that Bella Wright was competing in any sort of cycle race against Light, and her words to George Measures suggest she may indeed have done so; or if she was riding hard because she was trying to escape her assailant, then the condition of the bicycle that she was riding at the time becomes of some importance.

In a case where one particular bicycle played such a prominent role, it is perhaps surprising that the condition of the cycle that the victim rode on that last ride seems to have been overlooked. The cycle was examined by Hall, but only for the presence of blood. There is no evidence that the cycle was examined for fingerprints which, by 1919 was a well-established procedure.

It has always been assumed that the bicycle Bella rode on that last journey belonged to her, probably because it was described as a lady's cycle. It may be, though, that this was not the case. James Evans told the police early on that while at the cottage Bella told him of some work that had recently been done on her own bicycle, yet the machine she rode to Gaulby was clearly in need of attention. While at Gaulby Bella had herself borrowed a spanner, and attempted unsuccessfully to correct a fault on the bicycle she rode. James Evans told the police that before she set out on the journey home he said to her: 'I'll call at your place at Stoughton in the morning and repair the freewheel.' Evans deposed that Bella had replied: 'I'll stay in then but I am going to see Louie [her sister] during the day.' Evans's concern over the condition of the bicycle does not seem to have been shared by the police, who appear to have shown a singular lack of interest in it throughout the enquiry.

On 3 June 1920, less than a week before Light was due to stand trial, the police received an indication that Bella's young brother Philip wished to add to his statement. He deposed that 'the freewheel of his bicycle was broken and the machine was not safe to ride. He had not mentioned this to his sister Bella but had told her when she asked him to go for a ride'.

There may be several reasons why Philip felt the need to inform the police that his own cycle was unsafe to ride at the time of the murder. It could, for example, have been helpful in substantiating an alibi, but surely he could have told the police of the fault with his machine at the outset of the enquiry. It is significant that by the time Philip did mention his faulty bicycle to the police Light had already been in custody for some weeks. Only a few days remained before his trial opened, and by then the police had no interest in the alibis of anyone else for the night of 5 July. Why then should Philip feel it incumbent upon him at such a late date to inform the police of his faulty cycle? Can it be that he felt the police ought to know that on that last journey Bella was riding his bicycle, which was 'not safe to ride'. Perhaps it was only as the trial drew near that he felt guilty in not telling the police absolutely everything, whether or not it seemed to be relevant to their case. Seemingly only as a result of Philip's new deposition, Det. Supt. Taylor paid another call on the Wright family, where he would have been able to examine Philip's bicycle. Eight months had passed since Bella's death, during which her father had kept her bicycle untouched.

If the cycle was in a poor or dangerous condition on the night of Bella's death, it was almost certainly still in that same condition on 3 June 1920, yet there is no evidence that the cycle was examined by the police in any detail; for Det. Supt. Taylor's visit seems to have been primarily taken up with another item perhaps not unconnected. The item was an oilskin coat belonging to

Bella, which she had worn or carried with her when she first set out for the post office at Evington. But for Philip's wish to add to his statement, that oilskin would have remained untouched and unexamined by the police at the Stoughton cottage. In the pocket of the oilskin Taylor found a few coins, three sixpences and $4\frac{1}{2}d$ in coppers, probably change given to Bella by Kathleen Power when she sold her the stamps. It is quite clear that during her final visit to her home Bella decided to leave behind the oilskin coat, and also exchange her jacket which her mother had noticed as Bella left the cottage for the post-office for the raincoat she was wearing at the time of her death. Given that Bella's own cycle had recently been overhauled, that James Evans believed the fault on the bicycle that Bella was riding to be serious enough to warrant a special journey to Stoughton to repair, and also that he promised Bella he would 'repair the freewheel', is it unreasonable to think that during her brief visit to her home after posting her letters Bella exchanged not only her clothing but also her bicycle? Perhaps it was the change of bicycle that necessitated the change of coat. Though it cannot be categorically stated that this was so, it is possible that at the time of her death Bella was actually riding her brother's bicycle, on which the freewheel was broken. Bella was the eldest of the Wright children, used to taking some care of her younger brothers and sisters, so perhaps she intended that Philip would after all be able to go out that night, riding her own recently repaired machine. She may have considered herself more competent than he to cope with riding a difficult machine over rough roads or she may simply have been expecting to make a shorter journey than her young brother, who seems to have been of a mind to ride into Leicester for the evening.

What, then, might have been the result of Bella setting out from Gaulby on an unsafe bicycle, believing she could easily 'get in front' of Light? If the freewheel was faulty, it is possible that it could have jammed when travelling over a hard or rutted road, such as the lane on which Bella was found. This could have caused Bella to fall from her bicycle. The fact that she was travelling slightly downhill at this point may also have contributed to the accident. That it was indeed an accident that threw her to the ground is borne out by the trajectory of the bullet, and the presence of the particulate pattern around the wound.

The fatal bullet entered below the level of and slightly behind the left eye, making its exit behind and a little above the right ear. Had Bella still been mounted on her bicycle when the shot was fired, that trajectory would indicate her killer was crouched on the grass verge several feet ahead and to the left of the girl as she rode along the lane. Such a position, though, would not have resulted in the presence of the particulate pattern, as a muzzle position of no more than 6 ft from the victim's head is indicated by that. Given that the hedge is 9 ft from the roadway it would have required the assailant to take up his position without cover, and to crouch in full view of his victim. The lane is straight at that point, which means that anyone riding a cycle in the direction of Leicester would have had a clear view ahead: this would mean that Bella rode straight into the face of danger without taking any avoiding action whatever, which is difficult to imagine.

Bella's injuries could just as easily have been caused if she were attempting to avoid danger from behind. Had she turned and looked over her right shoulder, and her attention been diverted from the poor state of the roadway, the wheel rut across which she was found may well have been the cause, of her being thrown from a faulty machine to land on her left side, thus sustaining injuries to the left side of her face, to her left hand and wrist and possibly including the two small contusions at the right-angle of her mouth.

The trajectory of the bullet as it passed through Bella's head, the presence of the particulate pattern around the surface of the wound and the position in which she was found all go to indicate that the fatal wound was inflicted almost immediately after her fall from the bicycle. It might be expected that the victim was at least dazed by her fall; she may not have been able to rise immediately. By simply lifting her chin to look in the direction of the adjacent hedge she would have placed her head in a position where the trajectory of the bullet could have been achieved by an assailant standing within a few feet of her. The bullet would, however, have travelled downwards, rather than upwards as the prosecution believed. Bella might well have been thrown backwards to come to rest in the position in which Cowell found her, and her clothing accordingly escaped heavy blood staining when blood was channelled through the exit wound and directly on to the roadway. Any signs that a small calibre bullet travelling at supersonic speed had embedded itself in the roadway would soon have been lost – livestock, farm carts or even the float on to which her body was lifted may have served to expunge any tell-tale sign.

What part if any the larger calibre bullet produced by Hall had in Bella's death it is impossible to say. How it came to be lying, as Hall claimed, trodden into the surface of the lane must remain a subject for conjecture. It is significant, however, that Light disposed not only of live rounds of .455 calibre but also of spent cartridges which he had apparently retrieved after their discharge, no doubt with a mind to reloading.

Errors of judgement, inexcusable carelessness and unexplained oversights undoubtedly resulted in the prosecution's case being lamentably weaker than it might have been. That the Crown sought to prove malice aforethought when they so clearly could not, and never attempted to, present to the jury even the flimsiest evidence of a liaison or acquaintance between accused and victim might be construed as a case doomed to failure from the outset.

Evidence of a previous relationship between Light and Bella could not in itself have proved malice aforethought. Such evidence would, however, explain perhaps why Light waited for Bella in Gaulby for so long, but there may have been a secondary reason why Light was prepared to wait. In later years Archibald Bowker, Marshall Hall's clerk, wrote that Bella had told Light she could obtain bicycle tyres at cost price. This information could perhaps have come from Marshall Hall's brief, implying that the information had been given by Light himself. Although new tyres were not found on the green bicycle itself or in Light's possession, while he waited in Gaulby, could he still have been hoping that Bella would eventually supply him with the much-needed tyres? It is hard to envisage an accidental discharge of a firearm resulting in the fatal wound to Bella. The very position that the murderer would have had to take up in order that the shot would result in the particulate pattern and the known trajectory of the bullet indicates an attitude of dominance, of standing over the girl in a threatening and menacing manner, and in the deliberate and probably careful aim of a small bore revolver.

Light's apologists would claim, no doubt, that if indeed he did kill Bella then he must have done so while still suffering from the effects of shell shock, quite incapable of making a rational decision and probably hardly knowing what he was doing as he fired his revolver. There is one more fact, much overlooked, that undermines the theory that the killer panicked and made a hasty retreat, as a man suffering the effects of shell shock would perhaps do. When the body was discovered the bullet's entry wound was largely obscured by bruising, and Bella's head lay in a pool of blood. The bullet had exited behind and slightly above her right ear. Bella's hat was quite undamaged, so clearly could not have been upon her head at the time of the fatal shot. Therefore someone, and it was not Joseph Cowell, placed the hat upon her head as she lay dead. Such an act on the part of any killer takes a cool nerve. Every second spent at the scene of the crime increases the chances of detection. The inference must be that the hat was placed in position by the murderer to conceal the exit wound, which for over twenty-two hours remained known only to Bella's killer.

CHAPTER 20

Aftermath

After his acquittal Ronald Light returned by bus to his mother's Leicester home, where later that evening mother and son were interviewed by a reporter from the *Daily Sketch*. Both spoke of their confidence in the outcome of the trial and Catherine apparently expressed her delight that Ronald was back home. On the following day a photograph of Light in profile and wearing the uniform of a Second Lieutenant in the Royal Engineers appeared on the front page of the *Daily Sketch* along with photographs of Bella and Catherine. The acquisition of a photograph of Catherine Light was something of a coup for the *Sketch* reporter, and even the *Leicester Chronicle* was unable to match this. Over the weekend Light was interviewed on several occasions and always displayed an air of apparent satisfaction. One photograph taken in the backyard of his home shows him with a broad grin on his face, and a national newspaper printed a photograph of him cuddling his mother's dog.

Light's letter of thanks to Marshall Hall was written during the following week, and Marshall Hall's reply probably arrived about ten days after Light's acquittal. There is some reason to believe that Light was interviewed by the police shortly after his release, but no charge of perjury was brought against him, although it was seriously considered.

A rumour that surfaced in the early 1930s suggests that Light spent some time in Canada, and it may be that he was there for some time. It is too early to say if he declined to register under the census of 1921, but any reporters wishing to track him down would have found that his old address in Highfield Street had no telephone installed, and Mary Webb had departed. Light's mother continued to live at the house and it would be another ten years before another maid, Harriet Turrell, was listed along with that of Catherine Light on the electoral roll. Ronald Light's name did not appear on the roll.

While Light enjoyed his regained freedom the Wright family returned home convinced that their daughter's killer had walked free. Sally and Gertrude Ward kept in touch with the family, and in years to come Gertrude expressed concern for the plight of Mary Wright immediately following the trial of 1920. Her burden was twofold; not only was she still mourning the death of her eldest daughter but her youngest daughter, Elizabeth, aged only fourteen, and described as 'simple minded', had herself given birth to a mentally retarded child. It had fallen to Mary to bring the child up as if it were her own. Gertrude believed the father of Elizabeth's child was unknown, but recalled, however, Mary Wright's abiding fear of Light. On one occasion Bella's mother commented that she felt afraid to go and hang out the washing because she feared Light would strike again.

Recent research would seem to indicate that the holiday of which Light spoke after his release may have taken him east to Kent, and eventually led to a permanent move there. By 1928 he was living at a house which, considering Light's life, was aptly named The Folly, in Manor Way, Leysdown, on the Isle of Sheppey.

The Isle of Sheppey, divided from mainland Kent by the River Swale, is a remote backwater just 10 miles long and 5 miles wide. Leysdown, some nine miles south-east of Sheerness is the most easterly village on Sheppey and must have provided in the 1920s the ideal bolthole for any man wishing to disappear from the public gaze. In that and one other respect the area suited Light's purpose particularly well, for the presence of the nearby R.A.F. establishment at Eastchurch and the summer influx of visitors meant that the local inhabitants were quite used to seeing unfamiliar faces, and paid little attention to them. But for Light the sheer isolation was not enough. He lived for many years, certainly until 1938, under the assumed name of Leonard Estelle – and was perhaps advised to change his name to ensure privacy and anonymity.

During those early years on Sheppey, Light was not alone but living with the woman whom he would eventually marry, and who in the years before their marriage shared Light's assumed name. She is listed in parish registers as Lilian Gertrude Estelle. Lilian Bower was born in Ibstock, Leicestershire. In 1928 her daughter Gwendoline (by her marriage to Ernest Lester, an electrician) was aged fourteen and appears to have resided with her mother and Light at The Folly, Leysdown. By 1934 Lilian was a widow and free to marry Light. The marriage took place at the register office on Sheppey on 11 December. Light gave his age correctly as forty-nine and his address as The Folly, Leysdown. His bride gave her address as Manor Way, Leysdown, but of her age she was less forthcoming, stating herself to be just forty years old when in fact she had been born on 3 February 1884, therefore being some twenty months older than Light. The only insight into Lilian's character was made recently, when she was described to this author as 'a bit eccentric'. One week to the day after the marriage of her son, Catherine Light drew up her will. She left small bequests to her maid, and to many of her masonic friends in Leicester. For Lily Light, as she was known to her new mother-in-law, there was a half share in Catherine Light's furs and wearing apparel, the remainder going to her niece. Charles Sale Bigg and Ronald Light, who was, as one might expect, the main beneficiary, were appointed joint executors. The will, presumably because Catherine at seventy-four years of age was too weak or infirm to do so, was signed on her behalf by a colleague of Bigg.

On 23 September 1935, just two days after the nineteenth anniversary of George Light's death, Catherine Light died at her Highfield Street home. Acting as executor to his mother's estate Light was careful to use his own name, but until March 1936, when his own will was drawn up, he continued to give his own address as No. 54 Highfield Street, with no mention whatever of his Leysdown address. Ronald and Lilian continued to be listed on the Leysdown parish civilian residence register as residing at The Folly until some time after Catherine's death, so it seems probable that Light spent only a short time in Leicester administering his mother's estate and having his own will drawn up by a solictor whom he trusted and knew something of his past life.

By 1928 the Lights, however, were ready for a change, but even after something over ten years, not to the extent of using their real names. They moved just a short distance to The Doones, again in Manor Way. It is at that address eight years later, in May 1945, that the local civilian residence register for the first time listed Ronald Light and Lilian Gertrude Light as the sole occupiers, Lilian's daughter, who married in 1941, having by that time left home.

It is difficult to say precisely at what point Light deemed it safe to revert to the use of his lawful name, but it seems that his decision to cast aside his alias coincided with the closing years of the Second World War. Perhaps this change took place because of the simple and mercenary reason that Lilian, as a result of newly passed legislation, would be eligible for a state pension from February 1944 if she provided birth and marriage certificates.

In the summer of 1964 Ronald and Lilian Light removed to what was their last home together, one of a pair of dwellings named Sunnyside Cottages, at Minster in Sheppey, a central area of the Isle sometimes known locally as Halfway Houses. This probably suited them admirably, as the cottage was on a bus route, and close to shops and a post office. The couple seem to have lived a very quiet life and Ronald Light, who was seventy-nine years old by the time of the move, is remembered as an elderly balding man, a heavy smoker who was often to be seen leaning on the gate of his cottage smoking a cigarette and watching the world go by. Even near neighbours had little to do with the couple, who are described by those who remember them as keeping very much to themselves. In keeping with Light's previous homes on Sheppey, there was no telephone installed in the cottage.

Sunnyside Cottages, No. 110 Minster Road, Isle of Sheppey. The final home of Ronald Light and his wife Lilian

Light was in his ninetieth year when on 15 May 1975 he died at the home of his step-daughter, at Kingsdown, Sittingbourne. The cause of death was given as senile decay. His mortal remains were cremated at Charing crematorium near Ashford, and his ashes were dispersed in the crematorium grounds. There is no memorial to Light other than an entry in the Book of Remembrance which states: 'LIGHT, Ronald Vivian B.Sc. Died 15th May 1975 Aged 89 years.'

Following the death of her husband, Lilian moved to be with her daughter, and it was there on 8 December 1975 that she died. While on this occasion her date of birth was given as 2 February 1884 (she was actually born on the third of the month) the place of her birth is inexplicably recorded as Derbyshire.

How much of Light's previous history was known to his family before his death is not certain. One source seems to indicate that nothing was known of the green bicycle case by his stepdaughter and her children until it was brought to their attention by Light's solicitors after his death in 1975. Perusal of Bishop Wakefield's account of the case is hardly likely to have given a true picture of the first thirty-five years of Light's life, and one wonders what was made of the decision taken to revert to their rightful names, when Light's stepdaughter was around thirty years old and in the early years of her marriage. It is quite obvious from Lilian Light's own well-documented perpetuation of their jointly assumed name of Estelle that she must have known something of Light's past, probably far more than she was ever willing to share with her daughter; possibly more than she cared to admit even to herself. Coming as she did from Ibstock, her father having been a colliery company secretary, it is virtually certain that Lilian at least knew all about the green bicycle case and of her husband's involvement in it. As to Light's court martial offences and his many other misdeeds, his wife may have been less well informed.

Did Ronald Light heed the warning and the plea in Marshall Hall's letter to him in 1920? Did he begin to take life for the serious affair Marshall Hall thought it to be? It is hard to believe that in old age Light would have been any less inventive or likely to lie to achieve his aims than he had been in his younger days.

How often when Light signed his name as Leonard Estelle, or as he smoked a quiet cigarette while he watched the traffic drive past his cottage, did he remember that wait in Gaulby village or that last ride with the labourers' daughter who had at first been so beguiled by his attentions? And what of his trial for her murder? How often did he wake in the middle of the night and remember those nights he had spent in Leicester Gaol? Light certainly did not lack imagination; so how often in those last years did he wake in the small hours to wonder what it would have meant if that verdict had gone against him? Even to guess what went on in the head of a man of such complex character as Light can only be folly.

For Light, every successive account of his exploits that appeared in print, each failing to reveal the true Ronald Light – the character that had existed for many years, before he ever saw a Flanders poppy and long before he met Bella Wright – must have made satisfying reading. In 1929 Edward Marjoribanks's life of Sir Edward Marshall Hall was published, in which the case of Rex v. Light was dealt with most diplomatically. This was the most popular legal biography to that date, and was reissued by Penguin Books in 1950. In the intervening years there had been, among other accounts, two volumes from Marshall Hall's clerk, Edgar Bowker. In 1948 he spoke of Light as a man who 'appeared to be a decent sort of chap, against whom nothing of an unpleasant character was known'.

Perhaps the only real cloud on Ronald Light's horizon in later years appeared in July 1964, when the B.B.C. televised a programme about the green bicycle case as part of their 'Call the Gun Expert' series, based on the work of Robert Churchill. For Light, who had been living under his own name for about twenty years, this must have come as quite a shock, and probably precipitated that final move to Sunnyside Cottages.

It is probable that no one except Light himself knew the full extent of his crimes and probably we will never know of all his deceptions and duplicity, but it is possible at least, now, to put the green bicycle trial in a fuller context – and allow you, the reader, to come to your own conclusions about what outcome there might have been at this famous trial had *all* the evidence been available to the jury.

Bibliography

Bancroft, G.P. *Stage and Bar* (Faber & Faber, 1939)

Birkett, Lord, of Ulverstone, *Six great Advocates* (Penguin, 1961)

Bowker, A.E., *Behind the Bar* (Staples Press, 1948)

Bowker, A.E., *A Lifetime With the Law* (W.H. Allen, 1961)

Freeman, A.B., *Bristol Worthies* (1907)

Goold Walker, Maj. G. (ed.) *The Honourable Artillery Company in the Great War*:
(Seeley Service & Co., 1930)

Jackson, Robert, *The Chief. A Biography of Gordon Hewart* (Harrap, 1959)

Marjoribanks, Edward, *The Life of Sir Edward Marshall Hall K.C.* (Gollancz, 1929)

Myatt, Maj. F. *Illustrated Encyclopedia of Pistols and Revolvers* (Macmillan, 1969)

Wakefield, H. Russell, *The Green Bicycle Case* (Philip Allen, 1930)

OTHER SOURCES

Public Record Office: CRIM 6/20.

                         ASS 1 12/112

                         ASS 1 13/50

D.P.P. File: DPP 1/61

War Diary and Intelligence Summary. 152. Field Comp. Royal Engineers.

The Times, Leicester Mercury, Leicester Post, Illustrated Leicester Chronicle, Daily Sketch, Coalville Times, Bath Chronicle, Western Daily Press, Bristol Times & Mirror, Church Times, Tally Ho.

Index

R.V.L. – Ronald Vivian Light

Aldridge, Horace, 164, 182
Allen, Barbara, 161
Allen, John, 183
Allen, Mrs, of Hinckley Road,
  Leicester, 5–6
All Saints' church, Kensington
  Park, 62
Ambrose, driver/batman to
  R.V.L., 164
Atkins, John Henry, 77, 80, 117

Bailey, P.C. John William, 51,
  71
Balfour, Arthur, 98
Bancroft, George Pleydell, 98,
  100–1, 114, 152
Bancroft, Sir Squire, 98
Barratt, Sgt. W, 24, 52, 55
Bates, W. & A., 6, 36, 49, 76
Beaver, John William, 2
Beaver, P.C., 174
Bell Hotel, Leicester, 59, 94, 111
Benton, Maj. Norman William,
  125, 134, 178, 180
Bigg, Charles Sale, 73 et seq,
  101, 189, 196
Bigham, F. Trevor, 45, 176
Birkett, Sir Norman, 73, 95, 100,
  103, 106, 109, 116
Birmingham Small Arms
  Company, 54
Bourne, Charles Henry, 58
Bouskell, George Edmund, 28 et
  seq
Bouskell, James Tempest, 28
Bowker, Archibald Edgar, 73,
  92, 98, 100–1, 124, 131, 151,
  194, 198
Bowley, Supt. Levi, 28, 30, 40,
  44, 49, 55, 73 et seq, 82, 98,
  123
Brookes, of Birmingham, 14
B.S.A. Cycles Ltd, 53 et seq
Buchanan, Robert ('Mr
  Leicester'), 100
Burton, Adjt. Lt., 178
Bywaters, Frederick, 15

'Call the Gun Expert' T.V. series
  (1964), 51, 198
Cavan, Valeria, 43, 61, 80, 109
  et seq, 132, 174
Central Technical College, 64
Chambers, Joseph, 71, 119
Chapel, Dr M. Kirkland, 167
Chapman, Joe, 8
Charing Crematorium, Ashford,
  197
Childs, P.C. R.B., 52
Churchill, Robert, 51, 176, 198
Clarke & Sons, 84
Clarke, Henry, 32, 84, 119 et
  seq, 148, 176
Clifton, Arthur Henry, 163
Clifton, Catherine Eleanor (née
  Mullins), 162
Clifton, Frederick, 163
Clifton, John Henry, 62, 162
Clifton, Robert Walter, 163
Codrington, Lt. Gen. Sir Alfred,
  169
Colman & Lewitt, Messrs, 6
Cowell, Joseph, 19 et seq, 29,
  32, 83, 107, 175, 194
Cox, Harry, 32, 44, 54, 59 et seq,
  88, 121
Crippen, Hawley Harvey, 15, 73,
  131
Crook, Arthur Henry, 163
Crook, Sarah Anne, 162
Cross, Henry Andrew, 162

Daily Sketch, 154, 195
Davis, Albert Sydney, 54, 88,
  117
'Davis' (R.V.L.'s first alias),
  166, 172
Deacon, Mr, 22, 175
Dean Close School, 56 et seq,
  69, 71, 82, 154, 161, 171, 190
Doones, The 196

Ellistown Colliery, 62, 163
Edmondson, Maj. A.J., 67
Estelle, Leonard (R.V.L.'s alias),
  196 et seq
Evans, Margaret Louisa (née

Measures) 12 et seq, 32, 40,
  45, 61, 90, 190
Evans, James, 12 et seq, 32, 40,
  46, 61, 82, 116, 190 et seq
Evington post office, 10, 20, 36
Evington Valley Mills, 44

Flecker, William Herman, 56 et
  seq, 161, 190
Folley, The, 195 et seq
Fowler, Edward George Bennett,
  74, 167
Foxton Locks, Grand Union
  Canal, 6
Freeman & Light, Birmingham, 63
Francks, Walter, 88, 122

Gales Photographic Studio,
  Leicester, 188
Garfield, Sidney, 54, 88, 117
Gibson, P.C. W., 93
Goodyer, Frederick, 28
Gordon, Dr Robert, 68, 171

Hall, P.C. 97 Alfred, 22 et seq,
  71, 83, 108, 175–7, 192
Hall, P.C. John Sidney, 61
Hall, Edward 'Teddy', 95, 111
Hall, Grace Ethel, 97
Harper, Annie M. (née Stretton),
  156
Harris, Watts & Bouskell, 28
Hastings, Macdonald, 51
Havelock Shoe Works, 6
Hawkins, Det. Ch. Insp. Albert
  V., 30, 45, 190
Healey, Sgt. W., 51, 71, 76, 78,
  87–8
Hewart, Sir Gordon, K.C., 75,
  94, 103 et seq, 184
Highfield Street, Leicester, (No.
  54), 69, 71, 82, 173
HMS *Diadem*, 7, 12, 36
Holland, Samuel, 53, 72
Holmes, Ch. Const. Edward, 28,
  31, 40, 45, 61, 75, 80–1, 86,
  166, 183 et seq
Honourable Artillery Company,
  66 et seq, 77, 170, 179, 181

Horridge, Sir Thomas Gardner, 98, 107, 116 *et seq*, 152, 154, 159

Illes, Det. Sgt. Harold Frank, 56, 60, 88
Illustrated Leicester Chronicle, 100
Imperial College, London, 169
Institution of Civil Engineers, 64, 170
Isle of Sheppey, 195 *et seq*

Jackson, Robert, 124
John Bull Rubber Company, 44
Jones, Edward Brooke, 163

Keay, William, 83, 106
Keite's of Leicester, 109
Kerr, Mr of Keythorne Lodge, Tugby, 4
Key, Mr, 9

Leicester Daily Chronicle, 42
Leicester Daily Post, 113
Leicester East Aerodrome, 10, 17
Leicester Mail, 100
Leicester Mercury, 39, 42, 44, 80, 130, 139
Lester, Ernest William Arthur, 193
Lester, Gwendoline, 193
Light, Catherine Louisa (née Clifton), 56, 62 *et seq*, 69, 70, 140–1, 154, 157, 161 *et seq*, 195–6
Light, Eleanor (Jnr), 63
Light, Elizabeth (née Blake), 163
Light, George, 163
Light, George Henry (or Harry), 62 *et seq*, 161, 167–8
Light, Revd John, 62
Light, Lilian Gertrude (Lester, née Bower), 196 *et seq*
Light, Ronald Vivian: birth, 57, 62; education, 63 *et seq*, 161 *et seq*, 169; employment, 64, 76, 164; army service, 64 *et seq*, 76, 164–6, 168 *et seq*; arrest, 57 *et seq*; trial, 103 *et seq*; acquittal, 153; marriage, 196; death, 196–7
Lloyd George, David, 1, 5, 94, 124
Lumbers, John, 100

Mackintosh, A.W.P., 38
Maddocks, Henry, K.C., 95, 114, 118, 131 *et seq*, 157 *et seq*, 174, 178, 182, 189
Maltby Main Colliery, 12, 61
Mannock, Tommy, 100
Marjoribanks, Edward, 156, 158–9, 198
Marshall Hall, Sir Edward, K.C., 69, 73, 96, 100 *et seq*, 156, 176, 189, 194–5, 198
Measures, Agnes Olive, 13, 19, 61
Measures, George, 10 *et seq*, 31 *et seq*, 35, 43, 60, 80 *et seq*, 114, 152, 191
Midland Railway Company, 64, 164
Million Cycle Factory, 156
Moira Colliery Company, 39
Moore, Dr C., 92
Morris, Frederick Charles, 55, 88, 116
Morris Tubing, 182

Naylor, Mr., 22, 175
Newell, Maj. C.L.N., 51
Newton, Arthur John Edward, 73
Newton, S.W.A., 107
Nourish, Thomas Edward, 43, 61, 80, 113
Nunney, Albert Henry, 109
Nunney, Muriel Edith, 43, 61, 79, 109 *et seq*, 174
Nutt, Farrington, 69

Oakham School, 63, 159, 161–2
Orton Bros, Derby, 54 *et seq*, 58, 64, 88
Orton, Joseph, 55, 88, 117
Owston, Dickenson, Simpson & Bigg, 73

Palmer, Charles, 12, 31, 43, 61
Palmer, Elizabeth, 12, 43, 61, 80, 90, 114
Parker, Mr of Stocking Farm, 4, 80
Park View, Granville Road, 63, 164
Phillips, Dr Edgar Vaughan, 27, 30 *et seq*
Pick, Everard & Keay, 83, 106
Pinero, Sir Arthur Wing, 158 *et seq*
Power Kathleen, 10, 20, 113

Rawson, John Compton, 4
Richardson, Bill, 38
Rowe, Mr, postmaster, 36
Royal Engineers, 65 *et seq*, 76
Royal Engineers' School of Mechanical Engineering, Buxton, 65, 164
Royal Hotel, Leicester, 75
Rudyerd, Lt. G.W., 165
Rugby School, 159, 161
Russell & Sons, B., 6
Rundall, Maj. C.F., 65, 165

St Mary's and All Saints' church, Stoughton, 7, 35
St Mary's Mill, 6, 9, 36, 46, 49, 79, 84, 186
St Peter's church, Leicester, 168
Saint's dairy, 4
Salter, P.C., 58
Saunders, William East, 53, 88
Sims, Francis J., 61, 75 *et seq*, 111, 132, 157, 166, 178, 183 *et seq*, 192
Soar, River, 5, 49
Spinney Hill, Leicester, 174
Stanley, Clifford R., 23
Straight, Douglas, 97
Steele, P.C. Tom, 51
Stephens, Det. Sgt. William, 30, 45
Stephenson, Guy, 75, 132
Stoneygate Preparatory School, 63
Strand, magazine, 158
'Stretton' bicycle, the, 154
Strettons Ltd, 156
Sunnyside Cottages, Minster, 196

Taylor, Det. Supt. Herbert Chiltern, 30, 45, 54 *et seq*, 154, 156, 176, 183, 192
'The Light that Failed', Rudyard Kipling, 159–60
The Times, 100
Thompson, Edith, 15
Thurnby, Leicester, 166, 172
Timperley, A.E., 86
Tunnicliffe, Ethel Mary, 64 *et seq*, 86–7, 116, 164, 166, 178 *et seq*, 183
Turner, Alfred, J.P., 73 *et seq*
Turner & Jarvis, 73
Turrell, Harriet, 195

Uppingham School, 63

Victoria Park, Leicester, 62, 166, 174

Wakefield, Rt Revd H. Russell, 197
Ward, Archibald, 7, 10, 12, 36, 46, 123, 186
Ward, Gertrude, 7, 36, 50, 186 *et seq*, 195
Ward, John William, 49 *et seq*
Ward, Sally, 7, 36, 50, 186 *et seq*, 195
Watson, Capt., 169
Webb, Mary Elizabeth, 56, 69, 70, 72, 79, 89, 117–18, 157, 172, 188 *et seq*, 195
Webley & Scott, 84, 180–1
Welford Road cemetery,

Leicester, 168
Westmore, Revd W.N., 35 *et seq*
Wharncliffe War Hospital, 68, 171
Whitehouse, Enoch Arthur, 49 *et seq*, 71, 88, 118, 176
Whitwick Colliery, 69
Wightman Powers, George, 76 *et seq*, 101, 116, 154
Wild, Sir Ernest, K.C., 97, 169–70
Williams, Dr Edward, 22
Williams, Dr Edward Kynaston, 22 *et seq*, 30 *et seq*, 39, 76, 85–6, 112–13, 118, 175–6, 180
Williams, Montagu, K.C., 114
Winning, Norman, 133
Wood, Norman, 6
Wood, William Bertie, 6, 32

Wright Annie Bella: birth, 2; education, 2 *et seq*; employment, 4 *et seq*; death, 19 *et seq*; inquest, 28 *et seq*; funeral, 35 *et seq*
Wright, Elizabeth, 195
Wright, Kenus Emblin, 1, 9, 32 *et seq*
Wright, Leonard, 36
Wright, Louie, 3, 192
Wright, Mary Ann (née Beaver) 2, 9, 20, 26–7, 29, 32, 36 *et seq*, 107, 190 *et seq*, 195
Wright, Philip, 2
Wright, Philip (Jnr), 7, 9, 10, 26, 36, 192
Wright Thomas, Henry, 36

Young Hugo, K.C., 133